WATCHDOGS
OR
VISIONARIES?

WATCHDOGS OR VISIONARIES?

PERSPECTIVES ON THE HISTORY OF THE EDUCATION INSPECTORATE IN WALES

EDITED BY
ANN KEANE

UNIVERSITY OF WALES PRESS
2022

© The Contributors, 2022

All rights reserved. No part of this book may be reproduced in any material form (including photocopying or storing it in any medium by electronic means and whether or not transiently or incidentally to some other use of this publication) without the written permission of the copyright owner except in accordance with the provisions of the Copyright, Designs and Patents Act 1988. Applications for the copyright owner's written permission to reproduce any part of this publication should be addressed to the University of Wales Press, University Registry, King Edward VII Avenue, Cardiff CF10 3NS.

www.uwp.co.uk

British Library Cataloguing-in-Publication Data
A catalogue record for this book is available from the British Library.

ISBN   978-1-78683-940-4
eISBN   978-1-78683-941-1

The rights of the Contributors to be identified as authors of this work has been asserted in accordance with sections 77 and 79 of the Copyright, Designs and Patents Act 1988.

The University of Wales Press gratefully acknowledges the funding support of the Books Council of Wales in publication of this book.

Typeset by Marie Doherty
Printed by CPI Antony Rowe, Melksham

CONTENTS

Notes on Contributors — vii
Preface — ix
Glossary — xi

Introduction — 1
Ann Keane

1 Origins and Development of the Inspectorate in Wales, 1839–1907 — 21
   Russell Grigg

2 Owen Edwards, the Welsh Department and the School Curriculum, 1907–1925 — 47
   Ann Keane

3 The Inspectorate in Wales between 1925 and 1970: Responses and Reactions — 77
   Alun Morgan

4 Inspecting and Reporting in a Changing Educational Climate, 1970–1992 — 103
   Roy James

5 Challenge and Transition: The Inspectorate in Wales, 1992–2020 — 131
   Barry Norris

6 Women in the Inspectorate in Wales — 159
   Sian Rhiannon Williams

7 Devolution, Education Policy and Inspection in Wales: A Policy Analysis — 187
   David Egan

| 8 | Inspection in Wales and Internationally: Some Comparisons
Russell Grigg and Ann Keane | 205 |

The Future   225
Ann Keane

Appendix I: The Statutory Basis of the Inspectorate   235
Appendix II: List of Senior or Chief Inspectors in Wales   239
Appendix III: List of Key Milestones   241

Select Bibliography   247
Index   259

NOTES ON CONTRIBUTORS

David Egan
David is Emeritus Professor of Education at Cardiff Metropolitan University. His career has moved from teaching history in a secondary school to leading a large University School of Education and developing a profile as a policy researcher focused upon the education system in Wales since devolution.

Russell Grigg
Russell is an education inspector for the Ministry of Education in the United Arab Emirates, having previously worked for Estyn and Ofsted. His research interests are in the history of education.

Roy James
Roy taught mathematics in secondary schools before joining HMI (Wales) in 1970. Since retiring as chief inspector in 1997, he has undertaken research and consultancy work and has been External Professor at the University of Glamorgan and Visiting Research Fellow at the University of Wales Institute Cardiff.

Ann Keane
Ann taught in secondary, further and higher education sectors, in Wales and England, before joining HMI (Wales) in 1984. Since her retirement as chief inspector in 2015, she has been a Welsh Government Board member and has undertaken consultancy and research work.

Alun Morgan
Alun is a native of Merthyr Tydfil and a graduate of UCW Swansea. He has taught in every phase of education other than primary and was an HMI in Wales from 1983 to 2011.

Barry Norris
Barry started his career in education as an English and drama teacher. He was an HMI in Wales from 1991 to 2020 and led many inspections across pre-16 and post-16 sectors. He was Estyn's lead officer for inspection policy until his retirement in 2020 and lead officer for quality assurance from 2010 to 2018.

Sian Rhiannon Williams
A former Senior Lecturer at Cardiff Metropolitan University, Sian has published on various aspects of social and women's history in Wales. She is co-editor of the *Gender Studies in Wales* series (UWP) and Welsh language editor of *Llafur*. She is active in Archif Menywod Cymru/Women's Archive of Wales and the Purple Plaques Group.

PREFACE

I am grateful to those authors who have contributed chapters to this history of the education inspectorate in Wales, not only for their individual chapters but also for their generous support in the many contributions they have made to the process of the book's production by means of discussion, re-writing and the joint editing of each other's work, and including in particular the contributions of Russell Grigg and Roy James to the drafting of the introduction. Feedback from reviewers on the initial typescript submitted to the University of Wales Press has also proved to be invaluable in the preparation of a final draft.

I would like to acknowledge the willing support we have received from Estyn, the Wales inspectorate, notably from former Her Majesty's Chief Inspector (HMCI) Meilyr Rowlands, who made the historical files of the inspectorate available to us in addition to sharing his thinking about the shape of the future. Thanks too to his successor, Claire Morgan, for her continuing support and to Michaela Benjamin, Executive Assistant to HMCI, for her unfailing help in arranging access to the inspectorate's files and hunting down relevant documents. Librarians at several libraries and archives have been of notable assistance to us including those at the National Library of Wales, the Welsh Government Library (in which the old Welsh Department of the Board of Education collection of reports is stored) and the National Archive. There are several other individuals to include in our list of acknowledgements because of the valuable information they have provided to us as authors and the oral, and occasionally written, contributions they have made to the production of this book. They are as follows: retired HMI Sam J. Adams, R. Alun Charles, Gareth Wyn Jones, Robert O. Taylor, the late Dorothy Selleck, Peter C. Webb and the late M. J. F. (Peter) Wynn. Thanks are also due to other retired HMI who responded anonymously to the questionnaires featured in Chapter 6. Their readiness to assist is much appreciated.

Two academic authors have also been generous with their advice: Emeritus Professor David Reynolds offered valuable early support and challenge to the group; and Emeritus Professor Hazel Walford Davies, author of several publications about O. M. Edwards, has offered helpful support and advice. I would also like to thank the Welsh Government for the assistance they have provided to enable the production of this book and to record my gratitude to William H. Howells for his prompt preparation of a comprehensive index.

The chapters in this volume draw on a study of both primary and secondary sources; notable among primary sources are those archives held by Estyn, the National Library of Wales, the Welsh Government Library and the National Archive at Kew. The chapters also draw on the authors' direct engagement with the practices of inspecting the provision of education and training in Wales (including initial teacher education).

Ann Keane

GLOSSARY

Aide-memoire A series of questions to support interviews on inspection, including surveys.

Assistant Inspector Historically, there had been other grades of assistants to HMI, such as sub-inspectors and junior inspectors before they were subsumed into the grade of assistant inspector (AI) in 1912. After the Second World War, Martin Roseveare (as Senior Chief Inspector in England) abolished the rank of AI and existing AI became HMI. AI were paid around half the salary of HMI.

Associate Assessors Teachers and managers from further education institutions (FEI) who were invited to work as inspectors in FEI inspections from the mid-1990s. Later known as peer inspectors.

Board of Education In 1899 the Board of Education replaced the Education Department, Department of Education and Science and the Charity Commission as the British government's administrative body for education. In 1944 the Board became the Ministry of Education and then the Department of Education and Science (1964), Department for Education (1992), Department for Education and Employment (1995), Department of Education and Skills (2001), Department for Children, Schools and Families (2007) and Department for Education (2010).

Central Welsh Board This was created in 1896 as a national body responsible for inspection and examination arrangements in secondary schools created under the Welsh Intermediate and Technical Education Act (1889). It was succeeded by the Welsh Joint Education Committee (WJEC) after the Second World War.

Chief Inspector The chief inspector (CI) has been responsible for directing the work of the inspectorate in Wales, including: after 1992, the administration of the Office of Her Majesty's Inspectorate (OHMCI Wales); having oversight of the educational standards and provision in Wales; and liaising with/reporting to government.

Chief Woman Inspector This post existed from 1905 in England until 1938 when the position ceased, as part of a process of integrating women inspectors into the mainstream structure of the inspectorate. Women inspectors in Wales were answerable both to the chief woman inspector and the Wales chief inspector.

Committee of Council on Education (CCE) The CCE was established in 1839 as the British government's administrative body in education and was responsible for appointing early HMI. Its last official meeting was in 1880 although publications in its name continued being issued until 1899.

District Inspector HMI with responsibility for the oversight of inspection in and information about education and training in specified districts.

Divisional Inspector Divisional inspectors were appointed in Wales between 1920 and 1928 to take responsibility for inspection and inspectors in the Welsh Department at a time when the Welsh Department's permanent secretary took over the CI's administrative duties in Whitehall.

Education Department This British government office was created in 1856 to implement education policy and worked within the purview of the Committee of Council on Education. HMI were employed by the Education Department, although in principle they were independent of government policy in their reporting.

Estyn The inspectorate in Wales is currently named Estyn, the Welsh word for 'to stretch' or 'to extend'. Estyn is a non-governmental department of the civil service, independent of but funded by the Welsh Government.

HMCI Her Majesty's Chief Inspector.

HMI Her Majesty's Inspector. Originally grade 6 in the executive band of the civil service, this grade is often used to appoint specialists – such as lawyers, inspectors, economists – rather than career civil servants. There were three bands in the civil service structure before it became open in the late 1990s: clerical, executive and administrative, the latter of which constitutes the current senior civil service (senior civil servants at grade 5, or deputy director level, and above).

MHMI   Appointed at grade 6 in Wales in 2000, M(anaging)HMI were re-designated assistant directors in 2009.

NAfW   The National Assembly for Wales, established after the devolution referendum of 1999. Recently re-named the Senedd or the Welsh Parliament.

NoV   Note of visit by an inspector to a provider of education or training. This would be based on the notes made in situ that were used for feedback at the end of the visit. Revised and organised under a template or in response to an aide-memoire, it would end up in the file for the provider reported upon and might also be used to inform the findings of a published report.

OHMCI (Wales)   The Office of Her Majesty's Chief Inspector in Wales was created by legislation in 1992 in parallel with OHMCI (England) or Ofsted.

Peer Inspectors or Assessors   Teachers and managers from schools who were invited to work as inspectors on school inspections from the early 2000s as well as in post-16 providers.

Reporting Inspector   The title given to any inspector whose job it is to organise an inspection of an individual provider of education or training or a survey and to write and edit a report based on contributions from their team.

Senior Chief Inspector   This rank was reintroduced in England in 1926 although not in the Wales inspectorate because technically the CI in Wales, although independent in most respects and working to the Welsh Department and later to the Welsh Office Education Department and Secretary of State for Wales from 1971, was also nominally one of SCI England's team. (See Chapter 4.)

Staff Inspector   Responsible to the CI for a particular phase or aspect of education and training and a member of the senior management team and of the senior civil service. Nowadays (2021) designated a strategic director on Estyn's executive board.

Strategic Director   See Staff Inspector entry above.

Welsh Department   This was created in 1907 as part of the Board of Education, with responsibility for inspection in Wales. It later became part of the Welsh Office Education Department.

Welsh Government Previously known as the Welsh Assembly Government, this is the devolved government in Wales, established after the devolution referendum of 1999.

Welsh Office From 1964, the Welsh Office progressively assumed powers from Whitehall departments, including for education in 1970.

INTRODUCTION

Ann Keane

The education system in Wales is currently experiencing its most wide-ranging reforms since the nineteenth century. The reforms include a radical reconstruction of the school curriculum and arrangements for student assessment; reforms of initial teacher education; the introduction of new professional standards for teachers, leaders and support staff; and a realignment of school self-evaluation together with new arrangements for accountability. Notably, teachers have been given more freedom to plan their curriculum in the context of a framework that has been developed in full collaboration with a selection of so-called 'pioneer' schools. It is timely, in light of the current reforms and the decline in recent years in the academic study of the history of education in Wales, to reflect on developments in education as well as inspection over the period of three centuries during which the inspectorate has had oversight of the education system in Wales. One of the aims of this book is to examine the underlying structures and forces that have shaped the development of the inspectorate and the extent of its influence in the development of education. The book combines a chronological and thematic approach that spans the full period of the inspectorate's existence from 1839 to the present, in a collection of edited essays by seven authors.

This introduction starts with a summative overview of the chapters with a focus on what differentiates the Wales inspectorate from other UK inspectorates, that is, its existence in a country with a different and distinctive language and culture. The introduction continues by drawing out and reflecting on a number of themes from the rest of the book, starting with an outline of the structure of the inspectorate, its objectives and policy context, and followed by a consideration of its influence on education policy, its impact on provider improvement and its response to criticism. The introduction is organised under the following sub-headings:

1. Overview of chapters and the Welsh context
2. Background to the structure of the inspectorate, its objectives and the inspection policy context
3. The influence of inspectors on education policy
4. The impact of inspection on provider improvement
5. How the inspectorate has responded to criticism.

1. OVERVIEW OF CHAPTERS AND THE WELSH CONTEXT

Chapters 1–5 span the chronology of developments from 1839 onwards. The periods covered in each chapter vary in length, but all the chapters examine themes associated with how the inspectorate was organised to deliver its objectives, how its work evolved and what was important and influential in HMI reports on education in each period. Chapters 1–5 delineate the relationship between inspectors and the education providers they inspected, between inspectors and the central civil service departments they were part of until 1992, and their relationships with others in the education community.

Chapter 1 deals with the history of inspection in Wales at a time when the inspectorate was at its most integrated in the context of an 'England and Wales' infrastructure. It offers a wide-ranging perspective on the experience of school inspections in Wales and raises issues some of which resonate throughout the book, notably in relation to how the inspectorate dealt with the challenges of operating in the context of a territory where the language and culture were different from those in England and when most HMI were English-speaking Anglicans. The chapter also discusses the contribution of exceptional inspectors, such as HMI Longueville Jones, who was at odds with the notoriously critical *Blue Books*.[1] Written by English commissioners (inspectors) in 1847, this report represented an attack not only on poor educational standards but also on the religion, morality and language of Wales. It was not until the 1880s that a few HMI made a concerted effort to support the use of Welsh in schools. Even so, they had very limited impact.

Chapter 2 notes that, at the height of Empire, Wales HMI attended Imperial Conferences on education in London in which the colonies of the British Empire came together to share their common challenges as they tried to reconcile their schools to an education whose primary aim was to teach English to children. Owen Edwards[2] is the main focus of this chapter, as the first and most visionary of the chief inspectors (CI) of education and training in Wales, together with the Board of Education's newly established Welsh Department, the first ever British civil service department to be concerned solely with Wales. As Chapters 3, 4 and 5 continue the narrative, it becomes clear that the history of inspection in Wales is also a history of how the language, culture and history of Wales gradually gained recognition and a place in schools and other education providers. HMI had a role to play in respect of this and these chapters illustrate how HMI supported the strengthening of education policy in relation to the position of the language and culture of Wales in the curriculum and with advising government on local education authority (LEA) plans to establish Welsh-medium and bilingual schools. Chapter 4 records the role played by HMI in the development of Wales-only Subject Orders following the implementation of the 1988 Education Reform Act as part of the introduction of a subject-based National Curriculum, as a result of which, Welsh and the Welsh dimension (Y Cwricwlwm Cymreig) became mandatory for 5–16-year-olds in the maintained schools of Wales.

After the political devolution of powers to a National Assembly for Wales in 1999, the education system, including its inspectorate, became further divorced from England. The politicians of the Welsh Assembly Government became the new education policy makers, as discussed in Chapters 5 and 7. However, much of the primary legislation that governed inspection in 'England and Wales' still applies to Wales. The 2005 Education Act sets out what remain statutory requirements for inspection in schools while the Learning and Skills Act 2000 continues to apply to post-16 inspection in Wales (see Appendix I). After 2006, legislation on the inspection of education and training in Wales became a devolved matter.

Chapters 6–8 take a thematic approach and are intended to complement the chronological accounts in earlier chapters. Chapter 6 begins to uncover the history of how women became inspectors. They were few in the nineteenth and early twentieth centuries and, early on, women inspectors were borrowed from England. Even when appointed to the Wales inspectorate, they worked both to the Wales CI and the chief woman inspector (CWI) in England. Only gradually were women accepted as the professional equals of their male counterparts and it would not be until 1997 that a woman was appointed CI in Wales.

Chapter 7 is written from the subjective perspective of a respected academic who was also a political adviser to the first Minister of Education and Lifelong Learning in Wales. His chapter sets out a personal interpretation of post-devolution education and policy making in relation to the inspectorate. Chapter 8 draws some comparisons between the inspectorate in Wales and those in other European countries in the context of how inspectorates set and meet their objectives and how they have been affected by changes related to wider education reforms. Finally, the last section is not so much a conclusion to the volume as a meditation on a future that will inevitably be as conditioned by the past as much as it is a projection into that future.

2. BACKGROUND TO THE STRUCTURE OF THE INSPECTORATE, ITS OBJECTIVES AND THE INSPECTION POLICY CONTEXT

Structure

The structure of the inspectorate, the way it has been organised and managed, has changed over time in response to changes in political and social contexts. An early focus on value for money in the grant-aided elementary schools of the nineteenth century was expanded over the century to take account of the increase in the range of education phases, including secondary and technical education. The number of HMI was increased and, like their counterparts in England, HMI in Wales inspected adult education and institutes of further education as well as pupil teacher centres and teacher training colleges. (Appendix I lists the sectors that the inspectorate currently inspects.) A tradition of borrowing and lending HMI across the Wales–England border was a characteristic of the Wales inspectorate that was to continue until the mid-1990s, especially in relation to inspecting some of the more specialised provision in further and higher education.

While regional divisions were organised across the Wales–England border for most of the nineteenth century, by 1882, Wales (including Monmouthshire) was constituted as a separate regional division. Established in 1907, the Welsh Department gained a further degree of autonomy for the inspectorate and a new post was created of chief inspector of education for Wales. A Wales cohort of inspectors was identified, most of whom could speak Welsh, and a new administrative post was introduced at permanent secretary level. After a series of further minor reorganisations in the 1920s, the male and female inspectorates were aggregated from 1934 and, in 1944, Roseveare (senior chief inspector in England) introduced a significant and long-lasting reorganisation of the internal management structure of the inspectorate in both Wales and England. He abolished the posts of assistant inspector and chief woman inspector and created new senior management teams of staff inspectors (SI) with phase or specialist responsibilities, working to CI: in Wales that meant working to one CI across the phases of education.

The 1992 Education Act established the Office of Her Majesty's Chief Inspector (OHMCI) (Wales) and OHMCI (England) – known as Ofsted – which offered the inspectorates greater independence as non-Ministerial civil service departments. However, the requirement to outsource inspections also meant that school inspections would henceforth be undertaken by independent inspectors, and only exceptionally by HMI, who would instead regulate the new system. The internal management structure of the inspectorate in Wales did not change after 1992 although new posts were created to undertake the new administrative responsibilities created as a result of the Act. The Roseveare structure of CI, SI and HMI would continue in Wales until 2000, when, as a result of wholesale reorganisation, heads of division (later renamed strategic directors) replaced staff inspectors and a new tier of managing HMI was appointed, albeit at the same grade (6) as HMI. The inspectorate in Wales adopted the strapline of 'Excellence for all' and was re-named 'Estyn', a Welsh word for 'to stretch' or 'extend'.

Objectives

There has been a strong element of continuity in the iteration and reiteration of the objectives of the inspectorate since 1839 although the relative emphasis placed on accountability and advice has varied over time to reflect the wider political landscape. Chapter 1 tells us that the objectives of HMI in 1840 were to report on the quality of instruction and on the character and discipline of schools and suggest improvements but without interfering in the management of schools. Payment by Results, introduced from 1862, put a strong emphasis on schools' 'efficiency', a term whose usage was to continue into the next century and beyond but without exercising the punitive effects on its grant for any school whose pupils failed to pass the annual HMI examinations of the late nineteenth century. The power of HMI increased significantly between the 1860s and 1890s under this much-feared system but by the beginning of the twentieth century the emphasis had reverted to a gentler, more advisory approach according to which inspectors were given the objective of offering schools 'counsel, advice [and] encouragement' and offer 'more time, too ... for joint discussion and evaluation at the end of the inspection'.[3] Chapter 2 describes how, from 1907, HMI were expected to be the source of educational information and to disseminate criticisms and suggestions to teachers on the basis of their recorded observation in schools.

Chapters 3 and 4 record the outcomes of a series of reviews of HMI and their functions and the impact of the reviews on the objectives of the inspectorate in Wales. Chapter 3 indicates how the Roseveare inquiry of 1956 prioritised inspection visits and feedback to teachers over written reports and how this resulted in a less frequent rate of reporting. Subsequently, the balance between accountability and advice tended to prioritise an advisory role in HMI pastoral visits. In 1970, *HMI Today and Tomorrow* noted that HMI visited providers to observe and assess the quality of provision and to provide constructive feedback. They were to advise the Secretary of State while also acting as a link between central government and LEAs. From the mid-1970s, the work of inspectors in Wales was reinvigorated by new leadership although full inspection reports were still usually shared with only a limited range of stakeholders, that is, the head teacher, governors and LEA. Chapter 4 describes how, by the time of the publication of the largely supportive Rayner report in 1982, a more robust pattern of detailed reporting on full inspections had already been established. Although neither the 1944 Education Act nor the legislation that preceded it had clearly established the statutory role of HMI, Rayner maintained that, throughout history, the objectives of inspection had been interpreted as involving: 'a check on the use of public funds'; 'provision of information to central government'; and 'provision of advice to those responsible for running educational establishments'.[4]

Accountability became more transparent in 1983 after the Conservative government decided that all inspection reports should be published and made available to parents, the public and the press whereas previously they had normally only been shared with providers and LEAs. Accountability would continue to have priority in the broad objectives set for HMI from the 1980s and it remains at the top of the inspectorate's list of its current strategic objectives:

- providing public accountability to service users on the quality and standards of education and training provision in Wales
- informing the development of national policy by the Welsh Government
- building capacity for improvement of the delivery of the education and training system in Wales.[5]

Thus, the inspectorate provides the general public, parents, policy makers and other stakeholders with expert, independent evaluation of the state of education, which may also be used to inform policy making but also constitutes direct advice to providers on improvement since it is based on the inspection of individual institutions. However, it can be argued that, by now, one of the main arguments in support of inspection is that the service provides a form of external assurance for various stakeholders including parents and the general public, namely the first objective listed above. The inspectorate is thus a watchdog not only for the government that funds state education but for parents and for pupils who themselves often have very little choice as to which school they attend and can too often expect little redress if the standard of the service they receive is poor or only mediocre.

The inspection policy context

The wider context of governmental policy on inspection over the past forty years has involved intensifying the inspection of public services more generally and strengthening the focus on accountability and public assurance. There was an expansion in the use of audit, regulation, authorisation and certification of public services by the state over the period. Between 1976 and 1995 the number of government arm's length regulators increased by more than a fifth and spending on them doubled.[6] The Conservative UK government's Education Act of 1992 set up a more intensive programme of outsourced school inspections on shorter cycles than ever before, whose effects are described in Chapter 5. The publication for the first time of a detailed framework for inspectors offered more transparency about the criteria and methods of inspection.

Tony Blair's UK Labour government continued to expand the scope and managerialist thrust of inspection. In 2003 the Prime Minister's Office of Public Services Reform outlined the government's commitment to inspection, clarified what it meant by effective inspection, outlined the arrangements by which effective inspection could be achieved and stated its expectations of inspection. The statement applied 'to all UK government departments responsible for public services'.[7] Its definition of inspection as an external review, independent of service providers, that would provide assurance to Ministers, contribute to improvements, report in public and deliver value for money chimes with what would have been familiar to Estyn as well as to the other inspection, audit and regulation (IAR) bodies operating in Wales at the time.

After 2006, the Welsh Assembly Government (WAG) took responsibility for legislating on inspection and, in 2008, the WAG consulted the public on its own policy statement on *Inspection, Audit and Regulation in Wales*.[8] Reflecting the principles set out in the 2005 Hampton review as well as those of the Office of Public Services Reform, the 2008 policy statement also made a feature of value for money.⁹ This feature of inspection frameworks had already been revived in the 2004 Estyn common inspection framework and, before that, had been enshrined in the collaborative Best Value inspections of local government services since the mid-1990s. It was this collaboration between inspectorates, combined with the direction of travel in WAG policy thinking, that eventually led to the establishment of 'Inspection Wales' in 2011 on the basis of a strategic agreement between the heads of Estyn, the Wales Audit Office (now Audit Wales), Care and Social Services Inspectorate Wales (now Care Inspectorate Wales) and Healthcare Inspectorate Wales. The IAR bodies committed to working together in collaboration and created a forum for professional dialogue and the exchange of ideas both between inspectors and with service providers. Inspection Wales defined inspection as 'evaluating and publicly reporting on the standards and quality of public services and the impact this service delivery has on people'.[10] The publication of joint reports on the Inspection Wales website provides information to the public about the quality of education, local authority and health services.

The wider UK context has continued to be one of an expansion of IAR activity and there has also been an interest at both UK and devolved government levels in the rationalisation and amalgamation of IAR bodies and functions. In 2007, as part of a reduction from eleven to four 'super-inspectorates' in England, the remit of Ofsted was expanded to include those of three other inspectorates, including the inspection of children's social care services (a function in Wales that was offered to Estyn but turned down), adult learning (which was already within Estyn's remit) and the Children and Family Court (not part of Estyn's remit).[11] In Scotland in 2011, by comparison, Education Scotland was created, based on an amalgamation of Learning and Teaching Scotland, Her Majesty's Inspectorate of Education, the National Continuing Professional Development Team and the Scottish Government's Positive Behaviour Team. There would be a further external review of the IAR bodies in Wales in 2014 which involved consulting stakeholders on a common purpose, core functions and attributes for the four IAR bodies but there have been no published plans for their amalgamation.

3. THE INFLUENCE OF INSPECTORS ON EDUCATION POLICY

From an education policy perspective, Baxter argues that in the context of increasingly decentralised governance across Europe, inspectorates offer 'expertise and opportunity for governments to govern at arm's length'.[12] She contends that inspection plays a key role in the policy networks that have developed as countries move away from traditional, central bureaucratic forms of governance. In Wales, Estyn is part of the machinery of governance: it contributes to more than forty advisory groups, working parties and committees set up to develop and inform national policy and to facilitate its implementation. HMI advise on proposals for school and post-16 reorganisation; and they advise on the allocation of certain grants to education or service providers. HMI appear regularly before the Children, Young People and Education (CYPE) Committee of the Senedd (the Wales Parliament). They produce papers and oral evidence to inform committee scrutiny of legislation and they advise on the thematic reviews and investigations undertaken by the CYPE and other committees. Through their survey reports on themes commissioned in the annual Ministerial remit to Estyn (up to forty reports on various aspects of education provision are requested annually), HMI also provide the Welsh Government and Senedd with insight into progress on national policy priorities. In recent times the priorities have included: tackling child poverty and disadvantage; Welsh-medium education; and children and young people's well-being.[13]

In the complex interactions within the educational system, it is difficult to isolate and evaluate the impact on education policy making of such actions by the inspectorate at a national level, as is indicated in Chapters 7 and 8. Advice in the form of remit reports commissioned for publication by the Minister is published, but these reports often concern policy that is in the process of being implemented or the effectiveness of grants already allocated for specific purposes. Advice which is given as part of the earlier policy-making process is not made public and is protected in law as confidential. But by sharing their first-hand knowledge with Ministers and civil service officials – about the performance of individual schools, the outworking of policy and the state of the educational system in general – it is generally accepted that the inspectorate performs an important role in feeding evidence-led policy making.

Before the devolution of power to a Welsh government, education policy making was the prerogative of UK government Ministers and senior civil servants in Whitehall. HMI in Wales were for the most part relatively remote from their peers in London and limited in the direct contact they could have with civil servants and politicians. Even after the establishment of the Welsh Office in Cardiff in the 1960s, as indicated in Chapter 3, education policy makers remained at one remove from Wales and Welsh Office civil servants were mainly administrators. However, HMI in Wales always sought to inform and influence policy thinking, particularly in relation to those policies that concerned the Welsh language, bilingualism and the Welsh dimension of the school and post-16 curriculum. Their efforts in the nineteenth century did not meet with unalloyed success. In the 1850s and 1860s, although HMI Longueville Jones promoted bilingualism in schools, it was the censorship of his views in annual reports that led to the crisis which resulted in his virtual dismissal from office in 1864.[14] By 1907, as we see in Chapter 2, CI Owen Edwards succeeded in imposing on the Codes for both elementary and secondary schools his vision for a more bilingual curriculum. However, even for that most ambitious and visionary of CIs, it was a challenge to influence policy beyond that which applied narrowly to Wales.

Chapters 3 and 4 offer a vignette that exemplifies how concerns about policy might have been better addressed through inspection. Formal inspection of secondary schools was suspended for much of the 1960s and early 1970s, nominally to ease the pressure of reorganising grammar and secondary modern schools into comprehensive schools, following the issue of Circular 10/65. The difficulties that sometimes arose from the over-hasty planning that failed to adapt teaching strategies to the new environment might have been ameliorated had HMI been allowed to intervene more robustly by means of full inspections.

Chapter 4 describes how, in the same period, there was no central direction for HMI pastoral visiting and no systematic harvesting of information to inform policy thinking. Although surveys were undertaken to monitor a few areas of policy concern, not all surveys led to published reports. Rather, the focus was on supporting individual schools in responding to new reports like the Gittins report on primary education and the initiatives linked to the raising of the school leaving age.

Chapter 7 questions the extent of Estyn's influence on post-devolution education policy. Estyn's reports certainly generated a considerable body of evidence about how well policy initiatives such as the Foundation Phase, the 14–19 Learning Pathways and the Welsh Baccalaureate were implemented and HMI were members of the steering groups involved in developing those policies. However, one of the results of the creation of the Office of Her Majesty's Chief Inspector Wales in 1992 as a non-Ministerial civil service department that was independent of the Welsh Office was to remove HMI from the mainstream civil service in Wales and from structural integration with policy civil servants. By the time that Wales gained the powers to make its own education policy post-devolution, the inspectorate was already both physically and structurally separate from policy departments. While there have always been examples of individual HMI secondments to government, the inspectorate has also been jealous of its status as independent of government.

4. THE IMPACT OF INSPECTION ON PROVIDER IMPROVEMENT

The relationship between inspection and school/provider improvement is relative and indirect and, of course, it is providers themselves that are the primary agents of change. However, HMI have not relied on inspection alone to promote improvement in education. They have published overviews of standards in annual reports and in regular reports on surveys of provision, as noted above. From the early twentieth century, HMI in Wales have published official advice on the curriculum, and in particular on the teaching of Welsh history and the Welsh language, as outlined in Chapter 2. Chapter 4 describes how documents such as *Planning for Progress* in 1982 offered advice on planning a broad and balanced school curriculum, thus prefiguring the National Curriculum of the late 1980s. In their annual and survey reports, HMI have offered detailed exemplification of successful learning, teaching and leadership strategies in schools and other providers. They have regularly hosted and contributed to in-service courses for leaders and aspiring leaders, drawing on findings from inspections. In more recent years, Estyn has held conferences based on published reports about 'journeys of improvement' in which schools have shared their experience of how they have coped with challenge and change. All survey reports have included increasing numbers of case studies that exemplify the detail of successful improvement, including the progress made by schools that had previously been identified by HMI as causes of concern.

As to the impact of inspection itself on individual provider improvement, some academics challenge the very assumption of 'improvement through inspection' while even supporters of inspection concede that there is not a simple cause-and-effect relationship between inspection and improvement.[15] Rather, they maintain that inspection can act as a catalyst for change. As Manès-Bonnisseau, President of the Standing International Conference of Inspectorates (SICI), acknowledges, judging whether inspections have direct impact on individual schools is very difficult to quantify because 'it cannot be shown how schools would behave if there were no inspection at all'.[16]

Over recent decades, there has been a sharper focus on the measurable outputs of pupils and the use of school-level output data to hold schools accountable and to evaluate progress or improvement over time. Chapter 7 identifies the implications of the focus on high-stakes accountability in schools, as summarised by the Global Education Reform Movement (GERM).[17] Despite reservations such as those expressed in Chapter 7 about the reliability of the Programme for International Student Assessment (PISA) tests of 15-year-olds, a series of disappointing results in reading, mathematics and science since 2006 has contributed to a wide-ranging educational reform agenda in Wales designed to raise standards.[18]

One view of the function of inspection that has become particularly prevalent over recent years is of an inspection system that should lead or contribute to school improvement as manifested in student examination outcomes, including in the form of PISA results. The growing focus on expanding the scope and managerialist functions of inspection has led to an expectation that inspection should be seen to 'improve' schools in a measurable and immediate sense. But inspection can never, by itself, guarantee an improvement in student outcomes although most HMI would be able to offer anecdotal evidence in favour of a view that they 'do good as they go' and the scope of inspections has always been wider than that of narrowly focused standardised tests of basic skills.

It can be argued that it is the full inspection of individual schools, colleges or service providers that offers the most direct means to influence improvement with its very externality providing a degree of objectivity. Inspection can act as any external consultancy would, either by supporting an agenda for change or by concluding that there is a need for that agenda and by going on to recommend actions to take. After 1992, schools were required by statute to produce post-inspection action plans for approval by HMI. More recently, schools have received follow-up inspections to evaluate progress in areas identified by HMI for improvement. Researchers have found that even when a school has already identified these areas, inspection feedback is still valued by leaders as a means of reinforcing their agenda for change. A study of primary and secondary school inspections in Germany reported that principals highlighted the usefulness of verbal feedback at the end of inspection as well as the written report. The majority of the 468 principals surveyed reported that developmental activity was taking place a few months after the inspection.[19] In another study of 2,300 principals across seven European countries, those principals who felt 'accountability pressures' were reported to be more active in improvement activities.[20] A survey of head teachers by Ofsted found that four times as many of the respondents reported that the benefits of inspection outweighed the negative effects.[21] The most positive effect among school leaders was felt to be the provision of an objective, external view and a clear focus for the school's future development.

Over recent decades, many publications have identified the importance of leadership and teaching as two important drivers for raising levels of student achievement.[22] Post-inspection school improvement is more likely to follow when leaders and practitioners are receptive to change and external influence. Inspection recommendations can serve as a focal point to galvanise individuals and when leaders and teachers are sufficiently motivated to see inspection as a process in which they participate rather than an event to be endured, they can engage fully with inspection findings and recommendations, and improvement is more likely to follow.

5. HOW THE WALES INSPECTORATE HAS RESPONDED TO CRITICISM

The criticism of inspectors' judgements as inconsistent was a charge first levelled against the inspectors of the mid-nineteenth century. More recently, in the few research studies conducted, consensus rather than difference over inspection judgements has been observed among inspectors. One small-scale study found that when two trained inspectors independently observed the same lesson, they identified the same strengths and weaknesses in the teaching and arrived at similar conclusions about its overall quality.[23]

Estyn has made concerted efforts to respond constructively to any substantiated criticism about inconsistent practices on inspections and has attempted to address anxieties about what inspectors expect of providers by publishing guidance to explode myths about inspectors' expectations. The inspectorate has regularly updated its code of conduct and guidance for inspectors and for provider self-evaluation. Since the 1990s, as described in Chapters 5 and 8, the gradual introduction to inspection teams of peer inspectors from the education sector and nominees recruited from the provider being inspected has added credibility and transparency to the inspection process, while building professional development capacity and capability within the system. School leaders have reported that this has helped improve their analytical skills.[24]

In 2010, Estyn moved from outsourcing its school inspections to bringing them back in-house, as described in Chapter 5. After identifying a trend of awarding over-generous judgements in the 2004 inspection cycle, despite the fact that progress in improving GCSE outcomes was waning, Estyn moved to phase out the use of external contractors and re-establish direct control over the selection and conduct of inspection teams in 2010. Since then, too, the design of software to create a 'virtual inspection room' (VIR) in which inspectors have been able to share freshly recorded evidence and evaluations in real time during inspections has enhanced the corporate approach of inspection teams (Chapter 5 expands on this). The VIR has also enabled a more comprehensive process of post-inspection scrutiny and challenge as part of the quality assurance of reports before they are published.

However transparent the process of inspection is, and despite the involvement of peers on inspection teams, a degree of anxiety in anticipation of inspection is natural. This can sometimes be a positive factor because it can galvanise action. However, where major shortcomings are identified or a school is identified as causing concern, some studies have suggested that school leaders may face post-inspection challenges in rebuilding morale among individuals who have been collectively categorised as low performing.[25] The Wales Institute of Social & Economic Research, Data & Methods (WISERD) reported in 2018 that many teachers believed that anxiety over inspections was a major inhibitor of school improvement. But WISERD also reported that the majority of governors, parents and other interested members of the public who responded to its survey felt that Estyn had an important role in promoting improvement in the educational system.[26] It is worth noting that despite WISERD's 'call for evidence' asking for examples to substantiate the views of stakeholders, very few actually provided examples of poor practice amongst inspectors or provided examples of inspections that they believe captured an inaccurate evaluation of a setting. The authors reported that no alternative forms of accountability were suggested by stakeholders. Moreover, on balance, respondents considered Estyn to be 'very important for improving the quality of education in Wales'.[27]

Over recent years, the view that external inspection represents the best way to improve the quality of education has given way in Wales and elsewhere to a much stronger impetus for internal self-evaluation by schools and providers that enables those who work in them to take more responsibility for their own improvement without being 'managed' by inspectorates. Elmore, Hargreaves and Fullan, among others, have advocated pursuing policies based on promoting teacher professionalism and leadership, encouraging collaborative practices and trust-based, internal accountability in schools rather than traditional forms of external inspection.[28]

In his 2018 review of Estyn, Professor Graham Donaldson acknowledged the difficulty in striking a balance between accountability and improvement.[29] Donaldson also noted that concerns about the inspectorate tended to be subsumed within the broader discussion about the accountability culture, which he perceived as limiting the kind of creativity necessary to underpin a self-improving system. There have been attempts to acknowledge and reconcile the tensions between internal external evaluation in Wales, as in the rest of Europe (Chapter 8 expands on this). Estyn has worked with schools and other providers for over twenty years to combine external and internal aspects of quality assurance by using self-evaluation reports as a starting point for external evaluation and by routinely including peers and nominees (teachers and managers) in its inspection teams. Nevertheless, tensions remain between the vision of a school or provider in which professional autonomy alone generates the drive to improve quality in a self-improving education system and the perceived need for external checks.[30]

ENDNOTES

1. Committee of Council on Education, *Reports of the Commissioners of Inquiry into the State of Education in Wales 1847* (London: HMSO, 1848).
2. O. M. Edwards was known as Owen Edwards in the civil service.
3. Department of Education and Science (DES), *HMI Today and Tomorrow* (London: HMSO, 1970), pp. 12, 26.
4. Derek Rayner, *A Study of HM Inspectorate in England and Wales* (London: HMSO, 1982), pp. 7–8.
5. Estyn, *Annual Plan 2019–1920* (Cardiff: Estyn, 2019), p. 3.
6. Referenced in Howard Davis and Steve Martin, *Public Services Inspections in the UK: Research Highlights 50* (London: Jessica Kingsley, 2008), p. 14.
7. The Prime Minister's Office of Public Services Reform (OPSR), *The Government's Policy on Inspection of Public Services* (London: OPSR, 2003), p. 2.
8. Welsh Assembly Government (WAG), *Inspection, Audit and Regulation in Wales Policy Statement* (Cardiff: WAG, 2008).
9. Philip Hampton, *Reducing administrative burdens: effective inspection and enforcement* (London: HM Treasury, 2005).
10. Inspection Wales, *Briefing: Audit, Inspection and Regulation in Wales* (Cardiff: Inspection Wales, 2016), p. 2.
11. Jane Martin, 'Inspection of Education and Skills: From Improvement to Accountability', in Davis and Martin (eds), *Public Services Inspection in the UK*, p. 55.

12. Jacqueline Baxter, 'School Inspectors as Policy Implementers: Influence and Activities', in J. Baxter (ed.), *School Inspectors: Policy Implementers, Policy Shapers in National Policy Contexts* (Cham, Switzerland: Springer, 2018), p. 2.
13. Thematic reports are available on Estyn's website.
14. H. G. Williams, 'Longueville Jones and Welsh education: the neglected case of a Victorian H.M.I.', *Welsh History Review*, 15/3 (1991), 416–42.
15. Peter Matthews and Pam Sammons, *Improvements through inspection: An evaluation of the impact of Ofsted's work* (London: Ofsted, 2004).
16. Chantal Manès-Bonnisseau, 'Introduction' to Adrian Gray, *European School Inspection and Evaluation: History and Principles* (Bookworm of Retford: Standing International Conference of Inspectorates, 2019), no page number.
17. Pasi Sahlberg, *Finnish Lessons* (New York: Teachers College Press, 2011); Pasi Sahlberg, 'The Global Reform Movement and its Impact on Schooling', in Karen Mundy, Andy Green, Bob Lingard and Antoni Verger (eds), *The Handbook of Global Education Policy* (Hoboken, NJ: Wiley, 2016).
18. Organisation for Economic Co-operation and Development, *Improving Schools in Wales: An OECD Perspective* (Paris: OECD, 2014); OECD, *The Welsh Education Reform Journey* (Paris: OECD, 2017).
19. K. Dedering and S. Müller, 'School Improvement through Inspections? First Empirical Insights from Germany', *Journal of Educational Change*, 12/3 (2011), 301–22.
20. Herbert Altrichter and David Kemethofer, 'Does accountability pressure through school inspections promote school improvement?' *School Effectiveness and School Improvement*, 26/1 (2015), 32–56.
21. Matthews and Sammons, *Improvements through inspection: An evaluation of the impact of Ofsted's work*.
22. Lee Elliot Major and Steve Higgins, *What Works?: Research and evidence for successful teaching* (London: Bloomsbury, 2019); John Hattie, *Visible Learning; a synthesis of over 800 meta-analyses relating to achievement* (London: Routledge, 2009).
23. Peter Matthews, Roger Holmes, Paul Vickers and Bep Corporaal, 'Aspects of the Reliability and Validity of School Inspection Judgements of Teaching Quality', *Educational Research and Evaluation*, 4/2 (2010), 167–88.
24. Robert Hill, *The Future Delivery of Education Services in Wales* (Cardiff: Welsh Government, 2013).
25. Jane Perryman, 'Panoptic Performativity and School Inspection Regimes: Disciplinary Mechanisms and Life under Special Measures', *Journal of Education Policy*, 21/2 (2006), 147–61.
26. Being 71.5 per cent, 361 of 505 respondents. See Chris Taylor, Sally Powell and Rhian Powell, *Independent Review of Estyn's Contribution to Wales' Education Reform Programme* (Cardiff: WISERD, 2018), p. 4.
27. Taylor, Powell and Powell, *Independent Review of Estyn's Contribution to Wales' Education Reform Programme*, p. iii.

28. Richard F. Elmore, *School Reform from the Inside Out: Policy, Practice and Performance* (Cambridge, MA: Harvard Education Press, 2004); Andy Hargreaves and Michael Fullan, *Professional Capital: Transforming Teaching in Every School* (New York: Teachers College Press, 2012); and Michael Fullan, *The New Meaning of Educational Change* (London: Routledge, 2015).
29. Graham Donaldson, *A Learning Inspectorate* (Cardiff: Estyn, 2018).
30. OECD, *Developing schools as learning organisations in Wales* (Paris: OECD, 2017), pp. 16–18.

Chapter 1

ORIGINS AND DEVELOPMENT OF THE INSPECTORATE IN WALES, 1839–1907

Russell Grigg

The aim of this chapter is to provide an overview of the key developments that affected inspection in Wales from its beginnings in 1839 until the establishment of the Welsh Department of the Board of Education in 1907. It is organised in three broadly chronological sections: the first considers the origins of the inspectorate against a backdrop of a rapidly changing Wales in the 1830s and 1840s. The second explores how the role, scope and experiences of inspection in Wales developed in the years between 1850 and 1880, when the Education Department was established. The third discusses how the Welsh Division of the inspectorate, created in 1882, responded to the distinctive educational needs of Wales. The chapter concludes by assessing the contribution of the inspectorate in its formative years to advancing the educational system in Wales.

ORIGINS AND WIDER CONTEXT

As is the case in many countries, the notion of inspecting educational provision in Wales has religious origins. Licences to teach were originally issued by the medieval church whose bishops visited schools to determine the professional competence of its schoolmasters, who trained to become priests. These visitations, which considered both the private and public lives of teachers, were the earliest form of inspection. This tradition continued in a modified form through to the nineteenth century. The Society for the Promotion of Christian Knowledge (1699), the Anglican National Society (1811) and non-denominational British and Foreign School

Society (1814), all employed inspection-agents, such as William Roberts ('Nefydd') who visited British schools in south Wales, to check that their subscribers' money was being used as intended to impart religious instruction. The nature of such instruction, however, bitterly divided the Anglicans and Nonconformists. These tensions were accentuated in many rural communities where the only weekday schools available to children from poor Nonconformist families were run by Anglicans who insisted, according to their school trust deeds, on teaching the catechism.

These religious rivalries also manifested themselves when in 1833 the state offered grants for the building of elementary schools, provided subscribers met half the costs. In 1839 the Committee of the Privy Council on Education (CCE) was established to oversee the spending of such grants and with this came the principle of inspection based on accountability for spending public funds. Dr James Kay (Kay-Shuttleworth after his marriage in 1842), the CCE's able first Secretary, was keen not to offend the various denominations and so secured a compromise which meant that the appointment of inspectors was subject to their approval.

Nonetheless, some Nonconformists suspected that state aid would shore up the interests of the Anglican church, which was already better resourced than were the Nonconformist chapels through the political and financial support of Anglican landowners. But neither the National nor British Societies could keep pace with the fast-changing industrial south-east of Wales. Between 1801 and 1841 the population of Monmouthshire alone increased threefold.[1] Moreover, for social reformers and missionaries, the youthfulness of the population presented an urgent need to rescue the children of Wales from the social and moral temptations of an industrial age. While industrialisation raised standards of living overall in Wales, it also brought overcrowding, the breakdown of traditional mores and a perception that moral laxity was widespread among the poor. Children, in particular, were seen as increasingly vulnerable to what one newspaper article described as 'coarse language, vulgar habits' and other 'animal passions'.[2]

It is not surprising therefore that the social and moral condition of the poor was a recurring theme in the early inspection reports. The first report of the inspectorate for England and Wales, issued in 1840, had much to say about this. Its author, Hugh Seymour Tremenheere, had been assigned to enquire into the educational provision in the mining districts of south Wales, following the 1839 Chartist Rising in Newport. He visited thirty-five schools which were 'for the most part, dirty and close', one of which he found 'so filthy and disgusting that the inquiry had to be conducted from outside'. Few schools had sufficient books and equipment, and teachers kept classroom silence by 'loud exclamations and threats'.[3] Tremenheere estimated that two out of every three working-class children did not attend school in the district. However, he insisted that poverty was not the reason why parents sent their children to work rather than school. He pointed towards the decent working-class wages in the district and suggested that parents preferred to spend their money on pleasure such as drinking, smoking and gambling. Such habits were seen to be corruptible influences on the youth of Wales, with Tremenheere reporting that it was common for boys to boast that they were smoking before they were 12 years of age. The priorities of the 'modern Welshman', at least according to one middle-class newspaper editorial, was 'getting money, go to meeting, drink beer, and chaw [sic] tobacco'.[4]

As far as Whitehall was concerned, education was increasingly seen as a means of civilising the masses in such 'wild' parts of Wales. The fear of seditious activity undermining the social order was a real one, given the 1831 Merthyr Rising, the direct action of groups known as the 'Scotch Cattle' and the Chartist march on Newport. It was reinforced by the Rebecca Riots (1839–43). In the case of the latter, a Commission of Inquiry for South Wales reported that the children of both farmers and workers were 'almost beyond the state of any moral improvement' because of the shortage of schools in the district.[5] While the disturbances required a combination of what one historian has called 'repression, relief and reform',[6] education was regarded as the means of addressing the underlying ignorance among the Welsh working class. As HMI H. W. Bellairs put it in his report on schools in south Wales in 1843:

> an ill-educated, undisciplined population, such as exists among the mines of South Wales, is one that may be found very dangerous to the neighbourhood in which it dwells,

and that a band of efficient schoolmasters is kept up at a much less expense than a body of police or of soldiery.[7]

In the same year, the leading Nonconformist educationalist, Hugh Owen, called upon the people of Wales to support the setting up of British schools. Despite a positive response, the scale of the challenge is indicated by the estimated 40 per cent of Welshmen and 70 per cent of Welshwomen who in 1845 could not write their names.[8]

Wales had a well-respected and successful Sunday school tradition, which focused on teaching people to read the Bible rather than write. What it lacked in comparison to England was a strong middle class to support day-school provision. Put simply, the social demarcation lines in Wales separated landlords who identified with the English gentry in style, language, affiliation to the Anglican church and political support for the Tories, with the disenfranchised working-class, who were mostly Welsh-speaking and associated with Nonconformists, or of no religious affiliation. The historic contribution of the Anglican aristocracy and the religious societies to education in Wales was important but not sufficient. Wales lagged behind England in terms of the proportion of children attending school. One rough estimate is that in 1821 about 85 per cent of children aged between five and fifteen were *not* in school in Wales (compared to 70 per cent in England) and, despite state grants and the concerted efforts of the voluntary societies, even by 1851 this figure was still not much lower than 70 per cent (compared to 55 per cent in England).[9]

It is only within this wider political, religious and social background that the origins and early development of school inspection in Wales can be fully understood. Industrialisation increased the demand for a literate and numerate workforce; social concerns highlighted the need to civilise the masses; and schooling was a means of inculcating religious, moral and cultural values that formed the fabric of society. Given the inadequacies in educational provision, it was argued that the state had a responsibility to intervene. The inspectorate was thus part of the broader educational structure that was being created to establish schools and to ensure that they conformed to state regulations. What was unique about the school inspectorate was that achieving the approval of inspectors was a condition of grant, unlike the inspectors who operated in factories, workhouses and public health. Gradually, the religious difficulties would move to the background as the influence of the churches declined, the inspectorate established itself and the value of weekday education was increasingly recognised by the population.

THE ROLE, BACKGROUND AND APPROACH OF SCHOOL INSPECTORS

The role of the early inspectors, as envisaged by Kay-Shuttleworth, was a supportive one at a time when many areas of England and Wales had poor or no educational provision. He directed Tremenheere and John Allen, the first two Her Majesty's Inspectors (HMI) of schools in England and Wales, to cooperate with local efforts. Their remit was to report on the quality of instruction, the character and discipline of schools and suggest improvements, but not to interfere in the management of schools. They received detailed guidance embodied in the annual Minutes of the Committee of Council on Education. These took the form of *Instructions* and in 1840 they ran to around 10,000 words, including a bank of 140 standard questions.[10] The questions covered a wide range of subjects, including:

- the physical environment: for example, 'Are the schoolrooms sufficiently ventilated and warmed?'
- religious and moral discipline: 'Are the children assembled and dismissed every day with a psalm or hymn, and with prayer?'
- teaching methods: 'How far is the interrogative method used?'
- the teachers: 'state your opinion of the teachers as respects their character; and methods of conducting the school'
- children's attendance and appearance: 'Is punctual and regular attendance enforced?'; 'Do the children appear to be clean? neat?'
- discipline: 'Are corporal punishments employed?' and
- aspects of governance such as finance: 'What amount was expended last year in repairs?'

The inspectors were also provided with specific questions to ask when visiting infant schools such as 'What amusements have the children?' and 'Are the children trained in walking, marching, and physical exercises, methodically?' The range of questions indicated the breadth of the inspection.

Inspectors were appointed with the necessary social and educational standing to engage with managers. Typically drawn from the legal profession or the church, inspectors were well-educated, often Cambridge or Oxford men. Tremenheere's family had a long tradition of public service. He was an Oxford graduate and a practising barrister. John Allen, son of a Pembrokeshire rector and educated at Cambridge, was appointed to inspect church schools in Wales and could at least claim some previous experience in teaching. He had, for example, worked as a teacher (albeit in a privileged proprietary school in London) for two years and acted as examining chaplain to the church's Bishop Otter Teacher Training College in Chichester.

For the Education Department, which was created in 1856, the lack of elementary school teaching experience among inspectors was not seen as a drawback. Rather, it was far more important that they were socially and intellectually respected. Allen, whose brother was the Dean of St David's, relished in-depth conversations about church history and matters of religious instruction, such as whether children could be taught to interpret the scriptures themselves. He was often entertained by prominent patrons to church schools that he inspected, and this was not seen as potentially compromising. They were all gentlemen and expected to behave as such. The much-talented Harry Longueville Jones, who was appointed in 1848 as the first Welsh-speaking inspector and whose duties covered the whole of Wales, co-founded *Archaeologia Cambrensis* (1846) and the ensuing Cambrian Archaeological Association. He also wrote books such as the *Illustrated History of Caernarvonshire* (1845) as well as articles for *Blackwood's Edinburgh Magazine* and other leading periodicals.

Jones's career as a school inspector spanned a period of significant change and illustrates important broader themes in the early history of the inspectorate in Wales. Kay-Shuttleworth hoped that Jones, born in Beaumaris, would demonstrate 'a competent knowledge of the colloquial idiom of the Welch language', pointing out that this was 'a very different thing from a grammatical acquaintance with that language'.[11] Such comments reflected a wider sensitivity around the Welsh language, given the controversies surrounding the publication of the 1847 (Blue Books) *Report of the Commissioners of Inquiry into the State of Education in Wales*. The commissioners' derogatory comments about the morality of the Welsh people and the Welsh language cast a long shadow over a detailed picture of educational poverty.

As barristers, the commissioners Ralph Lingen, Henry Vaughan Johnson and Jelinger C. Symons seem to have viewed their task as 'the preparation of the case for the prosecution'.[12] Jones did his best to present the case for the defence in refuting their claims. On his first inspection tour, in 1849, he visited 190 schools and was impressed by the general teaching quality. His report includes descriptions of teachers who were 'very able', 'studious', 'clever', 'well informed', 'alert' and 'well respected' and a few were exceptionally gifted, like the teacher near Pwllheli who taught Latin to his ablest pupils, or the musically inclined master at Llanidloes whose '*forte* lies in his music' and '*piano* in his temper'.[13] While Jones was not reluctant to criticise teachers, particularly those who treated their position as a stepping-stone to better posts, he understood the pressures teachers faced in a life of 'trial and incessant watchfulness'.[14] His major contribution as an inspector was to advocate the importance of bilingual teaching as a response to the distinctive educational needs of Wales. Jones saw the potential for schools to develop a bilingual youth, which was against the grain of public opinion and the general views of the inspectorate.

Matthew Arnold, the most famous of nineteenth-century HMI, during his time as an inspector in Wales (1852–3) observed that Welsh children 'suffered from the drawback of having to acquire the medium of information as well as the information itself'. He argued that the British government should therefore insist on children acquiring the English language with Welsh preserved only on the grounds of 'philological or antiquarian interest'.[15] In contrast, Jones held the view that teaching Welsh alongside English would benefit children's acquisition of both languages. In his annual report for 1850, Jones wrote:

Although the greater part of the instruction given in Welsh schools is conveyed in English, at the express desire of the parents, yet it is found that the more the two tongues are taught concurrently, and so taught as to elucidate and explain each other, the greater is the progress made in the knowledge of each.[16]

However, Jones struggled to garner support. In his capacity as inspector of church schools, it was difficult for him to be seen as a credible, objective social observer among the Nonconformist communities, while his liberal views upset senior Anglicans such as Bishop Ollivant of Llandaff. Most significantly, Jones was never able to develop a working relationship with Ralph Lingen who was appointed in 1848 to replace an exhausted Kay-Shuttleworth as Secretary to the CCE. Lingen, one of the 1847 commissioners, pursued policies which have been described as a 'disaster' for Wales.[17] In 1852, for example, he refused to sanction the continued allocation of grants to the South Wales and Monmouthshire Training College (Carmarthen) to support bilingual instruction, a novel scheme that had been supported by Kay-Shuttleworth.

More generally, Lingen's managerial style sought to enforce a culture of compliance among inspectors. He took immediate steps to curb the length and scope of all inspectors' reports. And under the direction of Robert Lowe, vice-president of the CCE, in 1859 a stop was put on inspectors' annual conferences. These had been initiated in 1846, where it was customary for inspectors to meet, discuss and occasionally critique education policy. The combination of Lingen's managerialism and Lowe's drive for efficiency savings meant that the scope for inspectors to express their independent views was significantly reduced. By the 1860s, then, a climate of mistrust had developed between inspectors and the combined forces of Lingen and Lowe.[18] While Lowe resigned following a parliamentary inquiry (1864) into inspection reports, his legacy of introducing a system of paying schools by pupils' examination results and attendance remained in place until the mid-1890s.

The Payment by Results scheme followed on from the findings of the Newcastle Commission on Popular Education in England (1858–61), which had been set up to consider what measures, if any, were necessary to extend sound and cheap education to the masses. The appointment of the commission itself was a slight against the inspectorate. Rather than consult widely with inspectors, ten assistant commissioners were employed to gather evidence. Wales received token coverage through the report of John Jenkins, who focused on education in the districts in Merthyr, Neath and Merioneth. The commissioners also considered the question of school inspection. They reported that inspectors had been remiss in some of their duties, such as examining younger children in elementary schools. This provoked the likes of Longueville Jones, Joseph Bowstead and John Reynell Morell (inspectors for Anglican, British and Roman Catholic schools in Wales) to join colleagues in protesting directly to the president of the CCE.[19] One of the key recommendations of the Newcastle Commission was that, while inspection brought benefits, the focus should shift away from general inspection towards examination to test the efficiency of public education. Schools were to be judged on the examination outcomes of their pupils in reading, writing and arithmetic (the 'three Rs'), along with attendance rates. Lowe famously boasted that he would make the educational system either efficient or cheap.

Under the old system, an inspector would examine a sample of children in a class, asking them questions about their learning and general experiences in school, reporting his findings to the head teacher at the end of the visit. Under the Revised Code, inspectors heard *every* child over eight read but confined their questioning to the 'three Rs'. A glimpse of the interaction between inspector and pupils is indicated in the autobiography of HMI Sneyd-Kynnersley. He recalled seven-year-old Angharad who said in Welsh she did not know the answer to 4×4 ('nid wn i ddim') but he concluded that she might pass for her 'frankness, combined with good looks'. Such a comment, disturbing on several levels, reflects the idiosyncratic approach of inspectors irrespective of new regulations from central government.

Historians have discussed at length the consequences of these new changes embodied in the Education Department's Revised Code (1862). This was particularly so during this period when the grants allocated and teachers' salaries hinged on the inspection report. Such high-stakes inspection had the potential to ruin reputations. This is illustrated in the case of James Kelly, a schoolmaster who in 1863 left his post at St David's Roman Catholic school in Cardiff following a poor report. Kelly took the unusual step of making a formal complaint to the Education Department about the conduct of HMI John Reynell Morell. Kelly claimed that the inspector was in the school for less than twenty minutes, during which time the children sat quietly, before Morell hurriedly departed with the words: 'I will make a report sufficient for the grant.'[20]

The investigation that followed was an unsavoury business but illustrated the power of HMI and potential tensions with teachers. Morell drew upon his contacts to try to besmirch Kelly: a colleague informed him that Kelly had been previously suspended for misconduct at another school inspection, while a school manager revealed an incident where Kelly appeared drunk while teaching in Newport. Through such details, Morell presented Kelly as a 'mischievous' and untrustworthy man. Kelly countered by producing his own character references and threatened the inspector: 'I am in full possession of more than one case where your official kindness was such as might bring yourself into very serious trouble.'

The outcome of the investigation was that Morell was dismissed, having refused to resign. Angered at this, Morell sought support from other inspectors (including his cousin, J. D. Morell, a senior inspector) and privately published his own account including all the correspondence. Interestingly, Lingen set aside Kelly's complaints although he did ask Morell how it was possible to examine the standards achieved in eight classes across four or five subjects within such a short time. Officially, Morell was sacked for not keeping an accurate record of his itinerary for 1862 and failing to fulfil his school visits: he had missed 89 out of 153 appointments. In his defence, Morell's schedule was an exacting one. It extended across fifteen counties in England, including Lincoln, Devon, Kent and Warwickshire, as well as Glamorgan and Monmouth. Morell had calculated that between 1860 and 1864 he had travelled across 43,294 square miles, which was nearly equivalent to the combined distance of twenty-four other inspectors. It is not surprising therefore that Morell was tempted to seek shortcuts during inspection visits.

The logistical challenges inspectors faced in adhering to their annual schedule were considerable. The early inspectors had an average assignment of 275 schools a year to visit.[21] They travelled from one school to another, usually via a hired trap or carriage, and between towns using the embryonic rail system. Even by the 1900s, travel was not always a smooth business, particularly in rural Wales during winter. Abel Jones, a junior inspector in 1910, recalled travelling twenty-five miles by trap in the sleet and snow of the Radnorshire hills. Jones frequently slept away from home, finding it difficult to keep up a social life as a young man never knowing 'where and when the calls of the service' would take him away. He described his fourteen-hour working day on inspection, completing paperwork, such as observational notes and expenses, late into the evening. Inspectors were expected to maintain weekly diaries or notebooks and keep these up to date, which proved the downfall of Morell. Being separated from home for long periods and mindful that whatever inspectors said could be easily misconstrued, must have exerted considerable emotional strain. And yet the life of an inspector was generally a comfortable one. Inspectors such as John Allen loved travelling, seeing the beautiful scenery of Wales and the opportunity to meet friends in different parts of the country. The likes of Longueville Jones and Sir John Rhŷs took advantage of breaks in their schedules to explore their scholarly interests in the archaeology of Wales and Celtic inscriptions.

While Morell's case was an exception, in leading to a very public dismissal, the increasingly regulated system exacted its toll on both inspectors and teachers. In the more private worlds of schoolrooms around Wales, the day of inspection was a tense affair. Teachers faced the temptation to fiddle pupil attendance records or add a few marks, knowing the significance of high levels of attendance and attainment levels to the award of the annual grant. The Education Department directed inspectors to remind teachers that, if detected, fraudulent activity would have serious repercussions. In several cases, the officials sought to make an example of false registration by reducing grants or ordering dismissals. Inevitably, a 'cat-and-mouse' relationship developed as teachers sought to outwit inspectors. In such a climate, the tenacity of some inspectors undoubtedly irritated teachers. The headmistress at Llwynypia Colliery Infant School (Glamorgan) was directed to provide the birth certificates of children whose ages the inspector doubted. It transpired that nineteen out of twenty-four children were over the age of eight and therefore, as an infant school, it was not eligible to receive particular grants. To make matters worse, children who were absent were recorded as present and the class register was destroyed in 'a very suspicious circumstance'.[22] The mistress was given a formal warning and lost two-thirds of her grant.

For inspectors, the Revised Code signalled a shift in their wide-ranging role of evaluating the overall quality of provision to narrowly focusing on examining outcomes. Their duties, set out in 1863, were threefold: to examine religious knowledge (where necessary); to examine the subjects prescribed by the Code; and general inspection of the school. However, in practice, examination surpassed inspection. The difficulty for inspectors, as Longueville Jones had found, was that they were caught between toeing the corporate line and expressing their own concerns about their new role. Naturally, there was reluctance to criticise Education Department policy under Lingen and Lowe's regime. This might explain why the benefits of the Revised Code were highlighted in the inspectors' reports from Wales in the 1860s and 1870s. Arguments were put forward that examination data provided a more objective measure of the teacher's effectiveness than relying solely on the subjective views of inspectors. And the Code focused teachers' attention on raising standards in the grant-earning subjects when concerns over pupils' literacy and numeracy skills were widespread.

In the Welsh context any discussion about education was invariably sharpened by heated denominational disputes. And the Education Department could not immunise inspectors from these experiences. Joseph Bowstead, who inspected British schools in south Wales, suggested in the mid-1850s that 'South Wales is a land of Dissenters' where 'the schools best suited for such a population are those based upon the unsectarian principles of the British and Foreign Schools Society'.[23] Such controversial views raised questions over the impartiality of inspectors. A decade later, Bowstead revealed the extent of the conflict between church and chapel: 'a case of contest occurs on almost every application for a building grant', which presented 'great difficulty as to what to do under those circumstances'.[24] Bowstead, who was being questioned by a select committee on the working of the Education Department, refused to be drawn on whether the inspectorate had made wrong decisions as a result. However, he admitted that they were sometimes unable to verify conflicting claims. He cited the example of the village of Trecastle (Carmarthenshire) in which the church claimed three in four villagers were Anglicans, while the Nonconformists countered by saying that four out of five were not. In this particular case, the Education Department issued the grant to build a church school subject to a conscience clause, which was meant to permit Dissenters' children to opt out of religious instruction. The Nonconformists responded by building their own school. The farcical upshot was that, as Bowstead put it, 'there are two schools standing on opposite sides of the road, in a little place which is barely huge enough for one school'. This was not an exceptional case. In 1862 the Rector of Llanfairfechan (Conwy) expressed his anger and incredulity at the Education Department's refusal to grant an extension to the village National school on the grounds of 'wounding the imaginary conscience of an imaginary Dissenter', and queried whether church schools are to be 'crushed out in Wales'.[25]

While such enduring rivalries hindered educational progress in Wales, it is important to emphasise that in the minds of most school supporters, religion was central to their efforts. And inspectors were at the front end of school managers, teachers and others they met who had something to say about education policy and practices. Sometimes, inspectors acted as mediators and arbitrators. In 1857, for example, both Jones and Bowstead were sent to conduct a joint enquiry in Llanelli to try and gather facts to settle sectarian disputes over a school building application.[26] Moreover, HMI views were cited to suit the arguments of different parties. In the case of Llanfairfechan, for example, the Rector had no qualms about pointing to the recommendation of Longueville Jones that the school should be extended in his correspondence with the Education Department.

Clearly something had to be done to address the inefficiencies associated with the denominational basis of school inspection. In practical terms, the system meant that inspectors of National, British and Roman Catholic schools crossed paths when visiting in the same neighbourhood. While HMI continued to inspect church schools, after the 1870 Education Act the inspection of religious instruction was left to diocesan inspectors. The Act also empowered school boards to appoint their own inspectors to, among other things, check that local and central regulations were being followed by the newly established board schools. HMI commented upon the variable quality of the newly elected school boards in Wales. In 1876, the Reverend E. T. Watts lamented the deplorable apathy which characterised the majority of school boards in Anglesey, with ten out of twelve boards formed compulsorily since 1871. Watts privately described the challenges he faced as 'Anglesey curses' as he steered his way through church-chapel disputes, idle school boards and the politics of triennial school board elections.[27] Also, in 1876, HMI William Williams deplored the 'lack of independence and moral courage' among small school boards in rural south-west Wales in enforcing by-laws on compulsory attendance.[28] As the agent of Lord Powis told a Parliamentary Inquiry in 1902, the problem in mid Wales was compounded when the school board officers themselves, as small-scale farmers, employed their own children in the fields, while magistrates were reluctant to convict. He estimated that during the harvest between 40 and 50 per cent of children were absent from schools in his Welshpool district.

The third section of this chapter discusses changes in HMI role, composition and activity in the late nineteenth and early twentieth century. These were commensurate with an expanding educational system and gradual recognition of the distinctiveness of Wales, particularly in areas of language and culture.

THE WELSH DIVISION

Reflecting the need to accommodate the growth in the educational system and the distinctive needs of Wales, by 1882 there were 124 HMI and 123 AI to assist them, in England and Wales, under the overall guidance of ten chief inspectors.[29] Wales and Monmouthshire had its own division, sub-divided into ten districts: Aberystwyth, Cardiff, Carmarthen, Caernarfon, Denbigh, Merthyr Tydfil, Monmouth, Montgomery, Pembroke and Swansea. Nine of the districts had their own assigned HMI and AI, while Merthyr and Aberystwyth each had a sub-inspector and William Williams headed the division as CI. He was a former agent of the British Society and principal of Swansea Training College, widely respected without the 'slightest breath of suspicion of unfairness or bias'.[30] In 1887, Williams had a total staff of twenty-two inspectors: nine HMI, two sub-inspectors and eleven assistant inspectors. While the bulk of inspection activity continued to focus on elementary schools, the scope of the inspectorate gradually extended to include provision in particular settings such as reformatories, industrial training ships, evening classes and special schools, for example the Swansea and Cardiff schools for the blind and deaf.

By the 1890s, the Education Department had recognised that the role of the inspector needed to return to one that was more like the role envisaged by Kay-Shuttleworth, when the emphasis was on providing advice and guidance to improve schools, rather than a preoccupation with 'proving' the success of the school through the narrow lens of conducting examinations and checking attendance rates. This had brought much despair, summed up by a schoolmaster in Wales writing in 1890: 'I feel heartless in trying to continue with such irregular attendance, and such discouraging report from the Inspector is enough to eat the very life out of a poor fellow.'[31] And for their part, most inspectors welcomed the end of Payment by Results. In 1896, HMI L. J. Roberts told an audience of teachers in Rhyl that he 'hail[ed], the advent of the more rational system with enthusiasm'.[32] In his report, he referred to the healthier tone in schools and inspectors who were much happier donning the role of 'friendly adviser' rather than 'mere assessor of grants'.[33] Despite the open support of inspectors for such changes, it took time, commitment and training for teachers to gain confidence and move away from teaching by rote and mechanical means of instruction. However, by the 1900s there were signs of more variety in teaching and the curriculum through, for example, field visits, local study, school museums and the creation of school gardens.

Throughout the period under consideration the post of HMI in Wales was confined to men. As Williams discusses in a later chapter in this volume, the Welsh Division borrowed female junior inspectors from England. In 1899, the Cardiff school board successfully lobbied the Education Department for the support of a female inspector. It pointed out that two-thirds of teachers in

Cardiff were women and the prevalence of domestic subjects such as sewing, cooking and laundry work, as well as growing interest in kindergartens, were seen as areas where women were better qualified than men to inspect. The Education Department responded by sending Katherine Bathurst, who had been appointed in 1897 as a sub-inspector in London, although her stay in Cardiff was a short one. In England, the creation in 1905 of a women's inspectorate under Maude Lawrence, as its CI, was a sign that the Board of Education recognised the need to extend its scope.

The continued expansion of the inspectorate was necessary to keep pace with educational developments in the closing decades of the nineteenth century. These included the introduction of free elementary education, compulsory attendance, the raising of the school leaving age and the setting up of higher elementary schools. The latter offered fee-paying pupils the opportunity to study in more depth specific subjects such as chemistry, mechanics, Latin and French. HMI William Edwards, at the opening of the Rhondda Fach Higher Grade School in Ferndale, suggested that such an institution would provide 'a finishing touch' for those leaving elementary school.[34] The editor of the *Cardiff Times* welcomed these schools as offering 'a leg up' for the working classes who could not afford to attend grammar schools.[35]

The development of evening classes in subjects which met the needs of districts, such as book-keeping, shorthand, cookery, woodcarving, ambulance work and handicrafts, represented another stream of work for inspectors. This was not a new initiative. As early as the 1850s, Longueville Jones had called for the setting up of evening navigational schools along the Welsh coast to teach seamanship skills, arguing that this would represent 'a really national boon' given that so many boys went to sea after leaving school.[36] As was his custom, Jones could not restrain himself from criticising what he perceived to be a lack of official interest in such ventures and the discouragement this brought to the Welsh people. By the end of the century, although progress had been slow and patchy, inspectors were reporting a more positive picture of evening school provision. In 1898, HMI Wakefield applauded the Cadoxton Evening Class where the school board arranged to repay students their fees if they met an attendance threshold of 85 per cent.[37] At Llangollen Evening

School, the visiting HMI in 1908 reported on excellent work in drawing and the advanced class in Welsh where students prepared for the Eisteddfod.

The increased provision of higher elementary schools and evening classes in Wales was symptomatic of the need for a system of secondary schools for the working classes. The Taunton Commission's report of 1868 drew attention to the serious lack of secondary schools: in Wales, twenty towns averaging a population of 11,000 had no grammar school, including the likes of Merthyr, Cardiff and Caernarfon.[38] The Aberdare Committee (1881) reiterated the urgent need for improvement in Welsh secondary education, particularly for girls. The subsequent passing of the Welsh Intermediate and Technical Education Act (1889), which was one of the first pieces of legislation to apply only to Wales, created a system of secondary schools thirteen years before England and is rightly regarded as a landmark in Welsh education.

Arrangements to inspect the new intermediate schools, however, were not straightforward. The Central Welsh Board (CWB) was established in 1896 to administer the schools' inspection and examination arrangements, under the direction of its own chief inspector, Owen Owens. The schools were also visited by London-based inspectors from the Science and Art Department. This presented schools with organisational problems, as the syllabuses for these two bodies differed. The question of what role the Board of Education inspectors (Welsh Division) should play within the intermediate school system was raised in parliament in 1906. Technically speaking, the Board's inspectors had the powers to inspect all schools under the Welsh Intermediate and Technical Education Act. They could also inspect the training of pupil teachers provided by the schools. In practice, however, most inspections were undertaken by CWB inspectors while the Board's inspectors concentrated on elementary schools and training colleges. Given these complications, at times, relationships between the different inspectors were strained reflecting contested priorities, different personalities, or political manoeuvring.

While much of the inspection activity within the Welsh Division focused on schools, inspectors also visited teacher training colleges. Since the opening of the residential colleges at Carmarthen (1848),

Caernarfon (1856) and Bangor (1862), inspectors had reported each year on areas such as the standards of student teachers' work, staffing, the curriculum, finance, resources and the management of the college. The portfolio of inspections widened with the opening of Swansea Training College in 1872, which first presented women with an opportunity to train as teachers in Wales, and the establishing of day training colleges in 1890 linked to the university colleges at Aberystwyth, Bangor and Cardiff.

Historically, the main route into teaching was through the pupil teacher training scheme. Originally introduced in 1846, academically able girls and boys (aged between 13 and 18) spent five years in school under the guidance of a head teacher, teaching classes and receiving daily training for a small payment. During their visits, inspectors examined the progress of pupil teachers and those who were successful at the final fifth-year examinations could enter a two-year training college programme. One of the concerns frequently raised by inspectors was the lack of time for pupil teachers to study. Hence in the 1880s, there was renewed support for pupil teachers to attend separate centres for half-a-day's training away from the schoolroom. This called for additional inspection time to visit such centres, but the move was broadly welcomed by the inspectorate. In both Swansea and Cardiff, inspectors initially reported improvements in the quality of pupil teachers as a result of attending the central day classes. William Edwards, however, was concerned that young and inexperienced first- and second-year pupil teachers were being asked to cover for those withdrawn to attend classes. There were also particular challenges for rural pupil teachers who, at best, made their way to the nearest intermediate school for their instruction. Others had to settle for correspondence courses. HMI L. J. Roberts in his report for the Denbigh district in 1901 spoke up for their 'staying power and reserve of unexhausted fertility of the native soil, which enables them to go farther in the long run'.[39]

This pupil teacher apprenticeship route into teaching was the subject of a major Departmental Committee review in 1896, chaired by the Reverend T. W. Sharpe, senior chief inspector of schools in England. Two years later, the report concluded that it was 'economically wasteful and educationally unsatisfactory' to leave the teaching of classes to 'immature and uneducated young persons'.[40] The Board of Education, established in 1899 as the main administrative body replacing the Education Department, introduced important reforms to the pupil teacher system. Through its 1903 regulations, the Board effectively put an end to the employment of pupil teachers in school to allow them to continue their fulltime education. It did so by raising the minimum age to sixteen, although fifteen was set as a lower limit in rural areas. Inspectors were therefore no longer required to report on pupil teachers in school. Replacement bursar and student teacher schemes put the emphasis on prospective teachers following an extended secondary education, teaching practice and college study.

As well as teacher training, university colleges (as well as schools) provided classes in science and art, which attracted grants and inspection. Originally, these had been administered by the Science and Art Department of the Board of Trade, based in South Kensington, until this was moved to the Education Department in 1856. By the 1890s, Captain T. B. Shaw, chief inspector for the sciences and arts, was suggesting that Wales was holding its own in secondary provision but admitted that it was lacking in technical instruction. He highlighted the example of the department of applied science and technology at the University College, Cardiff, which offered technical instruction to students who did not intend to graduate. The university authorities in Aberystwyth offered classes in a bewildering range of subjects, including machine construction, building, model drawing, monochrome painting, architecture, magnetism and electricity, hygiene and botany.

While criticisms were levelled against the intermediate schools for failing to promote the scientific and technical knowledge much needed by the Welsh economy, more than 10,000 children gained from a secondary education hitherto denied to them.[41] As HMI Legard put it, a bridge had been established between the elementary school and the university and, as far as Wales was concerned, it was pretty complete.[42] In 1904, the House of Commons was informed that the quality of education in ninety-one out of the ninety-five intermediate schools was either good or excellent.[43]

The passing of the 1902 Education Act led to the creation of local education authorities (LEAs) and administrative changes within the inspectorate. The eleven chief inspectors in England and Wales, including A. G. Legard, in charge of the Welsh division since 1896, were renamed divisional inspectors. In practice this meant they took overall responsibility for inspecting elementary schools within the LEAs as well as the training colleges. They were supported by district inspectors (DIs) and accountable to one chief inspector, who was the main channel of communication between the inspectorate and the Board of Education. The DIs were expected to play a key role in advising the new local education authorities.

One area in which the inspectorate could have played a more decisive role was in promoting the Welsh language among LEAs and their predecessors, the school boards. There were individual inspectors who echoed the sentiments of Longueville Jones. In 1877, for example, Robert Temple encouraged schools in Welsh-speaking areas of Monmouthshire to make full use of Welsh in teaching English instead of 'tabooing their mother tongue as English is tabooed in the French hour in a Young Ladies' Academy'.[44] Thomas Darlington, an accomplished linguist from Cheshire who had learned Welsh, was another inspector committed to promoting bilingualism. But the most notable inspectors in promoting the Welsh language in education were Dan Isaac Davies and William Edwards. Davies had been appointed in 1871 as an assistant to Edwards, affectionately known as 'Edwards of Merthyr'. Davies was regarded as one of 'the most progressive educationalists of his day' whose premature death was described as 'a national calamity'.[45] He was a key figure behind the Society for the Utilisation of the Welsh Language, set up in 1885 at the Aberdare National Eisteddfod. This proved an effective pressure group in ensuring that Welsh became a grant-earning subject on the curriculum, albeit an optional one and one that, where it was used at all, would be taught mostly to help pupils learn English.

Edwards, whose impressive inspection career spanned thirty-eight years (1877–1915), argued that, as Welsh was the home language of most children, it was expedient to teach the language correctly in school. Contrary to the traditional view that Welsh was a handicap to business, Edwards pointed out that a good grammatical knowledge of Welsh would benefit children when applying for jobs. He also maintained that bilingual instruction improved children's thinking and expression; the spread of English would not be affected because children would be required to translate using both languages. As the argument for bilingual instruction had already been won on the continent as well as in Scotland and Ireland, Edwards continued, Welsh children should not be culturally disadvantaged.

Despite such individual voices of support, the inspectorate was still not seen as a proactive body in support to the Welsh language. This was despite the fact that inspectors had been directed in 1893 to encourage bilingual teaching by themselves 'making use of Welsh in testing children's intelligence' in Welsh-speaking districts.[46] What was needed was stronger commitment at the senior level of leadership for the teaching of Welsh and not simply as a means of facilitating a better understanding of English. In 1896, following the sudden death of William Williams, Albert G. Legard, a Yorkshireman, had been appointed as a non-Welsh-speaking senior inspector for Wales. In the face of public criticism in the press, Sir John Gorst (Vice-President of the CCE) defended his decision on the grounds that Legard was assigned to the eastern part of Wales where Welsh was not widely spoken. He added that Legard's duties were to oversee the work of the inspectorate rather than examine pupils or inspect schools where, he acknowledged, a knowledge of Welsh was necessary in Welsh-speaking areas.

These arguments failed to convince Welsh MPs and other interested parties. Tudor Howells of Wrexham put it plainly: 'We must have a man who is capable of examining children in the language they speak.'[47] T. C. Thomas from Bedlinog regarded the matter as 'the greatest affront to the Welsh national sentiment' by the British government, adding that any Welshman holding public office in England would be expected to be fluent in English.[48] The *Merthyr Times* assumed more colourful language, regarding the choice as 'a serious blunder' and another example of 'the thick-headed Saxon stupidity and purblind, hectoring tyranny which had made England's name hated not only in Wales, but the world over'. The editorial regarded the appointment as a 'slap in the face' of Welsh nationality.[49] It was bemused that a serious candidate such as the Welsh-speaking and widely respected William Edwards was overlooked, concluding this was politically motivated because Edwards was neither a Tory nor a churchman. The editorial trumped: 'It is too late in the day to regard inspectorships as snug berths for any Tom, Dick or Harry who may happen to be able to pull the official wires.' The editor of *Wales* adopted a more measured tone. He acknowledged that it is 'taken for granted in some quarters that he will not follow the example of Mr Williams in encouraging the use of Welsh for the teaching of English and the general development of the mind' but he could not 'believe that an inspector of the reputation and experience of Mr Legard will strike such a blow at Welsh education.'[50] The editor in question was Owen M. Edwards, who was to replace Legard as CI himself in 1907 and whose outstanding contribution to Welsh education is discussed in detail in the next chapter. In stark contrast to the appointment of Legard, the news of his replacement was eulogised by one newspaper reporter: 'there is no living Welshman who has wider or closer knowledge of Wales or is more in sympathy with the national life'.[51]

CONCLUSION

During its first seventy or so years, HMI in Wales made an important contribution to shaping education at different levels. Their reports steered government policy by providing grounded knowledge based on classroom observations. And at times a few inspectors, such as Longueville Jones, were willing to question the direction of policy and legislation which they considered detrimental to educational progress in Wales. Particularly in the early period, when transport and communication were more limited, the inspectors acted as an important source of networked knowledge, linking the various agents to regional and central news. They exercised a form of discursive power, manifested through their conversations and reports. At other times, they were effectively arbitrators in disputes and had to tread carefully so as not to offend strongly held religious views. For most teachers, while the day of inspection undoubtedly created feelings of anxiety, there is also evidence to show that they respected the views of inspectors on the basis of their prestige and expertise.[52] This was particularly so when inspectors stood up for teachers in the days before the development of professional organisations or trade unions. For example, inspectors commented upon the inadequacies of teachers' pay and working conditions.

Perhaps only a few within the inspectorate received the lavish praise heaped on sub-inspector Edward H. Short, who 'won golden opinions from the teachers of North Cardiganshire' for his 'ability, courtesy and impartiality' and whose manner presented himself as a 'jovial friend' among younger children.[53] Still, as a body, the nineteenth-century HMI established the principle of speaking without fear or favour. For example, in 1882 the headmaster at Bistre school (Flintshire) was reprimanded by HMI Owen Morgan in front of the vicar and the whole school for inflicting what the inspector called 'unreasonable and cruel' punishment using 'the flat and short stick' upon a group of latecomers, despite the headmaster's protestations that this was 'lenient and human and not objected to by children or parents'.[54]

At various times through this period, individual inspectors also recognised and spoke up for the distinctive needs of education in Wales, such as the challenges facing isolated rural schools. And while the Welsh Division fell short in terms of coordinated support for the teaching of Welsh in school for its own value, inspectors were beginning to support a more distinctive curriculum in Wales.[55] It would take the vision, passion and commitment of a new CI to take this to the next level.

ENDNOTES

1. From 45,568 to 134,368. Neil Smelser, *Social Paralysis and Social Change: British Working-Class Education in the Nineteenth Century* (Berkeley, CA: University of California Press, 1991), p. 154.
2. *Monmouthshire Merlin*, 7 March 1857.
3. H. S. Tremenheere, 'Report of Mr. Seymour Tremenheere on the State of Elementary Education in the Mining District of South Wales'; Appendix 1, Minutes of the Committee of the Privy Council on Education, 1840 (hereafter, 'Minutes' and, after 1858, 'CCE Report'), 208–18.
4. *Cardiff and Merthyr Guardian*, 26 September 1846.
5. *Report of the Commissioners of Inquiry for South Wales* (London, 1844), p. 116.
6. Smelser, *Social Paralysis and Social Change: British Working-Class Education in the Nineteenth Century*, p. 172.
7. Minutes 1843–4, Report by Rev. H. W. Bellairs, 108.

8. Gareth Elwyn Jones, *Modern Wales: A Concise History* (Cambridge: Cambridge University Press, 1984), p. 287.
9. Smelser, *Social Paralysis and Social Change: British Working-Class Education in the Nineteenth Century*, p. 160.
10. Minutes 1840–1, 1–15.
11. *The Times*, 6 January 1849, 5.
12. Frank Smith, *The Life and Work of Sir James Kay-Shuttleworth* (London: James Murray, 1923), p. 204.
13. Minutes 1849–50, 241, 539.
14. Minutes 1849–50, 606.
15. Marvin, F. S. (ed.), Matthew Arnold, *Reports on Elementary Schools 1852–1882*, Report for 1852 (London: HMSO, 1908), p. 11.
16. Minutes 1849–50, 511.
17. H. G. Williams, 'Longueville Jones, Ralph Lingen and inspectors' reports: a tragedy of Welsh education', *History of Education*, 25/1 (1996), 31.
18. According to Sylvester, 'Probably no man has been so universally condemned by educationalists as Lowe'. David Sylvester, *Robert Lowe and Education* (London: Cambridge University Press, 1974), p. 33. However, there are more sympathetic accounts of Lowe. For example, see Christopher Duke (1965) 'Robert Lowe – a Reappraisal', *British Journal of Educational Studies*, 14/1 (1965), 19–35.
19. Memorial addressed by certain Her Majesty's Inspectors of Schools to the Lord President, April 1862.
20. 'Copy of all correspondence relating to the Dismissal of Mr. Morell from the Office of Her Majesty's Roman Catholic Inspector of Schools', 1864.
21. John Hurt, *Education in Evolution* (London: Rupert Hart-Davis, 1971).
22. Log Book of Llwynypia Infants School, 21 November 1878 (GRO E/R 22/1).
23. Minutes 1854–5, 635–42.
24. Report from the Select Committee on Education, 1865. Evidence of HMI Joseph Bowstead, q. 3059.
25. Letter from P. C. Ellis to Ralph Lingen, 15 December 1862 in 'Copy of Correspondence Between the Education Department of the Privy Council and the Applicants for Grants towards Building or Enlarging Schools in the Parishes of ..., *Llanfairfechan*, *Winster*, and *Cwmamman*', 57.
26. Correspondence between the Committee of Council on Education (CCE) and the Promoters of National and British Schools and any other Parties, as relates to the Establishment of National or British Schools at Llanelly, Carmarthen, 1862.
27. David Petty, *Two Centuries of Anglesey Schools* (Anglesey: Anglesey Antiquarian Society, 1977).
28. CCE Report 1876–7, 647.
29. 'Return of Number of Inspectors of Public Elementary Schools, Scale of Pay and Average Attendance of Children', 1870, 1880 and 1889.
30. *The County Echo*, 3 December 1896.

31. Pamela Horn, *Education in Rural England 1800–1914* (Dublin: Gill & Macmillan, 1978), p. 129.
32. *Rhyl Journal*, 13 June 1896.
33. CCE Report for 1895–6, 10.
34. *The Pontypridd Chronicle and Workman's News*, 9 September 1892.
35. *Cardiff Times*, 21 October 1882.
36. CCE Report 1853–4, 588.
37. *Barry Dock News*, 1 April 1898.
38. *Report of the Schools Inquiry Commission*, 1868, Vol. 1/423.
39. CCE Report 1901–2, 51.
40. *Report of the Departmental Committee on the Pupil Teacher System*, 1898, 5.
41. Gareth Elwyn Jones and Gordon Roderick, *A History of Education in Wales* (Cardiff: University of Wales Press, 2003), p. 95.
42. CCE Report for 1897–8, 20.
43. Board of Education, *Report on the Administration of Schools under the Welsh Intermediate Act* (London: HMSO,1889), p. 7.
44. CCE Report for 1877–8, 566.
45. *Weekly Mail*, 4 June 1887; *South Wales Daily News*, 30 May 1887.
46. Board of Education, *Report of the Imperial Education Conference* (London: HMSO, 1911), pp. 256–7.
47. Cited by O. M. Edwards, 'Elementary Schools', *Wales*, IV/35, March 1897, 65. The Welsh-medium press was equally vociferous in its criticisms of Legard's appointment. See *Y Werin*, 20 March 1897; *Tarian Y Gweithiwr*, 31 December 1896.
48. *South Wales Daily News*, 26 December 1896.
49. *The Merthyr Times*, 31 December 1896.
50. *Wales*, March 1897, Vol. IV, 65.
51. *Weekly Mail*, 16 February 1907.
52. R. Grigg, '"Wading through children's tears": the emotional experiences of elementary school inspections, 1839–1911', *History of Education*, 49/5 (2020), 597–616.
53. *The Aberystwith Observer*, 3 January 1885.
54. J. C. Jones, 'A History of the Schools and Education in Buckley', *Flintshire Historical Society*, 55/15 (1954), 87.
55. For example, the Welsh Division encouraged the use of Welsh songs and poetry in 1893 and HMI L. J. Roberts composed hymns for schools. *Carnarvon and Denbigh Herald*, 26 June 1908.

Chapter 2

OWEN EDWARDS, THE WELSH DEPARTMENT AND THE SCHOOL CURRICULUM, 1907–1925

Ann Keane

Although Wales as a region in an 'England and Wales' inspectorate had had senior inspectors of schools before 1907, it was not until Owen Edwards[1] was appointed Her Majesty's Chief Inspector of Education in Wales that a distinct body of inspectors was allocated to Wales as part of a newly established Welsh Department. The appointment of Edwards – who had been an editor of the radical journal *Cymru Fydd* (*Young Wales*) – was seen as decisively political by MPs in a period during which there had been sustained but unsuccessful agitation both in Wales and in parliament for a National Council of Education for Wales. Had it been established, and established as envisioned by Lloyd George, this would have been a body that would have funded and overseen education in Wales independently of England. Despite further, persistent attempts to establish a devolved National Council both during and after the period between 1907 and 1925, Wales would continue to be governed from Whitehall and the two countries would share, for the most part, a common regulatory framework for education and inspection. Nevertheless, establishing a Welsh Department with its own inspectorate reflected an increasing degree of autonomy in practice. The Welsh Department was the first civil service department to deal with Wales separately from England. It was part of the Board of Education but had its own permanent secretary in Alfred T. Davies. At a time when Lloyd George was powerful in British politics, Welshmen could expect preferment and, of course, without the success of the Liberal Party in Wales and of Lloyd George, it is difficult to see how Edwards could have become CI in the first place and nor how the Welsh Department could have come into being.

The first section of the chapter deals with the role of inspectors in Wales between 1907 and 1920, including their approach to inspection, reporting and other responsibilities.

The second section of the chapter has a focus on the role of Edwards and his organisation of a new cadre of Welsh Department inspectors. The section goes on to describe the continuing attrition between the Welsh Department and the Central Welsh Board (CWB) whose duty to administer and inspect intermediate schools overlapped with the remit of HMI. This section also deals with the struggle between the Board of Education, whose perspective and values were those of an English hegemony, and a Welsh Department that was attempting to assert a Welsh identity for itself in relation to its parent body. The section ends with a summary of developments between 1920, when Edwards died in post, and 1925 when Davies took early retirement.

The third section of the chapter addresses the extent of the impact of Edwards on the teaching of Welsh and in Welsh, and on the inclusion of a wider Welsh dimension in a school curriculum that had long been anglicised. While Edwards took a strong stand on many matters to do with the school curriculum, teaching methods, examinations more generally, he was particularly concerned with the status of Welsh as a subject and as a medium for teaching in schools, particularly in Welsh-speaking areas.

A concluding section summarises the overall impact of Edwards's leadership and mission.

1. THE ROLE OF INSPECTORS: INSPECTING AND REPORTING

In 1907 the Board of Education's permanent secretary, Robert L. Morant, issued a *Circular to Inspectors* in which he outlined the 'province' of the inspectorate:

> it is the special province of the Central Authority, not merely to test the efficiency of all schools in respect of which it distributes Parliamentary Grants, but also and in particular to organise efficient sources of educational information, and

to disseminate in convenient fashion results, criticisms and suggestions, derived from continuous recorded observation of educational experiments and of the daily work of the various kinds of schools and teachers.[2]

Thus, a fundamental function of the inspectorate was to hold providers of education accountable to the state for the funding they received. Implicit in the use of the word 'efficiency' was the notion of 'value for money' and a school had to be recognised as 'efficient' to qualify for a grant. HMI had a continuing duty to report on compliance with state-set regulations that were updated annually. Morant added that inspectors were also to take note of the 'experimental' in addition to the presumably routine 'daily work'. Inspectors were to gather information that would inform government about the state of education as well as to offer criticism and suggestions to the education system on how to improve. 'Efficiency' and 'effectiveness' would continue to be key words in guidance for inspectors up to the twenty-first century.

One of the inspectors appointed by Edwards, Abel J. Jones, asserted in a memoir that 'the major part of an inspector's job was to inspect'.[3] He added that:

> Junior inspectors were expected ... to inspect schools for 10 half days each week ... After these inspections we would report on about one school in three, so that all schools would be reported on once in three years.[4]

Jones would spend additional time travelling and making notes beyond the ten half days in the schools themselves. The reports would be sent to the schools (where a summary would be recorded in school logbooks) and to the district inspector (DI). Jones commended the diagnostic and advisory role of inspectors:

> an inspector is a specialist and not a purveyor of patent medicines. He goes to the school, and after considering all the circumstances – the neighbourhood; the capacity of the children; the size of the classes; the qualities and qualifications of the teachers; the amenities of the equipment and

school buildings, etc., etc., etc. – he prescribes as a specialist the treatment he thinks best for that particular school. An experienced inspector feels that he is on safe ground when he follows this method.[5]

Inspectors recorded their findings in notes of visit (NoVs) and Owen Edwards's NoVs are based on the templates that were in common use across Wales and England.[6] Typically, the headings included whole-school aspects such as: staffing, school organisation, buildings, library, ethos; and specific curriculum subjects such as English, arithmetic, history and geography, music and drawing. The list of subjects might also include needlework, laundry, handicraft, hygiene and school gardens. Although there was some leeway, the pattern of school and provider visits was fairly standard and involved gathering information from lesson observations, the testing of pupils, scrutiny of their books and of the school's records (the course of instruction; approved syllabus; daily, weekly, monthly records of work done and progress made, by class and head teachers; including the reports of the latter to parents; and the examinations set, together with their results):

> Inspectors ... deal not only with tests and class attainments, but also with methods of teaching and school organisation, and [they] discuss with the teachers, from their wider and more varied experience of schools, matters of educational interest, and of progress in methods and results.[7]

In Edwards's handwritten inspection notebooks, those he used on school and college visits, he recorded in some schools the answers to an *aide memoire*:

1. Are children taught to think/speak?
2. Is Arithmetic suitable, practical?
3. Is local history taught?
4. Are examinations (1) held (2) records kept (3) results summarised: given to parents or children reported upon [?]
5. Are lessons prepared by teachers [?]

6. Handicraft (?) Manual work?
7. Playgrounds [.]
8. Connection with evening schools.[8]

Initial notes on schools were recorded in situ, in Welsh or English according to the language medium of lessons being observed. Inspectors would undertake one- or half-day visits to schools as part of their monitoring of individual schools and to inform surveys of wider provision. They also inspected teacher training colleges and technical, adult, art and design education (supported by specialists from England). Administrative control of the inspection of technical education in Wales was transferred to the Welsh Department from 1911 onwards.

In the 1910s, inspectors began to report on education provision within local education authorities (LEAs). Triennial 'area' inspection reports were published from 1910–11 onwards, with one aim being to bring 'the work of elementary, secondary and technical and further education in Wales to a closer relationship than has hitherto been possible'.[9] These reports were detailed and some progress can be traced in a comparison of standards between the first tranche of reports in 1911–12 and the second in 1913–14. Sir Lewis Amherst Selby-Bigge, the Board's permanent secretary from 1911 to 1925, promoted the benefits of a new approach to partnership working between HMI and LEAs, which had been established as decentralised bodies in 1902. Nonetheless, LEAs were occasionally reluctant to implement central directives or even legislation, and there were several instances of rebellion. As LEAs matured, they began appointing their own inspectors. Given that the Central Welsh Board already had its own inspectors working in intermediate schools at this time, this meant that HMI no longer had a monopoly of school inspection.

HMI had had less direct influence on the reduction or withdrawal of grants from elementary schools since the demise of Payment by Results in the mid-1890s. Introduced by Lowe's Revised Code of 1862, this crude and much-criticised system required HMI to test pupils annually, mainly on their attainment in the 'three Rs' through the medium of English. Welsh was not a grant-earning subject under the Payment by Results system until the 1890s and its use by pupils was criticised by most HMI and punished in many schools. Beriah Evans, in his evidence to the Cross Committee in 1887, admitted that 'I, as a schoolmaster did what was at one time an universal custom, and caned my boys for using in my hearing their mother tongue.'[10]

From 1907 the Welsh Department set out separate regulations for Welsh as a subject and medium in schools but there was no longer a direct link between the standards achieved, in Welsh or any other subject, and the payment of grants. As the role of HMI evolved to be more advisory than punitive under Morant and Selby-Bigge's leadership of the Board of Education in the early twentieth century, so did the influence of HMI become more diffuse. Inspectors were no longer the feared annual examiners on whose judgement of efficacy the sustainability of a school depended. HMI had become 'itinerant ambassadors of technical competence and good will'.[11] This change made it impossible for a new generation of HMI to strengthen the position of Welsh in the curriculum by threatening the financial sanctions that a failure to teach English would have inflicted under the system of Payment by Results. HMI now had to work more by means of encouragement and persuasion. The funding of schools still depended on an HMI judgement of them as efficient but the definition of efficiency was becoming ever more relative. Schools that did not teach Welsh would not be deemed inefficient on that score.

The role of inspectors: annual reports

Nowadays, the function of inspecting and reporting on standards has a greater focus on public assurance – the publication of reports for parents and the public more generally – than it did a century ago when reporting to government took priority. But even in the early twentieth century, annual reports on standards in education were being published and sold to an audience beyond civil servants and policy makers.

The Board of Education's annual reports, covering England and Wales, comprised a comprehensive account of standards in education, based on HMI judgements. A separate annual report was produced under the 1889 Welsh Intermediate Education Act on standards in intermediate schools in Wales. From 1907 onwards, the annual reports evolved from presenting a largely generalised set of findings for both England and Wales to presenting findings in separate sections. The Wales sections expanded gradually over time to being on a par in length and content with those for England. Although both countries had issues in common, the sections on Wales offered a platform to argue the separate concerns of the Welsh Department particularly in relation to the teaching of Welsh and the Welsh dimension of the curriculum, that is, the focus on Welsh history, geography, music and literature. These particular sections were not merely reports on standards; they became vehement exhortations to change and improve provision.

In his contributions to annual reports, Edwards was a tenacious critic of the teaching of both Welsh and English languages. He criticised an examination system that encouraged cramming at the expense of critical thinking; he argued for an expansion of school libraries; he promoted education in science and technology that was relevant to the industries local to schools; he encouraged schemes to improve facilities for practical work and physical exercise; and he was critical of an academic curriculum for the few who aimed to matriculate.

The wider roles of inspectors

Inspectors had a range of responsibilities beyond inspecting and reporting. Although they were commonly engaged during term-time in offering advice in schools, they also had an increasing role in overseeing grant-aided, in-service support for teachers in the form of short courses in various curriculum subjects and including, in 1915, a course on 'experimental pedagogy'. HMI also produced pamphlets containing guidance for teachers: on how to plan lessons in temperance (1910) or on the countryside as educator (1922), the latter being based on a summer course for teachers at Jesus College, Oxford, which had been organised and delivered mainly by Wales inspectors.

Inspectors would spend a few weeks annually administering the Labour Proficiency Examination in the 'three Rs' which allowed children who passed it to leave elementary school at twelve if they wished (until the 1918 Education Act raised the school-leaving age to fourteen). Inspectors also set and marked the examination papers in teacher training colleges as well as for pupil teachers in schools. (The CI himself inspected the training colleges in Wales regularly at this time.) Inspectors were also called upon to be members of Departmental Committees and to attend educational conferences. They acted as intermediaries between central and local authorities such as the CWB and LEAs. After the 1918 Education Act they were called upon to advise LEAs on new schemes and planned expenditure. They also advised other government departments on education and on the applications for grants to build new schools or to extend existing education premises.

The First World War imposed extraneous duties: some inspectors became Honorary Secretaries for War Savings for the counties where they served. Even while inspectors' duties were expanding, the inspectorate's capacity was being depleted as inspectors enlisted or retired. They were not always replaced and the rate of inspection slowed. In 1918, HMI L. J. Roberts noted that his district of Glamorgan 'could not be inspected with the fullness and thoroughness which it should have'.[12]

2. OWEN EDWARDS AS CI, AND HIS RELATIONSHIP WITH THE CENTRAL WELSH BOARD AND THE BOARD OF EDUCATION

Owen Edwards had been a critic of Wales's education system when he was a Fellow of Lincoln College, Oxford, well before he became CI. He was a popular author and publisher of books and periodicals which provided vehicles for his criticism. He would continue to publish journals (*Cymru* and *Cymru'r Plant*) and numerous books (such as *Cyfres y Fil*) while juggling a new existence as an inspector and Whitehall bureaucrat. This required considerable skills of organisation in dealing with a workload that was made heavier because of his decision to visit many schools himself. As CI, he was more a *primus inter pares* than what we would recognise today as a manager and administrator. In his role as leader and inspiration for others, both in the inspectorate and among the many readers of his publications, he was highly respected. Nonetheless, Abel Jones was critical of Edwards for his failure to delegate and reluctance to promote low-paid assistant inspectors (of which Jones was one). While Jones claimed that Edwards could be too patient with people, he also quoted an example where his upbraiding was swift and succinct:

> Once, after a couple of hours in a small school he asked the headmaster: 'Do you know what is the matter with your school?'
> 'Well, what is it?' asked the teacher.
> 'Dirt! On the floor and on the brain. Slovenliness generally!'[13]

Edwards appointed Welsh-speaking, Nonconformist inspectors like Abel Jones directly from teaching posts to the new Welsh Department rather than the English-speaking Anglicans who had been more common HMI recruits in the nineteenth century. From 1908, a List 6 for Wales allocated nine HMI to sectors across the thirteen counties together with a list of sixteen junior or sub-inspectors.[14] HMI were given district responsibilities and the junior/sub inspectors worked to their bidding. HMI from England would be made available to support the inspection of technical education and a 'Miss Sillitoe is at present employed in Wales under the direction of the Chief Woman Inspector of the Board of Education for Domestic Subjects'.[15]

Twelve years later, in 1920, in addition to Edwards, there would be twenty-seven inspectors in total, comprising '7 HMI (plus one vacancy), 6 sub-inspectors, 5 junior inspectors, 8 assistant inspectors'.[16] This meant that Edwards had not expanded the inspectorate's establishment in line with the increase in England and he had only promoted one junior/assistant inspector to the status of HMI during his thirteen years in post.

Unlike in England, Wales's inspectors were not designated as elementary, secondary, technical or further education specialists but worked more generically, a practice that was recognised as valid by the Board of Education, while allowing for some degree of specialisation. Although *Circular 532* argued in May 1907 in favour of specialisms in inspection, it also added that 'the fundamental principles of good teaching ... are practically the same for all grades of education (or perhaps ... of all education excluding the highly specialised or technical)'.[17] The group of inspectors allocated to Wales was small and Edwards dealt with them in a personal and direct way. He corresponded with them regularly and held termly conferences for HMI in different locations (Langland Bay and Llandrindod Wells were popular venues) to share and discuss findings, new regulations, and memos from the Board of Education.

Selby-Bigge, writing in 1926, described the conferences, re-established as common practice in divisions across England and Wales from 1882, as intended to 'secure substantial uniformity of judgement and practice throughout the country' and to agree 'common lines of action'.[18] He added that the conferences were 'also periodically attended by administrative officers, who explain and discuss with the inspectors developments in the Board's policy or its application'.[19] These conferences were to continue in Wales until the late 1990s. In 1927, one inference to be drawn from one of Selby-Bigge's observations, was to be apposite for many of those years: 'The charge of affection for uniformity, or dislike of originality, is probably one which can be least easily maintained against inspectors.'[20] The mechanisms to secure consistency in HMI judgements after their role became more advisory and less reliant on the outcomes of crude tests of basic skills or memory were never wholly successful. However, the Wales conferences and the constant interactions that Edwards maintained with his inspectors by means of meetings, minutes and letters achieved a strong degree of agreement on those aspects of education that Edwards felt strongly about.

Edwards never undertook a full-scale reorganisation of the inspectorate although he did appoint new inspectors and reallocate districts and responsibilities in response to pressures as they arose, such as the need to staff LEA area inspections across Wales. Edwards planned to reorganise the inspectorate more fully and he sent a memo to DI in 1918 to gather information about the range of their work and ask the following questions:

1. What are your E[lementary school] districts; how many depts. in each?
2. Have you any suggestions for a better distribution?

3. How are the schools inspected, how often, how apportioned?
4. What S[econdary] schools do you inspect, what T[echnical] work?[21]

These questions reveal a surprising degree of ignorance about the detail of how the inspectorate was organised and the extent to which leadership and responsibilities were distributed without detailed oversight. The quality and detail of returns from DI varied widely. One response, to question three, revealed the system of classifying schools on the basis of judgements about their 'excellent, good, satisfactory or defective and unsatisfactory' quality. This use of a four-point scale of judgements, or something very similar, was common practice and one that was to persist until the twenty-first century. In the north Wales district in 1918, around 10 per cent of schools were deemed excellent, 40 per cent good, 40 per cent satisfactory and 10 per cent unsatisfactory.[22]

Only one HMI – G. Prys Williams, then DI in Carmarthenshire and Pembrokeshire – returned a detailed proposal to reallocate schools into new districts to 'do away with disparity' and 'bring more congruity to the work of the HMI'. He also suggested that:

> the CI should be relieved of the detail work including ... having charge of a district, however small, reserving ... himself for the duties of generalissimo and for the broader phases of educational policy.[23]

In making this comment, Williams inadvertently revealed his view that Edwards's organisation of his own workload might be more effective, that he was doing too much front-line inspection at the expense of setting aside time to lead and organise the work of others. There is considerable evidence in Board of Education minutes to suggest that Edwards offered valuable and timely policy advice, but his record of inspection visits indicates that his overall programme of work was one that did not allow much time for managerial planning. For instance, HMI would often arrange their own temporary reallocations of inspectors although Edwards would be kept informed and he had the job of signing off all HMI diaries, which recorded the work done and evidenced claims for travel and subsistence expenses. After Edwards's death in post in 1920, Williams sent A. T. Davies an outline plan he had received from Edwards 'to reorganise the inspecting staff in Wales'.[24] But the inspectorate would eventually be restructured along different lines.

The relationship with the Central Welsh Board (CWB)

Tensions between the CWB and the Welsh Department were high for much of the period. Both bodies had a duty to inspect intermediate schools, and both had separate bodies of inspectors, led by two CI. This inevitably led to conflicts although these eased somewhat when William Edwards HMI was appointed CI of the CWB in 1915. His previous experience as HMI and his familiarity with colleagues might have helped to mitigate the tension but it was not to be entirely dissipated. That there was little sympathy between the Welsh Department and the CWB is evidenced by the fact that the CWB continuously agitated for the establishment of a National Council for Wales that they would lead, 'controlling all forms of education in the Principality other than University Education'.[25]

The battle between the two bodies is well illustrated in the furore over the 1909 report on intermediate schools and its outcome. Before the creation of the Welsh Department, the annual reports of the Board of Education on the intermediate schools of Wales had been based on the findings of CWB examiners and inspectors. The following comment is typical: 'The reports of the Examiners and Inspectors [CWB inspectors] are again satisfactory.'[26] Everything changed when Edwards used his first report on intermediate schools to reveal an astringent critique as part of his crusade for a better education system. Notwithstanding the fact that some of his criticisms echoed those of CWB examiners' reports, the power of his invective and the comprehensiveness of the attack on so many fronts in the report combined to elicit complaints from the CWB, from head teachers and from Welsh MPs. In that report he condemned the negative impact of examinations on the quality of learning in schools, arguing that:

the Central Welsh Board should now consider to what extent their rigid examination system may be the cause of the wooden and unintelligent type of mind of which their examiners complain ...There is a danger that the system of education in Wales may become stereotyped and ineffective.[27]

Edwards was critical not only of the CWB examinations but of the schools as copies of English grammar schools. He claimed that schools catered only for the fraction of children who required or could afford education. Its examinations elicited mechanical answers that repeated dictated notes and were more a test of memory than of understanding. The tendency for schools to choose CWB-set examination papers rather than to design their own prevented any differentiation in the curriculum to suit local conditions or to meet the needs of different groups of pupils. The examination system induced a fierce competition for certificates. Courses that should take four years were crammed into two for early leavers, whose sole aim was to gain certificates. The needs of the majority of children were ignored because of the university colleges' demands for rigidly academic standards and preference for academic subject combinations in the Senior/School Certificate. The Certificate was used for matriculation purposes that would apply in practice only to the minority who went on to university. The language and literature of Wales had less than second place. Many more pupils took French than took Welsh and too few schools offered Welsh. Edwards criticised the narrowness of the curriculum, the neglect of practical subjects and the effects of indifferent teaching. He exposed unsatisfactory standards in the use of English.

Edwards was supported by the Board in the battle that followed this concentrated volley of criticism. The CWB argued that he had no right to contradict the views of their examiners and inspectors. Edwards's argument in rebuttal was that his critique was based not only on the CWB reports but on evidence from HMI. And he claimed overriding authority for the Welsh Department and the Board over that of the CWB. In the next report a clear statement on this point was made in the preface:

> In order to prevent misconceptions about this Report, the Board think it desirable to make two observations. (1) The Report is based, as in former years, upon information supplied by their own Inspectors. Though the Inspectors are directed to use the Reports of the Central Welsh Board as far as possible, the responsibility for the accuracy of the facts and for the justice of the conclusions in this Report is entirely that of the Board of Education.[28]

The 1909 Report had significant repercussions. Its upshot may have been to privilege the judgements of HMI over those of more local inspectors but the consequences were not positive for subsequent relations with the CWB. The university colleges were heavily represented on the CWB and their representatives did not always appreciate Edwards's contributions in meetings (Edwards attended regularly in the early years but less often later on). Doubts were expressed about his abilities as a committee-man. One tribute written after Edwards's death judged that:

> He was far from being at his best in a committee and as a result he did not have the influence that he deserved to have. Committees are a must, and Wales is a land of committees, and many of her sons are well-versed in the craft of handling them, but Owen Edwards did not understand the basic elements of this craft. He was looked upon as a dreamer, and as one who lived in the world of imagination, and it was seldom that he could convince a committee of the wisdom and the attractiveness of his suggestions.[29]

Perhaps Edwards was not a great 'committee man' – and the brevity of his time as an MP tends to confirm that view – but he did exercise some influence on the CWB. And he was far from being a visionary who had no grasp of practical realities. His reports were full of practical advice which, while not always capable of immediate implementation, led to improvements when implemented. For instance, in 1910 he suggested that the CWB should use their examiners as inspectors in lengthier inspections so that the two perspectives could combine to offer a rounded view of standards.

He reported in the following year's annual report that this had been introduced with promising and more consistent results. Edwards also argued for a reduction in the burden of the four sets of public examinations set by the CWB in intermediate schools and they were eventually reduced to two.

R. T. Jenkins, the Welsh historian, later maintained that Edwards 'was led into arguments about details that it would have been better to avoid, and thus clouded the basic argument'.[30] It is true that Edwards's influence on the CWB was only partial in relation to the important issues he raised about examinations and the curriculum, but the 'basic argument' could not have been clearer. Although too much energy was expended on territorial squabbles, it remained part of the CI's job to hold the CWB to account. After all, it was public money they were spending. And even if Edwards had been able to exercise greater influence, the CWB itself had only limited capacity to change attitudes in schools and among parents at a time when most people believed that the overriding function of schools was to teach children to speak English and win certificates.

The relationship with the Board of Education

In a 1908 letter to Herbert Lewis MP Edwards refers to the 'autonomy offered by Mr McKenna' (then President of the Board of Education) in the form of a National Council for Education in Wales as proposed in the 1906 draft Education Bill before it was scuppered in the House of Lords debates.[31] Had the Council been established with the full range of powers envisioned by Lloyd George, Edwards would have gained control of the jurisdiction and resources that would have enabled him to have a much more direct impact on schools. However, what he actually encountered in the newly established Welsh Department was an overwhelming range of bureaucratic administrative duties, to which he added a heavy programme of inspection. He was soon disabused of the hope that his new post would allow him direct power to steer the course of education in the schools of Wales and he became unhappily aware of the constraints of working within the Board of Education. According to one of the inspectors he appointed:

His decisions in the early years of the Welsh Department were frequently questioned by officials in the English Department. They would tell him there were no precedents for his action. 'When they offer that argument,' he said to me, 'my reply is "I am here to make precedents and not to follow them."'[32]

Edwards was often at odds with the policy lines of the Board of Education: on issues such as the sharing of practical facilities between elementary and secondary schools, the introduction of post-matriculation qualifications in schools, and the limitations of an academic curriculum for Welsh secondary schools. His difficulties were sometimes exacerbated by the bumptious empire-building of A. T. Davies, the Welsh Department's permanent secretary, a colleague whom Edwards always respected, perhaps partly because of his continuing willingness to enter disputes in robust defence of their shared mission.

A 'Scheme of Educational Pamphlets' from the Welsh Department was met with disdain in 1909 by the Board, who refused to publish them, questioning the need for Wales to have separate publications.[33] Subjects for the planned pamphlets ranged from 'Temperance' and 'Thrift' to guidance on 'Welsh' and 'Practical Hints for School Managers and Others'. Henry Maurice, Secretary to the Board, described the proposal to the President (the Minister) as 'an absurd bid for self-advertisement' and insisted that it was the 'duty of [the] Welsh Department ... to have their minds directed outward ... not inwards perpetually towards their own peculiarities'.[34]

It is ironic that the Board for some years refused to publish pamphlets that were produced by someone who was already one of the most popular writers in Wales. But attitudes changed and, by the end of 1910, and after reading Edwards's rebuttal of the CWB's charges against him in the controversy surrounding the 1909 *Report*, Henry Maurice was writing of Edwards as follows:

> ... no one alive in all probability can speak with such authority on the subject of Welsh education, and ... Welsh education never had and probably never will have again a friend so entirely and enthusiastically devoted to its service.[35]

Soon the Board was allowing the Welsh Department to publish separate pamphlets for schools in Wales that reflected the curriculum interests of Edwards in language, Welsh history and rural lore, and many of these pamphlets were published partly in Welsh as well as in English.

1920–1925

After Edwards's death in 1920, A. T. Davies took on the CI responsibilities in Whitehall, supported by two divisional inspectors to whom he delegated the day-to-day organisation of inspection. They 'actively assisted in carrying out the duties of the CI since the death of the late Sir Owen Edwards'.[36] *Circular 153* outlined the new structure introduced in 1924, which allocated inspectors to districts in a way that reflected more fairly the distribution of a growing population and its schools. In addition to the two divisional inspectors (of north, mid Wales, Monmouthshire and Newport; and of Glamorgan to Pembrokeshire respectively), there would be twelve HMI, two HMI (Women) and eleven assistant inspectors (AIs). More AIs were to be appointed. The two divisional inspectors were Drs G. Prys Williams and William J. Williams, both of whom were later to become CI. The total establishment was reduced from twenty-nine to twenty-seven, despite the increasing number of schools, because, it was claimed, the use of cars and motorcycles made it possible for inspectors to cover more ground.

But after Edwards's death, the Welsh Department lost direction and leadership in pressing for curriculum innovation and new teaching methods that met the needs of Wales. Both the general annual reports and those on intermediate schools, after 1920, became increasingly a record of the technical statistics associated with the education sectors. After Edwards's contributions came to an end, there was less expiation on curriculum subjects in the annual reports and nothing specifically about Welsh or the Welsh dimension. However, before his early retirement in 1925, Davies was able to commission an inquiry into the position of the Welsh language. He took care to appoint to its committee members who could be trusted to take a sympathetic and informed view of the challenge before them. Their report on *Welsh in Education and Life* duly appeared in 1927.

Edwards's influence on Davies and on his HMI colleagues had been considerable. Prys Williams and William Williams both recognised the uniqueness of his vision and Prys Williams, in the biographical entry he contributed to the 1912–21 supplement to the *Dictionary of National Biography*, acknowledged the effectiveness of that vision in the context of Edwards's work as CI.

The CWB made further attempts to expand its empire during this period and the attrition with the Welsh Department continued. It proved difficult to find a solution to the long-standing problem of dual inspection in intermediate schools. However, a degree of cooperation was introduced in 1922 and, by 1926, dual control had been fully established in joint inspections.

3. THE IMPACT OF EDWARDS ON WELSH AND THE WELSH DIMENSION IN THE CURRICULUM

When Edwards became CI he found an important platform in his crusade for the Welsh language in education. At a time when many people in Welsh education had surrendered to the hegemony of anglicisation, Edwards asserted the benefits of bilingualism. In an address to the 'Imperial Education Conference' in Whitehall on 2 May 1911, he stated that: 'We do not regard bilingualism in our country as a disadvantage in any way. We look upon it as an advantage.'[37] This was a revolutionary stance when, for almost a century, most inspectors, including the authors of the infamous *Blue Books* of 1847 and eminent figures such as Matthew Arnold – HMI in Wales from 1852 to 1853 – had poured scorn upon the language, chapels and culture of Wales. Edwards himself had suffered corporal punishment for speaking Welsh as an elementary school pupil.

For most of the nineteenth century, with few exceptions, HMI had promoted the use of English in schools, as indicated in Chapter 1. Dan Isaac Davies, a junior inspector in Merthyr Tydfil, was among the few who took a different view. Davies played a prominent role in a campaign for bilingualism (he was a founder of 'The Society for the Utilisation of the Welsh Language for Educational Purposes in Wales' in 1885) and gave evidence to the 1886–8 Cross Committee on elementary education, as a result of which a small grant was made available to elementary schools during the 1890s to teach Welsh. However, no school was actually required to teach it and the curriculum, including any Welsh lessons, continued to be delivered in English. In 1899–1900, only 0.8 per cent of pupils in the whole of Wales took Welsh as a class subject.[38]

The main argument presented to the Cross Committee to justify the inclusion of Welsh in the curriculum was that its use helped the children to learn English. Edwards's ambitions went far beyond such a pusillanimous argument. It was his mission to achieve universal acceptance of a view of Welsh and the Welsh dimension as authentic and essential to the curriculum and ethos of the schools of Wales. In one of his early memos, he listed among his objectives: 'The bilingual problem ought to be faced squarely and so become a bilingual opportunity.'[39] This early statement of Edwards's ambition for universal bilingualism in schools was a sign of tensions to come. Once in post, Edwards soon realised that substantial changes were needed to curriculum and inspection policy and the training of teachers if schools were to reflect the changes that he wanted to make. He succeeded in setting out separate regulations for the curriculum of schools in Wales in 1907 that strengthened the emphasis on Welsh and the Welsh dimension, especially in elementary schools. And he was supported in his ambitions by his HMI, notably William Edwards (who would subsequently become CI of the Central Welsh Board), L. J. Roberts, G. Prys Williams and W. J. Williams. They, among others, invested considerable energy in the campaign to change the direction of the school curriculum in Wales. The accounts given in annual reports and codes for the years that follow offer a measure of their joint success in practice.

Elementary schools

In the 1908 *Code* for elementary schools, Edwards wrote: 'In last year's Code a definite place in the curriculum of the School was provided for the Welsh Language.'[40] He went on to explain the difficulties that arose when no use was made of the mother tongue in the early years of education:

> in several Schools, the infants are taught through the medium of a language that they do not understand, or ...

they are taught to read and write two languages at the same time. The result is unintelligent reading; the children get into the habit of repeating words without attending to the meaning of them. The Board have, therefore, introduced a provision that infants should be taught through the medium of Welsh where Welsh is their mother tongue.[41]

He added:

> The Curriculum should, as a rule, include the Welsh Language. Any of the subjects of the curriculum may (where the local circumstances make it desirable) be taught in Welsh, but it is not necessary that the Welsh Language should be taught in every School or in every Class.
>
> Provision should also be made for the teaching, in every School of Welsh History and the Geography of Wales, and Welsh Literature should also be included in the Curriculum of Higher Elementary Schools.[42]

It was optimistic to hope that all schools would be able to follow these recommendations. The LEA inspection reports that were published from 1911 revealed that, in many urban local education authorities, the teaching of Welsh in elementary schools was rudimentary, where it existed at all. In Swansea, Radnor, Neath, Newport and other mostly urbanised areas, there was either very little or none. But in the more rural county of Carmarthen, where Welsh had been taught in only a quarter of schools in 1903, by 1911, Welsh was being taught at all elementary schools bar three.[43] In Merioneth it was being taught in all schools though not to a satisfactory standard in all of them:

> Welsh is taught in every school in the county; in some with an enthusiasm and skill which give to it that high educational value which the teaching of the mother tongue ought to have ...; in others it receives a half-hearted and casual attention which robs it of much of its worth. Here and there too, oblique references can still be heard even from teachers, which go to show that traces of the old prejudice

against teaching Welsh have not been entirely obliterated ... Let the child be taught to honour and revere the language of the hearth.[44]

In the 1913 annual report, Edwards expressed his regret that Wales was not reaching those standards of bilingualism that were common in other countries. In the elementary schools, he blamed too much teaching of 'grammar, dictation and translation when the teaching should be mainly ... conversation, reading and composition'. He added that:

> the difficulty of giving adequate instruction in the Welsh language has been accentuated by the existing scarcity of teachers, as it has not always been found possible to appoint teachers who were well enough acquainted with the language to teach it by modern methods.[45]

By the time of the publication of the triennial reports on LEAs in 1914, however, progress in the use of Welsh was being noted in the elementary schools of several authorities, including Monmouthshire (in Welsh-speaking areas); Aberdare (where all schools taught Welsh and 75 per cent of teachers were fluent in Welsh); Neath (where there had been striking progress in Welsh as a second language); Caernarvonshire (where a successful scheme for bilingualism had been implemented by zealous teachers); and Cardiganshire (where schools had responded positively to new guidance by the authority and exceeded the expectations of the Code).[46]

And HMI had been promoting the Welsh language and love of Wales in both tranches of triennial LEA reports, with a fervour that strongly reflected the influence of Edwards:

> The best teachers know that the highest aim of teaching of Welsh in a Welsh school is a moral one; the Welsh child must be taught to love his country and his language, and to admire the heroes of past history. This will increase his self-respect and self-reliance ... [so he can become] a worthy member of a noble nation.[47]

The 1927 *Report on Welsh in Education and Life* offers a measure of the impact of the Welsh Department on elementary schools:

> In areas in which Anglicisation is most complete e.g. Radnorshire, South Pembrokeshire, East Monmouthshire, parts of Flintshire and Denbighshire and in some schools in certain districts of Glamorgan, Welsh is not taught. In the remaining part of Wales its place is strongest in the Infant Schools.[48]

In no LEA was Welsh the main language of all elementary schools by the mid-twenties but the Welsh Department's regulations had been implemented to the extent that the language had become the medium of instruction in infants departments in Welsh-speaking areas of Wales and was commonly taught in Standards I–IV in the Welsh-speaking counties. It was also taught as a second language in some English-speaking parts of Wales. The 1927 report's overview of the state of the nation reflected a picture of the partial but increasing success of Edwards's mission.

Secondary schools

The 1907 regulations also enhanced the status of Welsh as a subject in secondary schools but not as a medium of teaching. By 1909, the regulations maintained that: 'this important subject is gradually attaining its proper place in the curriculum of schools'.[49] However, in 1910, Edwards reported that the numbers choosing to study Welsh were disappointing, because:

> the high standard demanded in this subject by the Central Welsh Board examinations, compared with the exceedingly low standard in French, makes pupils, especially in the English-speaking parts of Wales, choose the easier alternative.[50]

Welsh was being offered as an option that was set against French, a popular subject that was examined as a second or third language whereas Welsh was examined against first-language criteria.

Progress on the inclusion of Welsh as a subject in the curriculum was slow and there was little or no progress on the use of Welsh as a medium for teaching except in the lower school when it was needed in order to explain the meaning of English terms.

In 1913, Edwards complained that the medium of Welsh lessons was English. The teacher: 'apparently attempting to ignore the fact that the children speak the language already, teaches them grammar as if they were beginning to learn a language new to them and dead'.[51]

The 1918 report noted some limited progress:

> The Intermediate Schools which do not teach Welsh at all are now less than half a dozen in number ... But [Welsh] is far from getting its proper place ... the lessons are given in English, the examination questions are set in English and the answers written in English even in the higher Forms. Such methods should be condemned.[52]

In his last report on the intermediate schools in 1920, Edwards confirmed that there had been further growth in the number of pupils taking Welsh as a subject and acknowledged that the CWB by that time was setting different examination papers for first- and second-language pupils. However, he also recorded regret that Welsh was still not accorded its proper status: it remained an optional subject in an English-medium curriculum.

According to the 1927 *Report on Welsh in Education and Life*:

> ... in 1897, only 31 [intermediate] schools out of 79 offered Welsh in the [senior] examinations of the Central Welsh Board [but] in 1925, 96 schools out of a total of 116 offered the subject.[53]

Even so, by 1925, only around 40 per cent of the pupil cohort was being entered for examination in Welsh while 67 per cent of the cohort was entered for French (a small number of pupils were entered for both, but it was not possible to take both in most schools).

Official and public attitudes were slow to change in line with the changing attitude of the inspectorate to the teaching of Welsh and in Welsh in secondary schools. Opposition to Edwards's views about the importance of Welsh in these schools remained widespread during his lifetime and would persist for many years. The obstacles to its recognition were multi-faceted: the initial schemes of work outlined by LEAs for their intermediate schools had been modelled on the grammar schools of England with their English-medium curriculum and choice of subjects that favoured the classics; there was a generally accepted assumption, as expressed in many newspapers and periodicals, that the curriculum in secondary schools should be delivered and examined in English; many parents believed that schools should teach their children to speak English to 'get on in the world' and escape from local industries rather than be prepared to work in them; university college lectures – even on Welsh as a subject – were delivered in English; and few teachers were ready to teach through the medium of Welsh, having themselves been educated in an English-medium system.

4. THE OVERALL IMPACT OF EDWARDS'S LEADERSHIP AND MISSION

R. T. Jenkins maintained that: 'In the years when he managed education in Wales', Edwards 'did hardly anything to "perfect our education system", or to change (apart from the subject of Welsh) the content and methods of that education.'[54] However, Jenkins was mistaken to think that Edwards was in a position to manage or 'govern' (*rheoli* was the word he used) the education system in Wales. Edwards had been given to believe in 1906 that he would lead a new National Council for Education in Wales and that position would have given him the resources and jurisdiction to enable him to manage the education system directly. When the National Council failed to materialise, Edwards had to rely more on his power to inspire and persuade. He was able to make some important changes to the priorities and practices of inspection in his role as CI and to influence individual schools and LEAs. But the larger question to be raised here is about the limits of the direct influence that any CI can have. Edwards had a high-profile leadership role on an authoritative national platform but he had no direct power to change policy. And although he was allowed to change the Board's policy on the teaching of Welsh and the Welsh dimension of the curriculum, this would only have been with the tacit support of key politicians. Even after introducing new regulations for the use of Welsh in the curriculum, he could not implement curriculum changes directly. Successful achievement of his mission depended upon the agreement and actions of a number of other stakeholders, like the CWB and LEAs, whose duties overlapped with those of HMI. The essential role of HMI was to collect and collate information, report on compliance, publish judgements and offer advice, to providers, to other civil servants and to politicians. Edwards had neither the jurisdiction nor the control of resources that would have made it possible to change radically the nature of the education system as he found it. It is true that he enabled change but change on a larger scale would only happen when social and political attitudes changed.

If schools are agencies of socialisation, then, by the beginning of the twentieth century, generations of children in Wales had been socialised in the context of a language that was foreign to them and a culture that belittled their native culture and language. For many people in Wales, while Welsh was the language of hearth and chapel, English was seen as the language of education and social mobility.[55] Edwards devoted himself to a programme of normalising the use of Welsh in schools. On visits to schools, he invariably commented on the teaching of Welsh, Welsh history and culture, and sent his HMI to challenge and persuade schools and LEAs that did not meet his expectations. He saw it as his mission to convince the Welsh people that it was important to acknowledge and respect their own language and identity and understand something of their own culture and history. Edwards was a key figure in the creation of a new and more authentic Welsh identity for the schools, colleges and inspectors of Wales. He appointed Welsh-speaking inspectors who understood Wales. His reports on standards in Wales gradually gained equal and separate status in the Board's annual reports. His extension of the scope of the codes and regulations led to an increase in the teaching of Welsh and the Welsh dimension of the curriculum. Welsh gained ground as a subject and as a medium of teaching and learning in elementary schools; more pupils were entered for examinations in Welsh in secondary schools; Welsh became an option in Teaching Certificate examinations from 1909; and adult education classes in Welsh were funded.

It is ironic that, while the first two decades of the twentieth century saw a gradual increase in the use of Welsh in schools and in teacher education, the proportion of Welsh speakers in the population was still declining. The percentage claiming to speak the language in the 1901 census was 49.9 per cent. This fell to 43.5 per cent in 1911 and, by 1921, following the losses of the First World War, only 37.1 per cent claimed to be able to speak Welsh.[56] Nevertheless, support for the Welsh language intensified among the population during the 1920s and several influential national movements were established.[57] The Wales youth movement of *Urdd Gobaith Cymru* was established in 1922 by Ifan ab Owen Edwards, the son of Owen Edwards; the Welsh National Party (*Plaid Genedlaethol Cymru*, later *Plaid Cymru*) was established in 1925; and the Union of Welsh Teachers (*Undeb Athrawon Cymreig*, later *Undeb Cenedlaethol Athrawon Cymru*) in 1926. During the 1920s, the campaign to embed the Welsh language and dimension in the curriculum continued, although its success varied in relation to the influence of individual LEAs and head teachers. Some momentum had been lost to the inspectorate itself after Edwards's death in 1920 but A. T. Davies continued to undertake his administrative duties efficiently and HMI continued to uphold Edwards's priorities for education in Wales. Nevertheless, it would not be until the implementation of the 1988 Education Reform Act, as described in Chapter 4, that a National Curriculum that reflected his vision for Welsh education would become mandatory for all schools.

ENDNOTES

1. The name on his birth certificate was Owen Edwards and he reverted to this usage in 1907 on joining the civil service. In 1889 he had agreed to add 'Morgan' as a middle name to avoid confusion with a cousin of the same name. He became well known in Wales as O. M. Edwards or 'O. M.' due to the popularity of his many publications as author and editor.
2. Board of Education, *Circular to Inspectors Circular 532* (London, 1907), p. iv.
3. Abel J. Jones, *From an inspector's bag* (Cardiff: Abbrevia, 1944), p. 79.
4. Jones, *From an inspector's bag*, p. 80.
5. Jones, *From an inspector's bag*, p. 92.

6. Owen Edwards's notes of visit are archived in the National Archives (TNA) and in the National Library of Wales (NLW).
7. Board of Education Welsh Department, *General Report of HMI on Elementary Education in the Urban District of Mountain Ash for the period ended 31st July 1913* (London: HMSO, 1914), p. 16.
8. NLW, O. M. Edwards Papers BC 2/6, Notebook for July 1911–July 2013.
9. Board of Education, *Report of the Board of Education for the Year 1910–1911* (London: HMSO, 1912), p. 64.
10. Board of Education, *Evidence of Welsh Witnesses before the Royal Commission on Education 1887* (London: HMSO, 1888), para. 42,581.
11. Quoted in E. L. Edmonds, *The School Inspector* (London: Routledge and Kegan Paul, 1962), p. 140.
12. TNA ED 23/149.
13. Abel J. Jones, *I was privileged* (Cardiff: Abbrevia, 1943), p. 79.
14. Board of Education Welsh Department, *List 6 Wales: The Inspectors of the Welsh Department of the Board of Education as allocated in relation to the LEAs' Areas in Wales (including Monmouthshire)* (London, 1908).
15. Board of Education Welsh Department, *List 6*, p. 4.
16. TNA ED 23/152A.
17. Board of Education, *Circular 532* (London, May 1907), p. vi.
18. Sir Lewis Amherst Selby-Bigge, *The Board of Education* (London: Putnam and Company Ltd, 1927), p. 149.
19. Selby-Bigge, *The Board of Education*, p. 149.
20. Selby-Bigge, *The Board of Education*, p. 150.
21. TNA ED 23/149.
22. TNA ED 23/149.
23. TNA ED 23/149.
24. TNA ED 23/152A.
25. Central Welsh Board, *Today and Tomorrow in Welsh Education* (Cardiff: CWB, 1916), p. 5.
26. Board of Education, *Report of the Board of Education for the Year 1904–1905 on the administration of schools under the Wales Intermediate Education Act 1889* (London: HMSO, 1906), p. 6.
27. Board of Education, *Report of the Board of Education under the Wales Intermediate Education Act 1889 for the Year 1909* (London: HMSO, 1910), p. 19.
28. Board of Education, *Report of the Board of Education for the Year 1910 under the Wales Intermediate Education Act 1889* (London: HMSO, 1911), p. 23.
29. John H. Davies, 'Atgofion', *Cymru Y Rhifyn Coffa*, LX (1921), 23–4 (translation by author).
30. R. T. Jenkins, *Y Bywgraffiadur Cymreig hyd 1940* (London: Honourable Society of Cymmrodorion, 1954), p. 180 (translation by author).
31. NLW, Leslie Wynne Evans Papers 7/4, Owen Edwards letter to Herbert Lewis MP (14 October 1908).

32. Jones, *I was privileged*, p. 68.
33. TNA ED 24/585.
34. TNA ED 24/585.
35. TNA ED 24/589, letter from Henry Maurice, Secretary to the Board of Education to Mr Sanderson, 12 November 1910.
36. Board of Education Welsh Department, *Wales Circular 153 Circular to LEAs and Governing Bodies of Educational Institutions in Wales* (London, 1924). The reference here to 'Sir Owen Edwards' reflects the award of his knighthood for services to literature in 1916.
37. Board of Education, *Report of the Imperial Conference 1911* (London: HMSO, 1911), p. 256.
38. Board of Education, *Report of the Board of Education 1899–1900*, vol. III, Appendix to the Report (Elementary Education) (London: HMSO, 1900), Table 9.
39. Quoted in Wynne Ll. Lloyd, 'Owen M. Edwards (1858–1920)', in Glanmor Williams et al. (eds), *Pioneers of Welsh Education* (Swansea: University College of Wales Faculty of Education, 1962), pp. 83–99.
40. Board of Education Welsh Department, *Code of Regulations for Public Elementary Schools in Wales (including Monmouthshire) with Schedules* (London, 1908), p. iii.
41. Board of Education Welsh Department, *1908 Code*, p. iii.
42. Board of Education Welsh Department, *1908 Code*, p. xiv.
43. Board of Education Welsh Department, *General Report of HMI on Elementary Education in the Administrative County of Carmarthen for the period ending July 31st 1911* (London: HMSO, 1912), p. 7.
44. Board of Education Welsh Department, *General Report of HMI on Elementary Education in the Administrative County of Meirioneth for the period ending July 31st 1911* (London: HMSO, 1912), p. 14.
45. Board of Education, *Report of the Board of Education for the Year 1911–12* (London: HMSO, 1913) pp. 56–7.
46. See Board of Education Welsh Department, *General Reports of HMI on Elementary Education in the Administrative Counties or Urban Districts of Monmouth, Neath, Aberdare, Caernarvon and Cardigan* (London: HMSO, 1914).
47. Board of Education Welsh Department, *General Report of HMI on Education in the Rhondda Urban District for the period ending July 31st 1912* (London: HMSO, 1912), p. 22.
48. Departmental Committee Appointed by the President of the Board of Education to Inquire into the Position of the Welsh Language and to advise as to its Promotion in the Educational System of Wales, *Welsh in Education and Life* (London: HMSO, 1927), p. 92.
49. Board of Education Welsh Department, *Regulations for Secondary Schools 1908* (London: 1908), p. ix.
50. Board of Education, *Report of the Board of Education for the Year 1908–1909* (London: HMSO, 1910), p. 145.

51. Board of Education, *Report of the Board of Education for the Year 1911–1912* (London: HMSO, 1913), p. 86.
52. Board of Education, *Report of the Board of Education under the Welsh Intermediate Act 1889 for the Year 1917* (London: HMSO, 1918), pp. 6–7.
53. Departmental Committee of the Board of Education, *Welsh in Education and Life*, p. 92.
54. R. T. Jenkins, 'Owen Edwards', Y *Llenor*, IX No. 1/4 (spring 1930), 6–21 (translation by author).
55. Geraint Jenkins dispels the notion that the Welsh language was confined to hearth, chapel and eisteddfod and notes that Welsh was the dominant language of both rural and industrial workplaces for most of the nineteenth century. See Geraint H. Jenkins, '"Cymru, Cymry a'r Gymraeg": Rhagymadrodd', in Geraint H. Jenkins (ed.), *Gwnewch Bopeth yn Gymraeg Yr Iaith Gymraeg a'i Pheuoedd 1801–1911* (Cardiff: Wales University Press, 1999), pp. 1–34.
56. Source: *Census of Population for England and Wales: 1901, 1911,* and *1921.*
57. See Marion Löffler, 'Mudiad yr Iaith Gymraeg yn Hanner Cyntaf yr Ugeinfed Ganrif: Cyfraniad y Chwyldroadau Tawel' and W. Gareth Evans, 'Y Wladwriaeth Brydeinig ac Addysg Gymraeg 1914–1991', in Geraint H. Jenkins and Mari A. Williams (eds), *'Eu Hiaith a Gadwant'? Y Gymraeg yn yr Ugeinfed Ganrif* (Cardiff: University of Wales Press, 2000), pp. 173–205 and 331–56.

Chapter 3

THE INSPECTORATE IN WALES BETWEEN 1925 AND 1970: RESPONSES AND REACTIONS

Alun Morgan

The period from 1925 to 1970 was one of massive change in education in Wales and in society more generally. In 1925 the inspectorate was still a relatively new Welsh Department in the Board of Education. By 1970 a Welsh Office had been established in Cardiff with a much wider administrative remit and a Secretary of State for Wales. Comprehensive schools had largely replaced selective secondary schools and the school-leaving age was in the process of being raised. The Welsh-medium sector was still expanding in the primary phase and about to expand at a faster rate in the secondary phase. By 1970, the Department of Education and Science (DES) had replaced the Board of Education in Whitehall, but the policies of the UK Secretary of State for Education remained the dominating influence on education in Wales as in England, allowing for some variation in the application of regulations in Wales. The period between 1925 and 1970 was also one of change for the inspectorate, although many of the core themes from its previous history would continue to concern its inspectors and provide a focus for their reports. This chapter explores the structure and organisation of the inspectorate, the work of HMI, the reports they produced, and the important role of HMI as advocates of the Welsh language and culture in education.

THE STRUCTURE AND ORGANISATION OF THE INSPECTORATE

In 1920 the Bruce Committee had recommended the establishment of a unified inspectorate to replace the respective bodies of HMI and Central Welsh Board (CWB) inspectors. Although these two inspection bodies did not merge, by 1926 there were joint inspections of intermediate county schools by both HMI and CWB inspectors, reflecting better coordination and cooperation between HMI and the CWB. In addition, there were: 'periodical consultations ... between the Divisional Inspector of the Board of Education and the Chief Inspector (CI) of the CWB on matters of mutual interest ...' and arrangements were made so that:

> Inspectors of the Central Welsh Board may have opportunities of accompanying Inspectors of the Board of Education on their visits to Elementary Schools, Central Schools, Junior Technical Schools and Training Colleges ... not with a view to their taking part in the formal work of inspecting and reporting ... but for the purpose of familiarising themselves, at first hand, with the conditions of work in those Institutions.[1]

Between 1925 and 1926 there were changes to the leadership of both inspectorates when A. T. Davies, permanent secretary at the Welsh Department, retired in 1925 and William Edwards, CI of the CWB, retired a year later. This created opportunities for better partnership arrangements although 'the two sets of Inspectorates [would] continue to be subject to the general control of their own Boards [while] inspections themselves would be joint and unified inspections'.[2] This arrangement was to continue until 1948 when the CWB was disbanded and the joint HMI/CWB inspections of secondary schools ended. In that year the Welsh Joint Education Committee (WJEC), a consortium of local education authorities, replaced the CWB as the awarding body for public examinations in Wales secondary schools. While HMI became solely responsible for national-level inspection of all types of schools, they retained an advisory role in relation to public examinations through their role as assessors to WJEC subject panels.

Another structural change to the remit of the inspectorate was made as a result of a recommendation in the report on *Welsh in Education and Life* in 1927. The report was produced by the Committee appointed to inquire into the position of the Welsh language and to advise as to its promotion in education in Wales. The report recommended that a senior member of the Welsh inspectorate be given responsibility for 'the supervision of Welsh teaching in all grades throughout Wales'. As a result, HMI D. T. Davies became the first such special adviser to the CI, a post he held until 1936. For the rest of the twentieth century, a senior inspector – from the 1950s a staff inspector (SI) – was to oversee provision in Welsh both as a subject and as a medium of education while serving as a member of the senior management team of the inspectorate.

From 1928, the CI had an office in Cardiff and was supported by a female staff inspector, seventeen HMI (of whom three were women) and eight assistant inspectors, one of whom acted as an assistant principal in the offices of the Welsh Department in Whitehall. An inspector with special responsibility for teacher training provision in Wales was appointed for the first time. This work had previously been led directly by the CI.

From 1934, the women's inspectorate was formally unified with the men's inspectorate although marriage, for a woman HMI, would continue to result in the ending of her service. Gradually, such restrictions were relaxed, when the civil service marriage bar was revoked in 1946, and equal pay for male and female HMI was introduced in 1961.

In the late thirties and early forties, major reports on aspects of education in England and Wales appeared, taking the names of their chairmen, Spens, Norwood and Fleming. Evidence and memoranda from Welsh witnesses, including HMI, were represented in these reports, which included chapters dealing with the issues from a Welsh standpoint and often including a consideration of both the challenges and opportunities posed by 'bilingualism' in Wales.

In November 1941, *Inspectorate and Inspection Arrangements in Wales (including Monmouthshire)* set out the following staffing establishment details for Wales:

(1) The Welsh Inspectorate consists of one CI, one H. M. Inspector with special responsibilities, eighteen H. M. Inspectors, and nine Assistant Inspectors. In addition, two members of the Board's staff of Physical Training Inspectors have been seconded to the Welsh staff for duties in Wales.

(2) The CHIEF INSPECTOR, Mr W. J. Williams, is responsible for the organisation, control and co-ordination of the work of the Welsh Inspectorate as a whole. He is also the expert adviser of the Welsh Department of the Board on all educational questions affecting the Department ...
(3) The INSPECTOR WITH SPECIAL RESPONSIBILITIES, Mr Caleb Rees, discharges his duties as the Chief Inspector may assign to him as his deputy.[3]

The Department at this time included two women HMI and three assistant inspectors. Fifteen of the HMI served as district inspectors (DIs). Wartime circumstances saw the Board's headquarters moved from London to Bournemouth while also maintaining the office that had first been established in Cardiff in 1928. By 1950, the number of HMI in the Welsh Department had increased to forty-eight, a growth reflecting reform and expansion in the education system. However, this was, in turn, followed by political pressure to reduce numbers. In 1956, the report of the inquiry chaired by Sir Martin Roseveare of the Department of Education was issued. The working party undertaking the inquiry had thirteen members (nine were HMI, including Wynne Ll. Lloyd, CI for Wales) and two Joint Secretaries, one of whom was D. E. Lloyd Jones, also from the Wales inspectorate. Its terms of reference were:

> To review the functions and organisation of the Inspectorate in England and Wales and to consider the number of Her Majesty's Inspectors required for the effective discharge of its proper functions in relation to the present and future responsibilities of the Department.[4]

A clear message emerged from the first meeting of the working party that: 'There was more profit to teachers (and therefore to children) from the visiting of schools than from the writing of reports upon them.'[5] This view was further reinforced at the third and final meeting when CI Dr Browne (from the England inspectorate) was responding to questions. Asked which was the more important – the report or what HMI said to the teachers – Dr Browne chose the latter.[6] The clear implications were that HMI should spend far less time on formal inspection reporting or written advice and more time visiting schools and talking to teachers. The final report, issued in July 1956, stated unambiguously that 'a policy based on expanding numbers is not now practicable even if on some grounds it might still seem desirable' and it advocated 'a rigorous pruning of responsibilities'.[7] It went on to say that 'the amount of time spent by HMI on visits to schools for reasons unconnected with formal reports or special enquiries is not as great as we think desirable'.[8] It proposed reducing inspector numbers in Wales from forty-seven to forty-three by 1959, adding: 'Quite apart from the special difficulties arising from bi-lingualism, questions of balance and age range will have to be taken into account in securing this reduction.'[9] It recommended a 'general lowering of frequency of reporting'.[10] This, the report suggested, could be achieved by increasing the time between inspections of schools that were judged to be 'stable and soundly progressing'. For primary schools this would involve inspection around once every ten years; for secondary schools once around every twenty; for further education around once every ten to fifteen years; and there would be an end to the formal inspection of teacher training. Pastoral visits by HMI in their general inspector role (GI) would be greatly increased and time spent on formal inspection and advice on premises and other technical issues were to be reduced. These recommendations were implemented and shaped the way HMI were to work for the next decade or so.

The Fulton Committee, whose report was published in June 1968, had been tasked with examining the structure, recruitment and management, including training, of the Home civil service, and to make recommendations. The inspectorate in Wales, smaller than England's, was significantly less affected by the recommendations of this report. In England, discrete, specialist teams would be set up, based on subject and phase whereas in Wales HMI would continue to inspect across all phases because their more limited numbers required more flexible deployment.

Of more immediate significance to the shape, structure and operations on the inspectorate in Wales was the gathering pace of administrative devolution. This was reflected in the establishment of the Education Office for Wales in Cardiff in 1963, together with a degree of Ministerial responsibility for education in Wales, although the Secretary of State for Education in Westminster and the DES still exercised overall responsibility for education policy. When Labour came to power in 1964 the Welsh Office progressively assumed more localised administrative powers from a number of Whitehall departments. The Schools Council was established to coordinate the development of the curriculum and examinations in England and Wales, with a separate steering committee for Wales. In 1970 the Welsh Education Office, later Department (WOED) took over responsibility for education in Wales and came into direct relationship with Wales HMI and this had ramifications for their autonomy and accountability.

The most important structural change in the internal organisation of the inspectorate in Wales after the 1944 Education Act involved the creation of a team of staff inspectors (SI). By 1970 there were eight SI, responsible for particular phases of education, for planning, research, Welsh in education and territorial oversight in north and south Wales respectively. The Wales inspectorate had its own system of committees, panels and teams. Committees, usually chaired by SI, represented the main phases of education and met regularly to discuss the needs in these phases and to promote new developments in their respective fields. Panels were created to deal with the curriculum and its subjects. The Standing Reference Committee, comprising SIs and the senior female inspector, with CI as chair, was to review the work of the inspectors and to advise on inspection, research programmes, courses and relations with outside bodies. A government publication in 1970 stated that 'its most important current task is concerned with the redeployment of the inspectorate to meet changing circumstances generally and those involving Wales more specifically',[11] a clear reference to the requirements associated with administrative devolution.

By 1970 there were forty-seven HMI in Wales, all but two educated in maintained secondary schools and forty of them were Welsh speakers. A half of the most recent appointments had come from posts in England.

THE WORK OF HMI

Cassie Davies, who had been an HMI in Wales during the 1940s and 1950s, published an autobiography in 1973 in which she shared some of her inspection experiences:

> Ond rhan yn unig o waith arolygwr yw mynd i ysgolion, rhan bwysig a phleserus iawn yn fy mhrofiad i. Ynghlwm wrth hyn, y mae sgrifennu adroddiadau, ar y cyfan, yn waith llai pleserus o dipyn a llai pwysig i'm tyb i. Y peth diflasaf oll gen i oedd ceisio disgrifio adeiladau ysgol a rhoi'r holl fanylion y disgwylid eu cael yn ôl y 'Building Regulations'.
>
> *But going to schools is only part of the work of an inspector, a very important and pleasurable part in my experience. Linked to this, writing reports is on the whole less enjoyable and a little less important in my opinion. The most dismal thing, to my thinking, was trying to describe school buildings by giving all the details expected according to 'Building Regulations'.*[12]

Between 1925 and 1970, HMI undertook a wide range of activities. Their central role was to report on classroom practice and standards of achievement, and they published a range of advisory reports about provision and standards in the individual subjects in the curriculum. The HMI report on the teaching of art, commissioned by the University of Wales in 1928, was said to have influenced practice in schools for many years and was described as 'an excellent example of the tendency for the advisory role of the inspectorate to be more prominent than the regulatory in the whole of the inter-war period'.[13] In addition:

> More formal reports and surveys such as those on the educational problems of the South Wales Coalfield, on adult education, technical education in North Wales and on music also indicated that the inspectorate's concern was

by no means restricted to matters concerned with language and with the more usual surveys of elementary education.[14]

The main publications from the Board of Education were the annual reports. They followed one of two formats: one was a general report on all the education sectors covering both Wales and England, but in which the two countries would be reported upon separately, and the other covered standards in the intermediate schools established under the Welsh Intermediate Education Act of 1889. Reports in the latter category were very similarly structured, year on year, under the following sub-headings:

I. Amendments to County Schemes
II. Welsh Act Grant
III. Numbers of Pupils
IV. Leaving Age of Pupils – Boys/Girls
V. The Central Welsh Board
VI. A Report
VII. Appendices: Number of schools/Number of pupils

The reports also often included a section devoted to a particular theme or to a curriculum subject such as Greek (1924), physical education (1929) or modern languages (1929). The reports covered the range of provision, standards achieved and resources available. The report on physical education was especially critical of both facilities and provision.

HMI continued to inspect throughout the Second World War and generated notes of visits (NoVs) to schools, a significant number of them handwritten. However, there is little evidence of more formal HMI reports and the rate of pastoral visiting slowed. During this period, HMI with district inspector (DI) status continued to deal with applications for the approval of individual proposals involving capital expenditure of up to £500 on any of the following:

(a) adaptation of premises
(b) equipment
(c) furniture.

NoVs sometimes drew attention to the restrictions of wartime life. For example, one for Bishopston School (Swansea) in October 1941 referred to 'the construction of an incomplete air raid shelter'[15] and one HMI commented on 'damage to school property during the air raid on the night of Wednesday 19th February 1941/Thursday 20th February 1941' and gave details about the twelve schools affected and damaged.[16]

An HMI visit to Bontddu School on 26 July 1940 recorded:

> When I arrived here the school was empty, but open exercise books on the desks showed that it was in session ... I learnt that the Sen[ior] group had gone to the beach to get sand for sandbags, accompanied by the H.T.[17]

NoVs commented regularly on provision and outcomes for evacuated pupils, from which a mixed picture emerges. In Ysgol Rhiwfawr, HMI reported as follows:

> On the first day of the visit there were 41 Glamorgan children enrolled and 10 from London, Birmingham and Swansea. A certified teacher from the L.C.C. is in charge of the 10 evacuated pupils. Individual attention has been given to the evacuated pupils and good progress is being made.[18]

In Garnswllt:

> The number of pupils on the registers on the first day of visit was 74, of whom 14 were evacuated from Birmingham ... the evacuated pupils do individual work with the Birmingham teacher. Closer records of individual progress should be kept.[19]

An NoV on Reynoldston School recorded that:

> The average attendance has decreased from 81.8 in 1927–28 to 39.8 in 1941–42 ... The average attendance of the visiting pupils in 1941–42 was 41.3: they come mainly from the areas of the L.C.C., Ealing and Swansea Education Authorities.[20]

At Ysgol Abergynolwyn, HMI recorded that: '28 official evacuees are here from St James (C.E.) Birkenhead. The class comprises an age range of 5–12 with one teacher in charge.' The NoV added that the evacuees 'have affected the school heavily' and explained how '2 of Standard 3 & 4 complain of disturbance and inability to get much work done'.[21]

The disruptions of wartime were not confined to the evacuees: comments in a letter following a visit to Carmarthen Borough Roman Catholic School stated that toilet facilities in the church hall (used by boys and girls in a mixed school) were being used by soldiers based there. A strong objection to this was recorded together with a reminder that such practice had been prohibited by agreement with the local education authority and HMI.[22]

In the post-war period HMI took on a wider range of duties: as assessors to the WJEC, the awarding body that replaced the CWB, they supported and gave evidence to a series of inquiries. HMI acted as secretaries to the Central Advisory Council for Education (Wales) in its consideration of 'the content and development of Secondary Education in Wales under the Education Act 1944 and its relation to Primary Education on the one hand and Further Education on the other'. Several HMI served as secretaries to the Council over time and many HMI offered evidence and advice. HMI also worked closely with the Schools Council Committee for Wales and were involved in establishing the National Language Centre in Pontypridd. They contributed to the Gittins inquiry and its subsequent report (entitled *Primary Education in Wales*) on the future of primary education in Wales. Published in 1968, the report considered both the nature and scope of primary education in Wales and the transition of pupils from primary to secondary schools. It proposed a system of first and middle schools to help ease the difficulties of transition. It also recommended that Welsh should be included in the curriculum of all schools as either a first or second language. The inclusion of Welsh in the curriculum remained largely a matter for individual LEAs and their schools to determine.

The overall impression of the post-war period, especially the 1960s, was that HMI, while remaining influential, were largely 'busy behind the scenes' rather than leading change through their publications and influence on education policy which was still largely a matter for Westminster and Whitehall. In the 1950s and 1960s, the amount of formal inspection declined significantly, especially in the secondary sector. Full inspections of individual schools were suspended, as it was considered inappropriate to impose further burdens on schools at a time when they were undergoing major changes as part of comprehensive reorganisation. Consequently, the central inspection programme was skeletal and much of the visiting was left to the initiative of individual HMI. The rough guidance given was that HMI should spend one-third of their time on specialist work, one-third on district work and one-third pursuing their own educational interests. Thus, individual HMI enjoyed considerable professional autonomy but had little impact on individual schools and LEAs at a time when they would have benefited from thoroughgoing formal inspections by HMI teams. Visits to schools were still largely determined by the specific interests and expertise of individual HMI. The methodology and working practices on visits varied considerably. Anecdotal evidence indicates that some inspectors gave advice while others virtually issued commands. Most were content to provide a very brief written, and largely descriptive, summary of their visit.

This lack of any visible and direct impact from the work of HMI may be one of the reasons why the Review by the Parliamentary Select Committee on Education and Science in 1967 led to a reduction in staffing and a questioning of whether the role should be redefined. After this, the HMI role became even more advisory. Each HMI was assigned about 120 primary schools and around six or seven secondary schools. There was no central guidance or direction regarding the issues they should pursue so that some 'interesting' schools were over-visited whilst others were neglected. There was no system for harvesting the information gained from the visits and no standardised format for reporting on visits.

HMI REPORTS

From the 1920s until the end of the 1940s, inspection reports were issued by the Board of Education (Welsh Department) from addresses in London. Even in the 1950s, when the Board had become the Ministry of Education and when the Welsh Department was located in Cathedral Road, Cardiff, reports of inspections of technical colleges in Wales were still issued from Curzon Street, London. All inspection reports were confidential, but the teaching staff might see part or all of the report, at HMI discretion. Otherwise, the reports were shared only with the head teacher, governors and the LEA. They could be published but only in their entirety and at the express direction of the 'competent authority' for the school (or in the case of technical colleges, at the direction of the LEA). There is no evidence that any in Wales were ever published at this time. This practice was occasionally questioned. For example, on 26 November 1951, Peter Thomas, MP for Conway wrote to the Minister of Education, Kenneth Pickthorn referring to a letter from the editor of the *North Wales Weekly News, Conway* as follows:

> Most local newspapers cannot find space for a 2000-word report regarding one school, although most reports contain material of great interest to the locality ... let me know whether it would not be possible for the Local Authority to issue summaries of such reports embodying the main conclusions and recommendations for press publication.[23]

The Minister responded on 30 November as follows:

> My reply must be that we are not prepared to change our long-established practice. Experience has shown that extracts from reports on schools by H. M. Inspectorate can be selected in such a way as to give an erroneous impression of the nature of the whole report. For that reason we ask that reports should be published in full, if they are published at all.[24]

Following the reorganisation of secondary education after the 1944 Education Act, the incidence of inspection changed but shows that HMI inspected secondary modern schools less often than grammar schools and that grammar schools were inspected more intensively. In 1947–8, there were twenty-two full and thirteen semi-full inspections of secondary schools. The inspections of grammar schools were undertaken by teams of around fifteen to twenty HMI, while those teams inspecting secondary modern schools had only around eight to ten members. Most inspection visits lasted for around three days and the reports were between eight and twelve thousand words long. There was a strong focus on the 'nature and scope of the school', 'general school activities and corporate life' and considerable coverage of 'premises and equipment'. Teachers, although not named, were easily identifiable from the text. A former SI wrote of 1950s reports, 'Full inspection reports always contained detailed observations of all subjects that are frank in their praise and criticism of teachers and teaching and free with recommendation and advice.'[25] He quoted examples:

> Every opportunity and encouragement is [sic] given to the responsible teacher to place this subject on a sure footing. Unfortunately, failure to grasp the subject's practical possibilities and inadequacy of presentation cause a general sense of frustration. (1952)
> The syllabus for the 'B' forms should be reconsidered in its entirety and redrafted on simpler lines. There is nothing to be gained, for example, from providing them with dictated notes which few will understand or study and which many cannot read. (1954)[26]

Primary school inspections, by contrast to secondary, usually involved a cumulative process carried out in several visits by the GI over time and leading to a report of two to three pages, with often only brief reference to pupils' standards. Both NoVs and formal reports could be directly critical of individual teachers. One stated:

> The H. T. has a jerky and fussy manner and his control of the class is very poor. There is ample evidence in the condition of the office that the general supervision is inadequate too.[27]

Another reported:

> Everything spoilt by HT's unpardonable mixing of W[elsh] & Eng[lish] in same sentence—constantly e.g. 'There's an old saying in Saesneg ...' He is obsessed with the idea

of giving these ch[ildren] as much Eng. as possible – has ordered the Inf[ants] Class teacher to speak as much English as she can, even at that stage. I counteracted this, as thoroughly uneducational and unpsychological. Another visit to this school is needed.[28]

However, there are also examples of reconsidered opinions:

> My first impression of the H.T. of this school was entirely wrong. I saw many good qualities of his teaching and influence today and realised how difficult it is to inform a correct judgement straight away.[29]

Up to the late 1950s, the main focus on standards in primary school inspection reports was on basic skills and, in secondary school reports, on preparation for public examinations. Recurring criticisms in reports concern the variable standards in mathematics and the unsatisfactory provision and standards in Welsh as a second language. HMI also raised frequent concerns about girls' take-up of mathematics and science subjects and the standard of their work in these subjects:

> Much attention needs to be directed to the provision of appropriate work in mathematics and science for girls. Indeed there is a strong need in most schools for a thorough investigation into the reasons why girls react so strongly against mathematics and science.[30]

The need for a broader and more accessible curriculum was another recurring theme:

> The question why the Intermediate Schools of Wales have developed so strongly on the academic side as to have led to the comparative neglect of what was defined in the Welsh Act as 'technical education' (but which could perhaps in these days be more appropriately described as practical education) has exercised the minds of teachers and administrators for many years.[31]

Between 1945 and the late 1960s, reports raise many concerns about the neglect of practical subjects. Since the early twentieth century, when Owen Edwards had criticised the resources and equipment in schools for practical work, HMI continued to raise issues about poor libraries and poor facilities for art, craft, physical education and music. A pre-war pamphlet on music, based on visits to 152 schools, described music teachers in these terms: 'He is the Pied Piper of pedagogy, and if he knows his craft the children will follow him—even to the enchanted mountain' before caustically concluding 'In old times Welshmen enjoyed music by taking part in it. All too often their descendants merely listen in.'[32]

Concerns also emerged about standards in 'hygiene' and 'health education'. In 1949, in *The Future of Secondary Education in Wales*, HMI suggested that 'more attention be paid to health education. It should not be the concern of one teacher in the school but of all'.[33] Reports frequently commented on poor basic facilities for hygiene. One report on a secondary school in 1957 commented that 'toilet paper was available in only two of the girls' twelve w.c.s. The doors and walls of every girls' w.c. were covered in rude scribblings.'[34]

Inspectors continued to stress that even by the mid-1960s, a significant majority of pupils continued to leave school at the earliest opportunity and with no recognised qualifications. Reports on secondary schools would comment on leavers' destinations. One 1946 report on a grammar school in Swansea stated that twenty-two of the original cohort of 106 went on to universities and training colleges, with five others going on to other forms of education.[35] A 1958 report on a grammar school in the mining valleys stated that only around 12 per cent of the annual intake went on to higher education and commented that: 'attention is drawn to the sometimes crude and immature response (stemming from a lack of aptitude for their studies) displayed by many boys and girls'.[36] The situation described in one school reflected the social and economic context of the mining areas: 'Sixty-five pupils left during the year 1955–56; most boys proceeded to employment under the National Coal Board and most of the girls entered factories and shops.'[37] A 1966 report on five comprehensive schools in urban South Wales, stated: 'there remains a substantial number of pupils entering the secondary schools, who, for a variety of reasons, have achieved only a very low standard in the basic skills'.[38]

Criticism of provision in both primary and secondary school reports were typically expressed in very direct terms. Reports often gave the impression that teaching methods had undergone only relatively minor changes for over half a century. Time and again, inspection reports criticise the practice of keeping pupils occupied with mundane tasks, especially with copying out dictated notes at the expense of more useful activities, as these extracts from inspection reports from 1959–69 testify:

> Music and physical education have not played a significant role in the life of the junior pupils ... In view of the excellent playground available more enthusiasm and opportunity for physical education and group games could be expected.
> Much of the written work tends to be copied from the blackboard or from prepared cards or workbooks.
> At present much of the written work is either copied from the blackboard or consists of answers to lists of prepared questions.
> It appears to be the main aim of the teacher ... to give information to the pupils rather than to rouse their enthusiasm, stir their imagination, or kindle their interest. Dictated notes appear to serve in some classes as the pupils' main source of knowledge.[39]

Inspectors were also concerned about pupils' access to a full and balanced curriculum. As late as 1968–9, a survey of science in secondary schools stated that 'all 17 schools allow substantial numbers of its more able pupils to opt out of science, especially physics or chemistry, after the second, or more often, third year'.[40] The survey report also stressed that 'the fairly widespread practice of allowing girls to drop mathematics needs to be discouraged'.[41]

There is enough evidence, particularly in inspection reports of the late 1960s and early 1970s about secondary school reorganisation, to suggest that this was a period that required more, not fewer school inspections. For example, one report stated:

In one school members of staff used the word 'floundering' to describe the state of some probationer teachers; and in nearly all schools senior staff spoke of the variability of quality and control and communications and leaders at Head of Department levels.[42]

Another report painted a picture of confusion, inconsistency and very poor organisation, with the two teachers in one subject department having never met because of too much time-consuming commuting between sites for them and others.[43] A report on a comprehensive school where the staff included teachers who had joined the newly reorganised school from posts in both grammar and secondary modern schools concluded: 'The school remains divided, with the two staffs unintegrated and pupils selected for different treatment in different surroundings.'[44]

A report on reorganisation in Newport in 1969 lamented that:

> there was evidence in some schools of a poverty of curriculum for remedial classes, deriving from too narrow a concentration on basic skills. Less able pupils require a rich and varied educational environment, adapted to their needs, as much as pupils of greater ability.[45]

The concern about provision for less academically able pupils in the new comprehensive schools was a recurrent concern in reports and in the 1960s HMI often criticised the lack of planning for provision for the less academically able:

> One of the most disturbing features of the new comprehensive high schools is their complete lack of appreciation of the needs of less able pupils. No evidence was forthcoming of any serious thought having been given to the educational problems involved with these pupils when the school leaving age is raised.[46]

Reports were also frequently critical about management in the comprehensive schools. One report in the mid-1960s identified weaknesses in managerial structures where a 'deputy headmaster

[is] ... overweighed with organisational details which might as well be done by an administrative or clerical officer'.[47]

Drawing on these findings, particularly the weaknesses they revealed, HMI went on to plan a programme of conferences and in-service courses for senior and middle management in secondary schools, which continued to be offered annually until the 1990s alongside parallel courses for primary leaders. These were widely credited as being very influential in redefining senior and middle-management roles and improving the quality of management and leadership. However, little direct evidence is available of the impact either of these courses or of the many inspection reports that identified specific weaknesses in educational provision in the 1960s. No studies were undertaken by HMI over the period on the impact of their trenchant criticisms of poor standards in individual schools and it was left to the school advisory service offered by local authorities to address failings and promote improvement in individual schools.

THE WELSH DIMENSION OF THE CURRICULUM

In one important respect, the inspectorate was an effective advocate. This concerned the Welsh language and the Welsh dimension of the school curriculum and the way in which the legacy of Owen Edwards continued its influence on the education system. HMI lent their weight and support to the following:

- bilingual education, Welsh-medium education and the teaching of Welsh
- teaching and learning about the history, geography and culture of Wales, and
- a strong focus in the curriculum on enabling pupils to learn about their locality.

An early example of the continuing influence of HMI in relation to the teaching of the Welsh language came in the 1927 report on *Welsh in Education and Life*, based on an inquiry into the position of the Welsh language and to advise as to its promotion in education. G. Prys Williams, who became CI in 1928, was a member of the inquiry committee, which also took evidence from a further six inspectors. There was general agreement among them as to the causes of the ineffective teaching of Welsh in many elementary schools: teachers in Wales had received practically all their education through the medium of English, although it was known that they would spend their lives teaching in parts of Wales where Welsh was the mother tongue of the children. Although many of the teachers themselves could speak Welsh fluently, English was the language used in schools. One HMI recommended in his evidence to the 1927 report:

> all teachers destined for schools or hoping to get posts in schools where a scheme of bilingual instruction is established should receive a training in Welsh which is comparable at least with that which they receive in English ... the proportion of those who have a sufficient knowledge of the language and the methods of teaching it to be enthusiastic and efficient teachers of Welsh is not high.[48]

The report concluded:

> We have to rid ourselves of the idea that a school in Wales must be the replica of a school in England with the exception that the former has undertaken the extra task of teaching Welsh because it happens to be in Wales.[49]

But although the report made many and detailed recommendations about the teaching of Welsh in schools in different and mixed mother-tongue catchment areas across Wales, most of its recommendations were not implemented and it did not recommend that Welsh should become a mandatory subject either in elementary or secondary schools.

However, HMI considered bilingualism an aspiration for all pupils in Wales. A pamphlet first issued by the Board in 1938 stated:

> It is to be regretted that Welsh does not occupy the place it should in the curriculum of Sixth Forms ... For all of us the means of bringing a pupil into close contact with his

environment and developing a lively apprehension of the culture and tradition which he has inherited, a study of the language in which the history of the development of that culture is recorded in prose and verse, is surely the most direct. A sympathetic study of the history and geography of Wales can do a great deal ... but there can ultimately be no substitute for a study of the language and its literature.[50]

The Welsh dimension could give life to an otherwise lifeless curriculum:

> It is possible for the curriculum of a Sixth Form to become 'academic' and lifeless by letting the syllabus of Examining Bodies define the whole scope of the work, and to show how, in one direction alone—possibly the most important one, the studies may be given vitality by an active effort to relate the work of the classroom to the cultural, historical and economic environment of the pupil. In this way, he will grow to understand and appreciate what is best in the culture of other nations. Not only will such studies not narrow his outlook, but they will help to widen it. Thus armed he may travel far, but he will not forget his home.[51]

Cassie Davies reflected much HMI thinking in these extracts from her autobiography:

> Roedd ysgolion y Rhondda yn ddarlun trist i mi o'r hyn sydd wedi digwydd ac yn parhau i ddigwydd mewn cynifer o ardaloedd yng Nghymru ... y diffyg gweledigaeth a'r diffyg argyhoeddiad ar fater mor sylfaenol bwysig a pharâd y genedl Gymreig a Chymraeg.
>
> *Schools in the Rhondda were a sad picture for me for what had happened and what continues to happen in a number of districts in Wales ... the lack of vision and the lack of conviction in a matter as basic as the continuation of the Welsh nation and Welsh language.*[52]

But, on a note of optimism, she went on to say:

> Does dim sy'n sicrach na hyn – fe all addysg ladd iaith a diwylliant cenedl. Mae wedi gwneud hynny mewn cynifer o fannau yng Nghymru ac mae'n dal i wneud mewn llawer lle. Ond mae'r gwrthwyneb yr un mor sicr – fe all addysg fywhau ac adfer iaith a chreu cyswllt byw â'r gorffennol.
>
> *There is nothing more certain than this – education can kill a nation's language and culture. It has done so in so many places in Wales and still does in many places. But the reverse is just as true – education can revive and restore a language and create a living connection with the past.*[53]

This reflects the sentiment in the 1927 report which stated that 'The salvation of the language depends on the schools, imperfect as they are ...'.[54]

Cassie Davies also bemoaned the failure of schools to reference the lived experience of pupils:

> Anodd credu y gallai athro roi gwers o lyfr ar waith glo yn Durham i blant a'u tadau bron i gyd yn lowyr, heb unwaith gyfeirio at hynny.
>
> *It is difficult to believe that a teacher could give a lesson about coal mining in Durham to children whose fathers are almost all miners, without once referring to this.*[55]

Throughout the period, HMI were critical of the status and standards of Welsh history in schools. The Board of Education's *Educational pamphlet 114* noted:

> Welsh history is gradually assuming more importance in the general curriculum of secondary schools in Wales, but it may be doubted whether it occupies the place it should occupy ...Welsh history is not only a desirable but necessary part of the curriculum they should follow.[56]

Inspection reports on primary schools often included recommendations to give: 'more attention ... to the History and Geography of Wales'.[57] This was in direct contrast to the jubilant account given by HMI in their 1948 report on Wales's first fully Welsh-medium primary school, Ysgol Gymraeg Aberystwyth:

> The School successfully reflects in the classroom and in its general activities the ideals set out by the founders. That ideal is the belief in the value of the rich, spiritual and cultural education based on a Welsh life and language as a best means of releasing the Welsh child to full capacity. With this ideal in mind the teachers help the children to live the Welsh life joyously through lively and varied activities with plenty of exercise for imagination and for creative work in language, in movement and in art. The children's growth is marked; they are stimulated to a desire for knowledge; their whetted appetites are satisfied and their memories are stored with treasures of Welsh lore, song and legend. The atmosphere is one of a lively Welsh community living together in freedom, joy and activity, learning to grow richly from their own native soil and later branching out to embrace a knowledge of English language, literature, song and story, and to some understanding of the ways of peoples of other lands.[58]

The Central Advisory Council for Education (Wales) 1947 report on *The Future of Secondary Education in Wales* reflected the concerns of HMI about the curriculum in Wales by stressing 'the need for beginning with the familiar Welsh scene' while also identifying 'the further need for the widening of the child's horizons'. The report went on to argue that 'the curriculum has been subject-centred rather than child-centred'.[59] The Council encouraged schools to visit local venues outside school and emphasised the need to take account of the variation in children's aptitudes and abilities when planning learning. The council expressed regret that French was studied more extensively than Welsh in secondary schools. They recommended giving child-centred conversation and oral work priority over written work and stressed that:

the study of the Welsh language has very special relevance to the life of the Welsh child, whether Welsh-speaking or English-speaking, it should not be neglected in the school.[60]

There was further HMI involvement in the Council committee on the curriculum in 1952 when the Welsh Department published a booklet entitled *The Curriculum and the Community in Wales*. It claimed that the Welsh language inheritance was also mediated by means of the study of the nation's history. A sense of place was central to pupils' understanding of their environment and Welsh children should know about the musical, artistic and poetic traditions of Wales.

HMI also contributed to the inquiry by the Central Advisory Council for Education (Wales) into bilingualism in schools, which led to the report on *The Place of Welsh and English in the Schools of Wales*, published bilingually in 1953. There were fourteen Welsh-medium primary schools in Wales at the time (this would not have included the naturally bilingual schools within Welsh-speaking catchments) with a total of just over a thousand pupils. Seven of thirteen counties and two of four county boroughs had no Welsh-medium schools. The report proposed that:

> The main concern of the teacher should be to establish every child securely in the control of his mother tongue, Welsh or English. At the same time it is an essential part of the work of the schools in Wales to relate all children to the two cultures that exist here side by side. To do this the schools will have to teach the two languages. Consequently ... the children of the whole of Wales ... should be taught Welsh and English according to their ability to profit from such instruction.[61]

CONCLUSION

Despite the eloquence and frequency with which advice about the teaching of Welsh and of the Welsh dimension of the curriculum was offered, its impact on practice was slow. Nevertheless, Welsh gradually gained ground in schools and became established as the medium of teaching in many primary schools in most Welsh-speaking areas. There are a number of possible factors to explain the relatively slower rate at which Welsh-medium secondary schools were established. These include the powerful emphasis on gaining academic qualifications in English as a means of social mobility; the persistent feeling in some parts of Wales that a strong focus on Wales was parochial; and a belief that learning foreign languages and about the wider world was the way forward. An inspectorate with a strongly Welsh-speaking and Nonconformist profile may also have encountered a lack of empathy in an increasingly English-speaking and more secular Wales, with very different notions of what Wales and Welshness represented. Nevertheless, it is the case that, in its promulgation of the Welsh aspects of the curriculum, the inspectorate was influential.

The history of the inspectorate between 1925 and 1970 is one in which the precise role of the inspectorate was left unresolved. Was its prime function to regulate or to advise? Should it be visionary or pragmatic? Were the visits to schools and the on-the-spot verbal feedback or the subsequent written document the more useful? To what extent did the very restricted circulation of most reports inhibit the changes and developments the inspectorate consistently advocated? Some aspects of these issues would be resolved in practice in the periods covered by the remaining chapters of this book.

ENDNOTES

1. Board of Education, *Report of the Departmental Committee on Education in Wales, 1919–1920* (London: HMSO, 1920).
2. Board of Education, *Education in Wales: Report of the Board of Education under the Welsh Intermediate Act 1889 for the year 1925* (London: HMSO, 1926), p. 8.
3. Department of Education and Science (DES), *HMI Today and Tomorrow* (London: DES, 1970), p. 30.
4. Board of Education, Welsh Department, *List 6: List of the Inspectorate and Inspection Arrangements in Wales (including Monmouthshire)* (London, 1941).
5. Roseveare Inquiry, *First Working Party meeting*, 16/17 January 1956, p. 1.
6. Roseveare Inquiry, *Third Working Party meeting*, 13/14 February 1956, p. 3.
7. Roseveare Inquiry, *Final Report* (HMSO: London, 1956), p. 3.
8. Roseveare Inquiry, *Final Report*, p. 3.

9. Roseveare Inquiry, *Final Report*, p. 3.
10. Roseveare Inquiry, *Final Report*, p. 8.
11. Roseveare Inquiry, *Final Report*, pp. 11–12.
12. Roseveare Inquiry, *Final Report*, p. 18.
13. David Egan, 'A Brief History of the Inspectorate in Wales', *The Welsh Journal of Education*, 8/1 (1999), pp. 14–15.
14. DES, *HMI Today and Tomorrow*, p. 31.
15. Estyn Archive (Cardiff), HMI 14–18–41. Note of Visit (NoV) to Bishopston School, Swansea, October 1941.
16. Estyn Archive, HMI 14–18–120.
17. Estyn Archive, HMI 33–68–18, NoV to Bontddu School, 26 July 1940.
18. Estyn Archive, HMI 14–18–116, NoV to Rhiwfawr Primary, 13 October 1940 and 4 November 1940.
19. Estyn Archive, HMI 48–18–75, NoV to Ysgol Garnswllt, 27 March 1942 and 16 July 1942.
20. Estyn Archive, HMI 48–1–90, NoV to Reynoldston/Knelston School, 1 April 1942 and 16 April 19.
21. Estyn Archive, HMI 33–18–65, NoV to Ysgol Abergynolwyn, 19 March 1941.
22. Estyn Archive, HMI 48–18–264, NoV to Carmarthen Borough Roman Catholic School, 11 March 1940.
23. The National Archive (TNA), ED 147/67, Peter Thomas MP, Conway, Letter to Kenneth Pickthorn (Minister of Education) 26 November 1951, citing letter from the editor of the *North Wales Weekly News, Conway*.
24. TNA ED 500/11, Reply to Peter Thomas from Kenneth Pickthorn.
25. Sam Adams, 'The Inspection System in Wales', *Welsh Journal of Education*, 5/2 (1996), 111.
26. Sam Adams, 'The Inspection System in Wales', p. 111.
27. Estyn Archive, NoV to a small school in the Swansea Valley visited in autumn term, 1940.
28. Estyn Archive, NoV to a small school in Merionethshire visited in summer term, 1940.
29. Estyn Archive, HMI 33–18–68, NoV to Bontddu Primary School, 26 July 1940.
30. Department of Education and Science (DES)/The Education Office for Wales (EOW), *Report by HM Inspectors: A Survey of Science Teaching in Seventeen Secondary schools in Wales undertaken 1968–1969* (London: DES, 1970).
31. Welsh Department, *Report of the Board of Education under the Welsh Intermediate Act 1889 for the year 1928* (London: HMSO, 1929), p. 7.
32. Welsh Department, *Report of the Board of Education under the Welsh Intermediate Act 1889 for the year 1936* (London: HMSO, 1937), pp. 5–8.
33. Quoted in *Estyn and the Centenary of the Welsh Inspectorate*, p. 13 (Cardiff: Estyn, 2007), p. 13.
34. *Estyn and the Centenary of the Welsh Inspectorate*, p. 13.

35. Ministry of Education (Welsh Department), *Report by HM Inspectors: Glanmor Secondary Girls Grammar School, Swansea, 6–8 May 1947.*
36. Quoted in *Estyn and the Centenary of the Welsh Inspectorate*, p. 6.
37. Ministry of Education/Education Office for Wales, *Report by HM Inspectors: Abercynon Secondary School, 27 February 1957.*
38. Quoted in *Estyn and the Centenary of the Welsh Inspectorate*, p. 7.
39. Quoted in *Estyn and the Centenary of the Welsh Inspectorate*, p. 8.
40. DES/EOW, *Report by HM Inspectors: A Survey of Science Teaching in Seventeen Secondary Schools in Wales undertaken 1968–1969.* Quoted in Estyn, *Estyn and the Centenary of the Welsh Inspectorate*, p. 10.
41. DES/EOW, *Report by HM Inspectors: A Survey of Science Teaching in Seventeen Secondary schools in Wales undertaken 1968–69.*
42. *Report by HM Inspectors: A Survey of Comprehensive Education in the Borough of Newport, autumn 1973.*
43. Ministry of Education Welsh Department, *Report by HM Inspectors: A Survey of Transition to Comprehensive Education in the Secondary Schools of the Ruabon Area of Denbighshire, 27–29 January 1969.*
44. Ministry of Education Welsh Department, *Report by HM Inspectors: A Survey of Transition to Comprehensive Education at Ysgol Emrys ap Iwan, Abergele, Denbighshire, 4–5 November 1968 and 20 January 1969.*
45. Quoted in *Estyn and the Centenary of the Welsh Inspectorate*, p. 5.
46. Quoted in *Estyn and the Centenary of the Welsh Inspectorate*, p. 12.
47. Quoted in *Estyn and the Centenary of the Welsh Inspectorate*, p. 11.
48. Board of Education, *Welsh in Education and Life* (HMSO: London, 1927), pp. 143–4.
49. Board of Education, *Welsh in Education and Life*, pp. 143–4.
50. Board of Education, *Educational Pamphlet 114: The Organisation of Sixth Forms in Secondary Schools* (London: Board of Education, 1938), p. 8.
51. Board of Education, *Educational Pamphlet 114*, p. 12.
52. Cassie Davies, *Hwb i'r Galon*, p. 126. Translation by author.
53. Davies, *Hwb i'r Galon*, p. 139.
54. Board of Education, *Welsh in Education and Life*, p. 173.
55. Davies, *Hwb i'r Galon*, p. 92.
56. Board of Education, *Educational Pamphlet 114: The Organisation of Sixth Forms in Secondary Schools*, pp. 9–10.
57. Estyn Archive, HMI 14–18–41, NoV to Bishopston School (Swansea) in October 1941.
58. Estyn Archive, HMI 48–18–78, NoV to Ysgol Gymraeg Aberystwyth.
59. Central Advisory Council for Education (Wales), *The Future of Secondary Education in Wales* (London: Central Advisory Council for Education (Wales), 1947), p. 9.
60. Central Advisory Council for Education (Wales), *The Future of Secondary Education in Wales*, p. 106.
61. Central Advisory Council for Education (Wales), *The Place of Welsh and English in the Schools of Wales* (London: HMSO, 1953), p. 17.

Chapter 4

INSPECTING AND REPORTING IN A CHANGING EDUCATIONAL CLIMATE, 1970–1992

Roy James

INTRODUCTION

The 1970s and 1980s were periods of considerable turmoil in education in England and Wales. The era began optimistically with the widening and enriching of the primary school curriculum following the publication of the Plowden Report (1967) and the Gittins Report (1968), the introduction of comprehensive schools to provide equal opportunities for all secondary pupils, the raising of the school leaving age (ROSLA) in 1973 and the expansion of further and higher education. These developments were supported by a profusion of exciting curriculum development projects under the aegis of the Schools Council and the Nuffield Foundation. There was, however, also a backlash against the so-called 'progressive' ethos of the late 1960s and early 1970s. This was pungently expressed in a series of articles in the *Critical Quarterly* between 1969 and 1977 by academics and authors known as the Black Paper writers. These articles triggered widespread public and political concern that the quality of provision was inconsistent across schools, that standards were falling especially in literacy and numeracy and that too many pupils were underachieving. This concern found expression at national level in James Callaghan's Ruskin College speech (18 October 1976), in which the Prime Minister called for a public debate (the 'Great Debate') about the nature and quality of school education. Political interest and action intensified in the 1980s, resulting in wide-reaching reforms including the introduction of the local management of schools, the incorporation of further education colleges, the reform of teacher training and the introduction of the national curriculum (NC). In Wales, particular attention was focused on the high percentage of pupils leaving school at 16+ with no or few formal qualifications and the discrepancy between the attainments of pupils in Wales and their counterparts in England in external examinations and other performance indicators.

The challenge for the inspectorate, throughout the period, was how best to gather information to inform and advise Ministers on issues related to policy in a rapidly changing social and educational environment, while at the same time providing constructive feedback to LEAs, schools, colleges and providers of youth and adult education.

This chapter describes the organisation of the inspectorate in Wales during the period, seeks to analyse inspectors' (HMI) working practices and assess their influence on the education system, including their responses to contemporary issues in the primary and secondary phases and their contribution to the development of Welsh-medium education.

THE ORGANISATION OF THE INSPECTORATE IN WALES

The Welsh Office (WO) took over responsibility for schools in Wales from 1970 and for further and higher education (FHE) from 1978. Policy making in education remained largely on an England and Wales basis. The political impetus came from the Department of Education and Science (DES), with the WO tweaking legislation and initiatives to meet the particular needs of Wales. Following the transfer of powers, HMI (Wales) were on permanent loan to the WO from the DES. For all operational and management purposes, the inspectorate in Wales was independent of its partner organisation in England, but strong links were maintained throughout the period. The chief inspector in Wales (CI) attended the senior management group of the English inspectorate and HMI (Wales) were represented on phase and subject committees in England and participated in induction programmes, conferences, training courses and overseas visits with HMI (England). There was also a limited amount of cross-border participation on inspections, especially in FHE.

The number of HMI in post in Wales remained fairly constant over the period, ranging from forty-seven to fifty-one in the early 1970s and from fifty-four to fifty-six in later years. The HMI complement had been increased from fifty-five to sixty following the transfer of FHE to the Welsh Office in 1978, but the numbers in post did not reach full complement during the period because of recruitment freezes. HMI were recruited from the body of practising teachers and lecturers, mostly from Wales; some, especially those appointed to work in FHE, had experience in industry and commerce. Appointments were through open competition, with posts advertised in the national and regional press. Discreet enquiries, using the HMI network, were made of candidates' suitability before drawing up a shortlist to be interviewed. The selection panel, chaired by a civil service commissioner, comprised the CI, other senior HMI, including an appropriate specialist, and a senior WO administrator. On the basis of the panel's recommendation the successful candidate would be formally appointed by Order in Council, a Crown appointment which recognised the inspectorate's professional independence from the executive. Appointees were normally aged between thirty-five and forty-five, but in the late 1960s and early 1970s there was a deliberate policy of appointing recruits of a younger age. On appointment, HMI served a period of a year's probation and were mentored by an experienced colleague. Although the HMI complement included a few head teachers, generally, appointees were those 'on their way up' rather than those who had reached the top of their profession. The inspectorate was predominantly a male organisation during the period, with women representing 18 per cent of the workforce in 1970 and 21 per cent in 1992.

The inspectorate was managed by a CI and eight staff inspectors (SIs). Seven of the SIs had responsibility for a phase or aspects of education. The eighth had responsibility for Welsh and Welsh-medium education. Three also had territorial responsibilities, for north Wales, south-west Wales and south-east Wales respectively. The CI had the right of direct access to the Secretary of State for Wales, but direct access to Ministers at the DES was the prerogative of the senior chief inspector in England.

HMI were generally appointed as subject or phase (primary or special education) specialists but were expected to develop expertise as general inspectors. HMI were deployed across Wales with small teams located in each local education authority (LEA). The responsibilities of some HMI, especially in FHE, straddled more than one LEA. Within each LEA there would be designated district inspectors, one for schools and another for FHE. The district inspectors had responsibility for liaising with LEA officers and for keeping CI/SIs and the Welsh Office informed about developments in their district. The schools inspectorate was not divided into primary and secondary teams as in England (numbers precluded this). Those appointed as subject specialists from secondary schools were required to play their part in primary school visits and inspections and had to learn quickly on the job. The FHE inspectorate, consisting of specialists covering ten broad vocational areas and two specialists in youth and adult education, were more separate but there was also some crossover with work in other phases. This increased as more tertiary colleges were established and vocational and pre-vocational courses were introduced in schools. The aim was a unified inspectorate with common standards and a shared ethos.

A shared identity within the Welsh inspectorate was fostered through its annual general conference and working practices were honed through phase committees (primary, secondary and FHE) chaired by SIs and subject or subject area panels usually chaired by HMI. These committees and panels were seen both as a source of professional development and as a means of directing the work of the inspectorate.

There were opportunities for HMI to be placed on secondments for two to three years to senior administrative posts in the WO or as Secretary to the Schools Council Committee for Wales (SCCW). In the early fledgling years of the Welsh Education Office, it was advantageous to have someone with an intimate knowledge of the education scene in a senior administrative post. Equally, it was beneficial to the seconded HMI and the inspectorate as a body to be aware of the pressures that administrators were under to respond to Ministers at short notice and the importance of being able to contact HMI in the field when urgent advice was required.

Similarly, the SCCW benefited from having as its Secretary a person with status in the educational world and a wide network of contacts. HMI gained experience of the curriculum development projects and an exposure to the politics of education by observing at first hand the uneasy partnership between central government, local government and the teacher associations.

THE WORK OF THE INSPECTORATE IN THE EARLY 1970s

A booklet, entitled *HMI Today and Tomorrow*, published in 1970, described the range of activities undertaken by the inspectorate in England and Wales and tentatively broached future developments in inspecting and reporting. It argued that the two traditional functions of HMI – the regular visiting of schools and colleges to observe and assess the quality of provision and, on the basis of this, providing information and advice to the Secretary of State on educational issues – remained valid and relevant. However, it failed to provide a clear blueprint for the future and debate continued on how the twin roles could be effectively and efficiently fulfilled.[1]

As indicated in Chapter 3, full/formal inspections (FIs), which covered all aspects of the work of individual schools and colleges, had been suspended in the 1960s, partly as a result of the ongoing debate regarding the most effective and efficient ways of deploying HMI resources and partly because it was considered that there was little to be gained in inspecting institutions formally when they were in a state of flux. As a result, the central inspection programme was skeletal and consisted largely of surveys. However, HMI were expected to visit the schools/colleges assigned to them on a regular basis, with the planning of the visits left to the initiative of the individual inspector. These visits were largely pastoral and advisory and, in FHE, they might be undertaken for reasons associated with course approval. They were regarded as a means of keeping a finger on the pulse of the educational system and of gathering intelligence to inform and provide advice to Ministers and their officials, including advice on the funding of new courses in FHE.

Individual HMI and the inspectorate as a whole gleaned much information from these visits. However, there was no central guidance or direction regarding issues that should be pursued; nor was there an agreed sampling process to ensure a wide and representative pattern of visits. There was no standard format for notes of visit (NoVs) and no system for harvesting information from school or college files. While HMI, through discussion, advice, exhortation and dissemination of effective practice, made a positive impact on individual schools and colleges, the visits were too short (day or half-day) and infrequent to have a major effect across a range of schools/colleges or on the system as a whole.

A number of surveys were undertaken to monitor developments and trends and to identify areas of concern. These included: primary/secondary links and transfer arrangements; schools' responses to ROSLA; the work and impact of teachers' centres; organisation and provision within open plan primary schools; and a number of subject surveys. The surveys provided a sharper focus for HMI work than pastoral visiting. They also provided a valuable baseline of information in some key areas. Not all these surveys resulted in published reports, as some were merely mapping exercises, but the findings were invariably shared with the LEA and the group of schools involved.

Relations between HMI and schools/colleges in the early 1970s were fairly relaxed, possibly because of the absence of formal inspections. *HMI Today and Tomorrow* stressed the importance of maintaining good relations with teachers, even going as far as to state that HMI were in schools 'neither to record weaknesses nor to reprimand but to advise and encourage'. Head teachers and college principals, especially those who received relatively frequent visits, regarded HMI more as an impartial, informed outsider, who could be relied upon to provide objective advice and support, rather than a feared critic.

The general thrust of the work during this period was to help schools and colleges meet the considerable challenges that they faced in an era of rapid change. The inspectorate sought to do this by providing in-service training courses in key areas, leading and participating in working groups, and working closely with LEAs and teachers, for example on the implementation of the Gittins report.

The directive to LEAs by central government in Circular 10/65 to reform secondary education along comprehensive lines was the major challenge in the secondary phase. Inevitably, the organisation and management (O and M) of large secondary schools loomed large in the thinking and practice of HMI. An 'O and M' team was established which ran courses for senior school staff and LEA officers on the organisation and management of comprehensive schools. HMI did not advocate any particular form of organisation but discussed different models, analysing the strengths and weaknesses of each in context.

The introduction of ROSLA meant that extra or improved accommodation was required in many schools, both in terms of classrooms and technical areas, and HMI were involved in advising on building requirements. District inspectors and specialist HMI worked closely with LEA officers in identifying these needs. ROSLA also posed curricular and pedagogic challenges. HMI were involved in working groups across the country designing relevant courses for that cohort of pupils who were not always overly enthusiastic about further compulsory attendance at school.

The period was a time of rapid and diversified development in the FHE sector. HMI were called upon to advise (the DES up to 1978 and the WO thereafter) on a range of issues including the general pattern of provision, particular courses, building projects and the purchase of major items of equipment. The initiation of all advanced courses in FHE establishments required the approval of the Secretary of State (SoS) and HMI played a crucial role in this process. In the light of their specialist expertise, discussions with colleges, LEAs and the regional advisory councils (the Welsh Joint Education Committee (WJEC) in Wales), HMI commented and made recommendations on these proposals. The final approval on the proposals would be made by the regional staff inspector (RSI) who would sign the approval letter on behalf of the SoS. Thus, the RSI had an executive role that was unique in the inspectorate of the time.

While HMI contributed valuably, at one level, to the education system in Wales during this period, it was apparent that working practices were in need of review. The lack of a consistent pattern and clear objectives for pastoral visits, with no systematic means of collating the evidence derived from them, gave rise to doubts about their effectiveness as a means of obtaining a dependable and valid evaluation of educational provision in Wales. The surveys undertaken gave a broad view of the quality of provision in aspects of education and subject areas and yielded much information that was potentially of considerable use to policy makers. The emphasis in both pastoral visiting and survey work tended to be more on reporting on the quality of provision than on standards achieved by pupils and students. The limited time spent in individual schools and colleges during these visits gave insufficient opportunity to delve deeply enough into levels of attainment.

There was also growing concern that, because there were few opportunities for intensive visits with an inspectorial edge, HMI were not fully apprised of the realities of education in a changing environment. The practices of the time precluded them from gaining a holistic view of the total experience provided by a school or college.

REFORM

In the mid to late 1970s, the inspectorate in Wales was reinvigorated when a number of factors combined to give a greater sense of purpose and urgency to the work of HMI. As indicated above, there was a sharp awareness of the inadequacies of current practices within the inspectorate in Wales. Major changes in working practices were afoot in England with a reorientation towards increased policy-related activity. Whereas the structural changes introduced in England were not replicated (nor necessary) in Wales, the general thrust away from pastoral visiting towards a sharper focus on current educational issues was embraced. The Prime Minister's Ruskin College speech in 1976 provided a further powerful stimulus to make the inspection regime more rigorous.

Regular FIs of individual schools and colleges leading to a confidential report to the school or college and the LEA again became the norm. Surveys of subjects and aspects of education became more robust. Thus, programmed inspection took a great deal of HMI time; pastoral visits decreased in volume but became more focused. The opportunities to work together in teams on FIs and surveys helped to develop a corporate spirit within the inspectorate.

By the time the Rayner report into the work of the inspectorate was published in 1982 the new pattern of HMI working was well-established. The general thrust of the Rayner report was supportive of the work of HMI, but it made a number of recommendations regarding working practices, management and organisation. The recommendations of particular relevance to the inspectorate in Wales are summarised below:

- strengthening cooperation with the Welsh Office, including giving officials the opportunity to contribute to the composition of the inspection programme to reflect Ministers' priorities;
- reducing the time spent on surveys within individual LEAs and increasing the time on national surveys;
- devising a system for collating evidence gathered from routine general inspector and specialist visits;
- producing reports on the provision made by individual LEAs;
- defining more clearly the role of the college general inspector with greater emphasis placed on inspection and assessment rather than on giving general advice in a 'college visitor role'; and
- reducing the involvement of HMI in the detailed administration of advanced course approval.[2]

The recommendations were largely accommodated as reforms were already under way, although the course approval function remained until the FHE colleges became independent institutions in 1992. The flow and quality of information from inspectors in the field to the centre were facilitated by standardising the format of notes of visit and providing clear guidance on emerging issues which needed to be explored.

INSPECTING AND REPORTING IN THE LATE 1970s AND 1980s

In the late 1970s and 1980s, school/college reports were very detailed and covered all aspects of an institution's work. School reports would include an introduction setting the school in its context, followed by sections on accommodation and resources, management, staffing, curriculum and organisation, pastoral care, the school as a community and its role in the community, and an evaluation of the standards of work in each subject area. Consequently, reports on large, complex comprehensive schools could run to eighty pages or more. The inspection team included specialists to cover most or all of the subjects on offer, but only six or seven core team members, who would inspect aspects of provision as well as curriculum subjects, spent a whole week in a school; others with subject responsibilities would only visit for two or three days. The team, especially the core team, met after school each evening to share findings, identify issues and, following intense discussion and analysis, form judgements. At the end of the week, the reporting inspector, accompanied by a member of the core team, provided oral feedback to the senior staff and, at a later date, reported to the governing body with a senior officer of the LEA present at the meeting.

The inspection of FHE institutions was even more complex because of the range and diversity of courses offered – from day-release, part-time courses to sub-graduate, professional-level courses – and because of the large number of staff and students involved. Inspections of the larger colleges would last for a two-week period and the report could run to over 150 pages. Because of this complexity and the related resource implications, the number of full inspections of FHE colleges that could be undertaken was limited to between two and four a year.

A written report would follow after all the evidence had been accumulated and a draft report scrutinised and approved by the relevant SI. This process would take time, sometimes up to a year for schools and even longer for FE colleges, because of the volume of information involved, the desire to be scrupulously fair and balanced, the need to produce bilingual reports, and the other demands on HMI time.

The general inspector for the school or college, who was usually the reporting inspector, invariably followed up inspections to check on the progress made on remedying identified deficiencies. While they encouraged and influenced action, they had no power to insist on changes. It was up to the head teachers, principals, governing bodies and staff to decide whether, and in what way, they would respond. Momentum was often lost because of the time lag between the inspection and the issuing of a report. The nature of the report could also impede action. While reports contained detailed description and evaluation, the volume of information could obscure significant issues, as it was a convention of the time to eschew direct 'recommendations'. However, matters requiring attention were drawn to the attention of senior staff and departments during oral feedback at the end of the inspection. It was probably the case that the process of inspection and the ensuing dialogue were of greater influence in securing improvements than the report itself as many of the improvements identified would have been put in train by the date of its publication.

Traditionally, to respect professional sensitivities, reports on individual institutions were confidential and available only to the school or college, LEAs and Ministers and their officials. Parents and the wider community did not have access to the reports and thus to independent evaluation of provision and standards in their local school. For this reason and to stimulate school improvement more generally, the Secretaries of State for the DES and for Wales decreed that the reports should be published from January 1983. As a result, schools and colleges became more open to public scrutiny than they had ever been before and both local and national news media began covering reports. There was, however, at that stage no requirement that reports be made directly available to parents. Consequently, especially in the early years of publication, parents and the community were more likely to be informed of the contents of the report from the press than by reading it themselves. This caused some consternation in schools and colleges, as the press were selective in their reporting and often quoted the more critical aspects of the report. Heads and principals, who would receive advance copies, often sought to counteract this by preparing their own, more favourable, interpretation for the press.

HMI, for their part, also had to adapt to the new situation. Hitherto they had written for a professional readership using terminology that was in common use by those in the education service but perhaps not well understood by lay people. With an expanded and different readership in mind, the reports needed to be more concise, free from unnecessary detail and jargon, and assessments needed to be unambiguous. This was achieved to a large extent without compromising the need to place a school or college in its proper context. Some success was also met in producing reports more expeditiously. It is difficult to assess whether this reform had the desired effect of raising standards as there were many other major factors in play, but it certainly increased transparency and accountability for providers and for HMI.

Surveys of individual subjects and aspects of education continued, with their range and scope increased. In addition to reporting on almost all subjects of the curriculum, survey reports were produced on a wide range of issues including provision in newly formed comprehensive schools, mixed ability teaching, small rural schools, the work of 'athrawon bro' (peripatetic Welsh teachers), pre-vocational education, enterprise education and school-industry links. In the FHE sector there were surveys of individual programmes, for example, engineering, construction and business studies and of Youth Training Schemes (YTS) sponsored by the Manpower Services Commission (MSC). These reports provided rich sources of information on, and evaluation of, aspects of educational provision at the time. There would be feedback to each establishment at the end of a visit and to a meeting of representatives of all the institutions surveyed following the publication of the report and to LEA officials if the survey was LEA based (as most school surveys were). All-Wales surveys were followed up by a national conference to disseminate the findings and to push for improvements.

The surveys set the tone and agenda for discussion and debate within and across LEAs and, as evidence accumulated, across Wales. The reforms introduced in the 1980s were directly influenced by the amassed HMI evidence. A significant example of a survey that had a major impact on the work of schools was the survey of the teaching of history in secondary schools which found there was very little teaching of the history of Wales. Following the publication of the report, the history syllabus in Wales was transformed, especially after the introduction of the National Curriculum (NC) in the late 1980s.

Following publication of the Rayner report in 1982, HMI embarked on a series of surveys of the total education provision within individual LEAs. These were based on recent inspections and surveys and the accumulated knowledge of the local HMI team, supplemented by specific surveys of aspects of provision where there were knowledge gaps. They involved close consultation with LEA officers and advisers. Although there were sections on local administration and finance, HMI did not stray outside their areas of expertise and the main emphasis was squarely on the quality and effectiveness of educational provision. HMI found the work demanding but satisfying in that it provided opportunities for local teams to work closely with each other. LEA officers for their part were most cooperative and seemed to welcome a review of their provision.

The range of surveys undertaken together with the formal inspection of individual schools and colleges placed the inspectorate in a strong position to advise Ministers and their officials in the WO on current and emerging issues and to provide feedback to the system through its publications and in-service training courses.

ADVICE AND SUPPORT FROM THE MID-1970s

Roughly half of HMI time (47 per cent in 1978–9) was spent visiting schools/colleges on centrally programmed inspections and on pastoral or specialist visits. The other half would be spent on activities related to inspection, including writing reports and NoVs, responding to requests for information and advice from CI/SI and the WO, running in-service courses for teachers, attending committees, courses and conferences and being assessors on various educational committees and panels. In the late 1970s and 1980s, an increasing amount of time was devoted to writing booklets and occasional papers in response to identified issues and to disseminate good practice in various aspects of education. These included: *Literacy and Numeracy*; *Years 1–3 in Comprehensive School*; *Years 4–5 in Comprehensive Schools*; *Good Practice in A-level Courses*; *Pastoral Care in Secondary School*; *Role of Senior Staff in Comprehensive Schools*; and *Assessment and Monitoring of Progress in Secondary Schools*. A consultation document on teaching methods and organisation in primary schools was issued as well as the *Planning for Progress* series of papers dealing with secondary school issues. These publications were based on the effective practices identified by HMI in the course of their programmed and pastoral visits, supplemented by specialist visits by one or more inspectors delegated to lead on a particular theme.

Advice to Ministers and WO officials would usually come through CI/SI, although WO territorial officers would often contact district inspectors directly. The CI/SIs obviously depended on the quality of information they received from the field and the district inspectors' local knowledge was crucial in forming advice on issues such as secondary reorganisation proposals, the establishment of grant-maintained schools, the closure of small rural primary schools and funding for the government's Technical and Vocational Education Initiative. As well as their work to approve courses in new occupational areas, HMI were involved in providing advice on the incorporation of FE colleges and on their subsequent amalgamation to provide more viable units.

A good deal of HMI time (12 per cent in 1978–9) was directed to providing in-service training for teachers, lecturers and school/college leaders. This included subject-based courses for classroom teachers and courses on curriculum and organisation for school leaders and potential school leaders in both the primary and secondary sectors. The latter made a significant contribution to the development of leadership skills in schools and many of those who attended the courses became influential head teachers. At the time, HMI were the sole providers of educational leadership courses in Wales and they were invariably over-subscribed. HMI were frequently invited to give keynote speeches or make other contributions at courses organised by LEA advisers and others. Towards the end of the 1980s, the involvement of HMI in in-service training decreased as inspection and survey work took precedence.

HMI contributed positively to the education system in Wales as 'assessors' on various committees dealing with curriculum, assessment and cultural matters. HMI were represented on all of the WJEC subject panels and on the SCCW and its sub-committees. FHE inspectors were associated with committees whose decisions affected the colleges, including qualification awarding bodies and the MSC and their successors, the Training and Enterprise Councils (TECs). The Rayner report indicated that, generally, the host organisations greatly valued the objective advice, based on their knowledge of schools and colleges, provided by HMI.

HMI were closely involved with the preparation for the introduction of the NC in Wales as assessors on subject committees. They played a prominent part in developing curricula in Welsh, art, geography, history, music and religious education which reflected the culture and traditions of Wales. The inspectorate in Wales was also represented on subject committees in England. The influence of HMI on the teaching and learning of Welsh and on Welsh-medium education was considerable and is discussed more fully later. This was a very productive time for the inspectorate. The volume of activity was considerably higher than in the late sixties and early seventies, with increasing demands and responsibilities, especially from the mid-1980s. The intensity of the work brought increased pressure for individual HMI. The ethos had changed within a decade from a somewhat unstructured *modus operandi* relying on the initiatives of able, enthusiastic individuals to a more professional, systematic approach with an increased emphasis on teamwork and a clearer, shared perception of the role of HMI. The development of teamwork was facilitated by the increase in FIs, the formation of working and writing groups and the effectiveness of phase committees and subject panels in exploring, debating and forming opinions on the complex issues of the period. HMI's extensive knowledge of educational provision in Wales, based on direct evidence from the field, enabled them to comment authoritatively and impartially on these issues and to work constructively with schools, colleges and LEAs in the drive for higher standards. HMI were required to be educators as well as inspectors, visionaries as well as watchdogs.

HMI RESPONSES TO THE ISSUES OF THE PERIOD

The dominant issues of the period were: teaching methods and classroom organisation in primary schools; underachievement in secondary schools; and the growth of Welsh-medium and bilingual education. The implementation of the NC and its associated assessments loomed large towards the end of the period. This section draws on NoVs, published inspection reports and other HMI publications to illustrate the HMI response to some of these issues.

Issues in primary education

Following the abolition of the 11+ tests for entry into the grammar school, there was concern that primary schools were neglecting the 'basics' (the 'three Rs') and indulging in informal teaching methods to the disadvantage of their pupils. However, HMI evidence indicated that this was a distorted view of what was happening in classrooms in Wales. A scrutiny of a random sample of HMI reports and NoVs of the period reveals that there were interesting examples of innovative work, often associated with Schools Council or Nuffield projects. For example, the Schools Council projects on Welsh in both primary and secondary schools provided stimulating and challenging programmes of work which gained a wide and enthusiastic take-up. However, there was very little of the so-called 'trendy' teaching methods decried by the critics.

The majority of schools continued to offer a traditional curriculum of language and mathematics in the morning and thematic work in the afternoon. Although the curriculum had expanded somewhat beyond the 'three Rs', pupils' learning experiences were still, on the whole, rather narrow. It was not that the 'basics' were not being taught but that they were not taught effectively as they might be in a wider curriculum context. HMI noted that in many schools the emphasis was on mechanical exercises in grammar and computation which were unrelated to other aspects of the work. There were few opportunities in mathematics for problem-solving, the work in science lacked an investigatory element and topic work often consisted of verbatim copying from reference books. HMI were critical of these narrow approaches and, through their reports, school visits and in-service training courses, they advocated a wider range of experiences for pupils and the development of a broader repertoire of skills.

The other major issue regarding primary education was classroom organisation. The majority of schools by the 1980s had ceased to organise pupils in rows of desks facing the front in favour of a more informal arrangement whereby pupils would sit in groups around three or four tables. This approach was criticised by some educators and politicians who had come to the conclusion, after looking at methods used in countries which scored well in international comparison tests, that the major factor leading to success was the high incidence of whole-class teaching in a formal classroom setting.

HMI, while agreeing that there was often insufficient direct teaching in primary schools, sought to explain that whole-class teaching *per se* was impractical in many schools in Wales. Children in rural areas were educated in small one, two or three teacher schools: in Dyfed, for example, more than half the LEAs' primary schools had fewer than seventy-five pupils on roll in September 1983. Teachers were thus faced with the difficulties of teaching classes containing two, three or four year groups and, in some cases, the whole primary age range within the same class. This meant that at least some of the work needed to be age-appropriate for different age-groups within the same classroom. Differentiation could not easily be achieved if whole-class teaching were the only teaching style.

HMI also drew attention to the other major factor affecting the organisation of primary schools: the coexistence of two languages as media of instruction and the wide range of competence in Welsh within individual classes. Welsh-medium streams had been established in a number of larger schools (usually containing more than one year group), but in the majority of schools pupils with widely different linguistic backgrounds were taught within the same class, a situation which demanded considerable organisational and pedagogical skills from teachers, especially when they also had to cope with a wide age and ability range.

HMI recognised that, in these circumstances, flexible grouping within classes was the only practical way to meet the varying needs of pupils. To help schools meet these challenges HMI drew attention to good practice and shortcomings in their survey reports, occasional papers and short courses. They advocated more direct teaching of knowledge and skills to groups, more opportunities for discussions within groups and the avoidance of the organisation of too many group activities simultaneously within a classroom.

Whilst others were being dogmatic about teaching methods and classroom organisation, HMI in Wales remained resolutely pragmatic, basing their judgements on observed classroom practice rather than on ideology or the prevailing political climate. This pragmatism is illustrated in the 1992 discussion paper entitled *Classroom organisation and teaching methods in primary schools in Wales*,[3] which drew on inspection evidence accumulated over a number of years. The paper stressed that, in practice, what distinguished the effective from the not-so-effective school was not the teaching methods themselves, but rather their suitability to the learning activity, the balance and relationship between them and the quality of planning and organisation underlying their implementation. Prior to the 1988 Education Reform Act and the introduction of the NC, primary school teachers had considerable autonomy on how and what to teach in their classes. This often resulted in a lack of progression and continuity in pupils' learning, especially in subjects other than language and mathematics. Following the introduction of the NC, expectations in terms of the knowledge, skills and concepts to be acquired by pupils were enshrined in law and curriculum objectives were no longer open to the same degree of interpretation by individual schools and teachers. The 1992 discussion paper encouraged greater cooperation between teachers and better whole-school planning to meet these challenges. It acknowledged the challenges faced by primary schools in planning the more subject-based curriculum stipulated by the NC and expressed concern as to whether the class-teacher organisation traditionally employed in primary schools was now fit for purpose.

The paper stimulated considerable action within LEAs across Wales to redress the expertise deficit, improve whole-school planning and schemes of work, develop the role of subject coordinators, encourage cooperative working between schools and introduce some specialist teaching, especially in years five and six.

Issues in secondary education

In the secondary phase, the main issue at the beginning of the period was the embedding of comprehensive education and the resolution of the associated problems of organising and managing schools that were much larger and more diverse than the grammar and secondary modern schools they had replaced. As the volume of inspections increased, it became evident that there were too many variations in the nature, quality and effectiveness of educational provision both between and within schools. HMI identified underachievement in pupils' day-to-day learning and a failure to master skills and concepts which should be within their capabilities. Pupils' examination results at 16+ were consistently inferior in Wales to those in England, with about a quarter of the cohort leaving school with no formal qualifications in 1980.

HMI responded to the widespread concern about pupils' standards of achievement by producing a paper on literacy and numeracy which provided the basis for a national conference in March 1978 and a series of Ministerial meetings with LEAs, head teachers, teacher associations, employers and trade unions. In 1980, an HMI working group including a senior WO official was set up to promote improvements in educational provision. The group produced eight occasional papers published by the Welsh Office commencing in 1982 with the general paper entitled *Planning for Progress*.[4] This was followed by:

- *Public Examinations in Wales: Attainment at 16+* (1982)
- *Homework in the Secondary School* (1982)
- *Home-School Links* (1983)
- *Assessment and Monitoring of Progress in Secondary Schools* (1983)
- *Response to Underachievement* (1984)
- *Departmental Organisation in Secondary Schools* (1984)
- *Attendance and Achievement in Secondary Schools* (1985).

The underlying theme in *Planning for Progress* was that the efforts of senior management were insufficiently focused on the core functions of the school, that is, on teaching and learning. Management structures in schools had, generally, been more successful in ensuring the smooth day-to-day running of the school and in providing effective response to short-term emergencies than in providing a framework for long-term planning and for evaluating provision. The paper stressed the role of senior staff in eliminating in-school discrepancies, in motivating colleagues and in creating an environment where effective learning flourished.

As in primary schools, there was a great deal of classroom autonomy in the grammar and secondary modern schools and the concept of working as a team towards agreed goals was underdeveloped. An informal approach to planning lingered on in the new comprehensive schools, even though the larger departments could have ten or more members. Schemes of work were sketchy, especially for less able pupils and departmental meetings tended to be concerned only with routine administrative matters rather than pedagogic issues and standards attained by pupils. The paper on departmental organisation sought to enhance the role of the heads of subject departments and emphasised their responsibility for the planning, execution and evaluation of pupils' learning programmes. While giving due prominence to whole-school and departmental policies in combating underachievement the *Planning for Progress* series recognised that it was the day-to-day pupil–teacher interaction that was of paramount importance. Effective practice was identified in the papers and the crucial role of continuous assessment and monitoring of pupils' progress emphasised. A recurring theme in all the papers was the critical importance of enhancing pupils' sense of self-worth and esteem:

> Pupils need to feel a sense of personal value and dignity arising from their dealings with the school if they are to derive maximum value from their experience there. This means more than a display of mutual respect between teachers and pupils in day-to-day relationships. It implies a sensitivity to the opinion of, and regard for a pupil expressed through many aspects of daily provision and routine – in the classroom as well as the quality of the environment and community life of the school as a whole.[5]

The findings and implications of the papers were disseminated and discussed in residential conferences for head teachers and their deputies and in consultations with senior officials and advisers in each of the eight LEAs.

In 1991–2 and 1992–3, HMI conducted a survey to follow up on *Planning for Progress*. The findings were published in an HMI Occasional Paper entitled *Achievement and Under-Achievement in Secondary Schools in Wales*.[6] The paper reported that curriculum planning, pupils' classroom experiences and external examination results had improved but that progress had not been steady or uniform. Whilst HMI deemed much of the work seen during the survey to be 'satisfactory', the incidence of 'good' work was relatively low and the amount of 'unsatisfactory' work remained too high. The paper stressed the fact that the work which was regarded as generally satisfactory was capable of improvement. Heads and senior staff in most schools were adopting a more active quality assurance role but remained excessively preoccupied by administrative tasks. The report concluded that much scope remained for a further shift of management attention, at all levels, to improving the effectiveness of teaching and learning. While modest progress had been made, many of the issues identified ten years earlier remained.

Welsh language and bilingualism

As indicated in the earlier chapters of this volume, the *raison d'être* for separating the inspectorate in Wales from that in England was to meet the needs of a country with a distinctive Welsh language and culture. From 1970 onwards, after the transfer of educational functions to the SoS for Wales in the WO, there was an increasing demand for professional advice and assessment specifically related to education in Wales. While HMI advice covered the whole spectrum of pre-university educational provision in Wales, there was a particular need for advice on the Welsh language and culture and on bilingualism.

The staffing profile of the inspectorate in Wales reflected the importance attached to the Welsh heritage: throughout the period roughly two-thirds of the HMI in post were Welsh-speaking, including the CIs of the time. The SI responsible for Welsh and bilingualism led a strong team of Welsh specialists. In addition to the Welsh subject panel, there was a separate panel on bilingualism which had cross-curricular membership. Its remit was to establish an understanding of effective bilingual practice in schools by drawing on the findings of inspections and surveys in order to advise the WO on provision through the medium of Welsh and the development of both languages side by side. To deepen their understanding of the bilingual educational context elsewhere, members of the panel visited Quebec to study the methods used to develop bilingualism in the French-speaking province. In May 1979, HMI were involved in organising, participating in, and reporting on a Canadian/Welsh three-day seminar on 'Teaching through the medium of a second language'.

Before the 1988 Education Reform Act brought transformational changes through the introduction of the NC, two major countervailing trends were manifest in the 1970s and 1980s:

- the dilution of Welshness in the schools of rural Wales due to an influx of English-speaking families
- the expansion of Welsh-medium/bilingual schools in urban areas where English was the predominant language.

The complexity of linguistic provision within the Welsh-speaking heartlands is illustrated in an HMI report published in 1977 – *Welsh in the primary schools of Gwynedd, Powys and Dyfed*[7] – based on a survey undertaken between 1974 and 1976. The report identified five categories of pupils' competence in Welsh, ranging from those who were Welsh first language speakers on admission to English speakers with no knowledge of Welsh at all. Almost all the schools visited during the survey were in mixed-language situations. The report's findings were salutary. In only a few schools were pupils' achievement in Welsh of a satisfactory standard, and serious shortcomings were found to exist in both first- and second-language teaching. Schools were finding great difficulty in preserving and improving the Welsh of Welsh-speaking pupils, especially if they were in the minority within classes. The teaching of Welsh as a second language served to give non-Welsh-speaking pupils an introduction to the language and some consciousness of Welsh culture and tradition, but only rarely did pupils achieve fluency.

The report concluded that more effective methods of dealing with mixed language situations should be sought. HMI, through organising in-service training courses, their membership of Schools Council and WJEC committees, their advice to the WO and diligent monitoring of provision and support to schools were in the vanguard of the effort to secure improvement in the provision for mother-tongue pupils and learners alike.

Survey and individual school reports published in the late 1970s and early 1980s acknowledged that, in mixed language situations in primary schools, the timing of the introduction of skills in the second language was a delicate professional decision. However, HMI evidence clearly indicated that, in those schools that used Welsh as the sole or main medium of instruction at the infant stage, standards in Welsh were enhanced. After being immersed in the language in the early years, Welsh learners often achieved oral, reading and writing skills in Welsh which compared favourably with their Welsh mother-tongue counterparts by the age of eleven. The strategy of total immersion in the Welsh language was successful in designated Welsh-medium schools (where children from English-speaking homes were often in the majority) as well as in naturally Welsh-speaking schools. However, HMI found the teaching and learning of Welsh as a second language in English-medium schools where Welsh was taught as a stand-alone subject to be largely ineffective.

HMI were aware, from their own inspection experience and from their contacts with educationists in other countries where two (or more) languages existed side by side, that true bilingualism could only be achieved when the second language was used as a medium of instruction for part of the curriculum. However, the provision of Welsh-medium streams in both primary and secondary schools was meeting with only limited success in promoting Welsh-medium education. On the basis of this evidence, HMI were unequivocal in their support for establishing officially designated bilingual/Welsh-medium schools even in areas where the Welsh language was traditionally strong but now losing ground.

One of the biggest challenges faced by bilingual schools was the dearth of Welsh-medium text and reference books. The relatively unstructured nature of the inspectorate's work in the early 1970s gave opportunities for individual HMI to be given special assignments to meet specific needs. For example, the secretary of the Welsh panel, Geraint Bowen, was given responsibility for organising courses on Welsh literature, held at each of the university colleges of Wales and at Jesus College, Oxford. Following these courses, four books on Welsh literature and culture, edited by Geraint Bowen, were published. Bowen, in collaboration with others, also provided translations of English books on science for primary and secondary pupils.

While direct involvement in producing materials was not possible in later years as the inspectorate concentrated more on its core functions, the influence of HMI on the teaching and learning of Welsh and on Welsh-medium education remained considerable and they continued to advise on the publication and translation of appropriate textbooks. They encouraged the setting up of the Schools Council projects on Welsh as a first and second language in primary and secondary schools and, through their assessorships on these projects' steering groups, they provided valuable support. They also played a key role in advising the WJEC and later the Welsh Books Council on the commissioning and publication of materials.

The inspectorate's underlying philosophy remained constant. It held as a central tenet that a child's linguistic development should be developed in the context of the nation's culture and that this could only be achieved within a bilingual context. Through formal and informal networking, professional dialogue with schools and LEAs, reports and publications and advice to Ministers and civil servants, HMI helped create a climate where this philosophy became widely accepted. Their contribution was acknowledged in an article by Colin Baker:

> Not only at the visible and formal level, but also in an informal manner, the inspectorate in Wales supported and influenced the development and expansion of Welsh-medium education. Their publications have contained implicit assumptions of the cross-curricular validity of the use of the indigenous language, perceptive and considered advice for the progressive evolution of bilingualism throughout the school, not just in the formal curriculum, but also in the culture and ethos of the school. It is perhaps easy to underestimate the legitimisation process effected by HMI.[8]

The Education Reform Act 1988, heralding the introduction of the NC, was widely regarded as the most important education legislation in England and Wales since the 1944 Education Act. In Wales, it was particularly significant in that it gave full national and official recognition for Welsh as a subject in the curriculum. It gave Welsh the status of a core subject within the NC in Wales in Welsh-medium schools (defined in the Act as 'Welsh-speaking schools'), and the status of a foundation subject in other maintained schools in Wales. Core and foundation subjects were mandatory so that Welsh, either as a first or second language, became a compulsory subject for all pupils in Wales up to the age of 14 in 1992. In the following year, Welsh became a compulsory subject for pupils up to the age of 16. The status of Welsh in the curriculum was a contentious and politically sensitive issue and had been subject to much debate. In this climate, the inspectorate's resolute and unambiguous advice to Ministers was crucial in ensuring that Welsh should be a core or foundation subject for all schools in Wales and that there should be a Welsh dimension across the curriculum.

At the start of the 1990s, HMI were closely involved in the deliberations of the curriculum and assessment bodies in England and Wales on the development of the NC, especially those aspects of it that related specifically to Wales. An HMI was appointed as secretary to the committee set up to produce the Curriculum Orders for Welsh First Language and Welsh Second Language. The SI responsible for Welsh chaired the committee. The inspectorate produced papers for the committee as necessary. Similarly, HMI were influential on the panel producing the Subject Orders for history and in ensuring that there was a Welsh dimension in the geography, art and music Subject Orders for Wales. Other Orders also included references to the Welsh dimension: for example, the English Orders where the categories of reading required the inclusion of authors from Wales. Thus was established what came to be known as the Cwricwlwm Cymreig, which embodied the notion of delivering a Welsh dimension across the whole curriculum. This was to realise officially Owen (O. M.) Edwards's vision that it should be the entitlement of all pupils in Wales to study the Welsh language and to learn about their heritage.

CONCLUSION

From the mid-1970s onwards, the *modus operandi* of the inspectorate was based on full inspections of an annual sample of individual schools and colleges, supplemented by surveys and focused general inspector visits. Its main objectives were to inform the Secretary of State on the state of education in Wales and to improve the system by disseminating good practice and identifying deficiencies in provision. As indicated above, HMI worked energetically and effectively to these ends. Towards the end of the 1980s, under the visionary and rigorous leadership of CI Illtyd Lloyd, the inspectorate in Wales was highly influential through its initiatives in seeking improvements in standards and its even-handed reporting on educational provision. As the Rayner report concluded, HMI was well-regarded as a professional body which could be relied upon for authoritative information, sound assessment and valuable advice.

Given the high standing of HMI in Wales, it is perhaps surprising that in the late 1980s and early 1990s another review of the inspectorate was in the offing. The impetus for this came from DES Ministers who wanted to monitor the implementation of the NC carefully. Kenneth Baker, the Secretary of State for Education at the time, expressed the view in 1986 that, once established, the curriculum would have to be inspected on a more regular basis than previously and that this would require a much enlarged inspectorate. The other driver for change was Prime Minister John Major's *Citizen's Charter*, which promised parents up-to-date information on schools by means of regular short inspection reports.

From the mid-1970s until 1992, the inspection regime was designed to provide an overview of the state of education in Wales; this it did effectively. However, the system did not ensure that all schools were inspected within a reasonable timescale or that individual schools took effective action to improve standards. The inspectorate, as constituted at the time, did not have the resources or the powers to achieve this. Given that progress in raising standards had been slow, there was a case for arguing that faster progress could only be made by shifting the focus of the inspection system towards more frequent inspection of individual schools and giving the inspectorate powers to ensure that schools took action to secure improvement.

Following separate (unpublished) reviews in England and Wales, the passing of the 1992 Education Act would radically transform the structure and working practices of the inspectorate. These changes are discussed in the next chapter.

ENDNOTES

1. Department of Education and Science, *HMI Today and Tomorrow* (London: HMSO, 1970).
2. Department of Education and Science/Welsh Office, *Study of HM Inspectorate in England and Wales* (London: HMSO, 1982).

3. HMI (Wales) Discussion Paper, *Classroom Organisation and Teaching Methods in Primary Schools in Wales* (Cardiff: Welsh Office, 1992).
4. HMI (Wales), *Occasional Paper: Planning for Progress* (Cardiff: Welsh Office, 1982).
5. HMI (Wales), *Occasional Paper: Response to Underachievement* (Cardiff: Welsh Office, 1984), p. 24.
6. HMI (Wales), *Occasional Paper: Achievement and Under-Achievement in Secondary Schools in Wales 1991–93* (Cardiff: OHMCI, 1994).
7. HMI (Wales), *Welsh in the Primary Schools of Gwynedd, Powys and Dyfed* (Cardiff: Welsh Office, 1977).
8. Colin Baker, 'Perspectives on Bilingual Policy in Wales', in R. Daugherty, R. Phillips and G. Rees (eds), *Education Policy Making in Wales: Explorations in Devolved Governance* (Cardiff: University of Wales Press, 2000), p. 119.

Chapter 5

CHALLENGE AND TRANSITION: THE INSPECTORATE IN WALES, 1992–2020

Barry Norris

INTRODUCTION

This chapter will focus predominantly on the following key aspects of the inspectorate during the period 1992–2020:

- the Office of Her Majesty's Chief Inspector (OHMCI) and the privatisation of school inspection;
- HMI inspection of post-16 education and training;
- challenges in the inspection of schools and changes to inspection arrangements;
- inspection grade inflation and performance outcomes in schools; and
- the inspection of Welsh and bilingualism.

OHMCI AND THE PRIVATISATION OF SCHOOL INSPECTION

The initial focus of the chief inspector (CI) in Wales in 1990 was on building upon the sound base established in the inspectorate's recent past, as described in Chapter 4. However, the UK Conservative government wanted more radical change and it established independent, separate reviews of the inspectorates in England and Wales. Neither report was ever published so it is unclear to what extent the subsequent changes made by the government reflected their recommendations. But there were big changes in train.

Even though HMI had been undertaking an extensive programme of pastoral visits to institutions which gave them a detailed overview of sectors, the inspectorate was still only publishing a relatively small number of full inspection reports on schools annually. Thus, an individual school might not receive an inspection leading to a published report for twenty or more years. The government wanted public services to be more responsive to the citizens they served, as reflected in the *Citizen's Charter* (1991) and the White Paper on *Principles in Public Service* (1991) with their emphasis on clear standards of service, openness, accessibility and choice for service users. The government wanted parents to receive more regular independent information on standards in schools in their locality in inspection reports that enabled them to make the best choice of school for their child. The theory was that this choice would drive up standards and quality as parents would decide to send their children to good schools and weaker schools would have to 'raise their game' to retain a viable number of pupils. Ministers also wanted each school to be inspected at least once during a child's time in school and for reports to be available to anyone who asked for them. However, HMI in Wales did not have the numbers of inspectors necessary to undertake the greatly increased number of inspections that the new system would require (there were fifty-six HMI in Wales in 1992). The same was true in England. Thus, a new system was introduced based on an outsourced model in which independent inspectors replaced HMI as the agents of direct inspection of schools.

Before the inspection of schools was privatised, there had existed a growing antipathy towards HMI among some politicians. This was clearly expressed by Kenneth Baker – Secretary of State for Education in the late 1980s – in his 1993 memoir, where he identified HMI as the 'priesthood' of a Department of Education and Science culture that was 'rooted in "progressive" orthodoxies' and 'presenting perfectly the theory of "producer capture", whereby the interests of the producer prevail over the interests of the consumer'.[1]

The Education Act 1992 introduced legislative requirements for a five-year cycle of inspections of every maintained school that would largely be undertaken by a cadre of independent inspectors, called Registered, Team and Lay Inspectors. These inspectors would eventually be deployed onto inspection teams by private inspection contractors who would tender for inspection contracts.

The functions of the CI within the Education Act 1992 were similar to those enshrined in previous legislation, including keeping the Secretary of State informed about: the quality of the education provided by schools in Wales; the educational standards achieved; whether the financial resources were managed efficiently; and how well the schools provided for pupils' spiritual, moral, social and cultural development. However, the Act's emphasis on establishing a system of independent inspection and promoting competition for contracts to inspect schools were new functions. Two new independent departments were set up: the Office of Her Majesty's Chief Inspector of Schools (England), which later became Ofsted, and the Office of Her Majesty's Chief Inspector of Schools (Wales), known just as OHMCI. In effect, the 1992 Act reflected the political reality that Wales required a separate articulation of the functions of its own inspectorate, even if those functions were substantially the same as those in England. Prior to this, the inspectorate in Wales, for all operational and management purposes, had been independent of England, but strong links with the inspectorate in England had been maintained even after the Welsh Office (WO) was formally constituted in 1965. This cooperation was to continue until the early 1990s. For example, the framework for inspection that Wales developed in the early 1990s drew heavily on the work undertaken by colleagues in Ofsted, with the Welsh inspectorate's version having additional sections relating to aspects of schools specific to Wales, for example on the Welsh dimension of the curriculum (Cwricwlwm Cymreig) and the Welsh language.

OHMCI (Wales) was established with less trauma than Ofsted partly because there was significant continuity of personnel in Wales. Immediately after 1992, the CI in Wales, his senior team and most HMI remained in post. However, in England, the inspectorate was cut rapidly by almost 50 per cent and a new CI was appointed. The argument for continuity of HMI in Wales after the 1992 Education Act was based on the risk to the education and inspection system in Wales of losing HMI expertise at a time when the efficacy of the new system had yet to be proven. Senior officers in the WO were generally supportive of the Welsh inspectorate and a smooth transition was achieved and the new department launched effectively with little fuss. (As the new inspection system became embedded, the number of HMI in post in Wales did reduce gradually, from fifty-six in 1992 to forty by 1997.) HMI were needed in the early stages to establish the new system, to produce the detailed framework for the inspection of schools to guide the new inspection teams and to select and train the new inspectors. OHMCI faced the challenge of managing a privatised school inspection system while also assuring the quality of the outsourced inspection teams at arm's length. At the same time, HMI continued to inspect teacher training, youth services and adult education outside universities, and further education colleges (on behalf of the Further Education Funding Council for Wales (FEFCW)). HMI also continued to undertake surveys and to publish survey reports, most of them commissioned by the Minister of Education in an annual remit letter to the CI. Up to forty of these surveys would lead to published reports each year on key aspects of education in Wales.

Within three years, OHMCI had recruited and trained over 600 new inspectors, including 150 Registered Inspectors (RgI) who were judged competent to lead the inspection of schools. These new inspectors were generally experienced educators drawn from local authority advisory services and teacher education institutions or they were retired teachers or retired HMI. After initial screening in an open recruitment process, candidates had to pass written tests and role-play assessments at the end of a rigorous week of training by HMI, followed by an assessment of their performance on an actual inspection, before becoming accredited by OHMCI as independent team inspectors. The inspectorate also trained just over 160 lay inspectors, a new category of inspector with no previous involvement in teaching or the running of a school who were expected to bring a fresh perspective to the judgements of the inspection team. Subsequent quality assurance procedures involved HMI monitoring of a sample of inspections undertaken by the new inspectors. Initially, this monitoring was extensive in order to provide support to new inspectors and to ensure the system was working as intended. The regularity of the monitoring and the sample size were significantly reduced over time.

The emergence of the privatised RgI system seemed at first to be an existential threat to HMIs, but it led to positive outcomes in the early days of the new system. The inspectorate had to produce cogent, detailed and publicly accessible guidance on inspection which made fully explicit for the first time the criteria used by inspectors in evaluating provision. The *Framework for Inspection* handbook set clear descriptors for making judgements and it became a bible for many schools in helping them to evaluate their own provision. Advanced notice of inspection dates (up to a year) gave schools the opportunity to 'get their house in order' prior to the inspection. Too long a period of notice could be said to allow time to set a stage for lessons that give a more positive view of standards than would normally be the case. However, it also energised providers to improve aspects of their work for the benefit of learners and to develop their self-evaluation and planning processes to deliver positive change. In the 1990s, more regular publication of inspection reports with clear judgements gave the public access to a wider range of information on school performance than they had before and created a much sharper accountability landscape within which schools had to operate. And, in the early years, the post-inspection plans produced by schools to address inspection recommendations had to be submitted for approval to OHMCI. This helped to secure post-inspection improvements in schools.

The outsourced inspection system was set up quickly and smoothly, but there were unintended and unforeseen consequences. The withdrawal of HMI from the direct inspection of schools resulted in an erosion of their knowledge and expertise over time. Over the years, HMI gradually ceded ownership of direct knowledge of schools to independent inspectors who took that knowledge with them when they left at the end of each inspection week. Reading the written reports of others was no substitute for the deep, first-hand understanding of the life of schools that HMI had built up over the years through direct inspection and which had always underpinned their expertise and advice.

There was a fundamental review of the inspectorate's management and staffing structure in 1999 and OHMCI was re-branded as 'Estyn', a Welsh word, meaning 'to extend' and 'to reach out'. The aim was to create a brand that projected an aspiration for the organisation and for the education system. A new strapline – 'Excellence for all' – further emphasised the mission of the inspectorate in driving up standards and quality.

The management review was conducted by an independent consultant.[2] Its conclusion was that the existing structure was 'no longer fit for purpose' and was 'not geared to take the organisation forward'.[3] The previous inspection management structure, which included five senior staff inspectors, was reduced to two inspection divisions. These reflected the subject committee structure of the National Assembly for Wales, that is, a pre-16 education division and a post-16 education and training division. The review created six new managing HMI (MHMI) roles: three to cover pre-16 and three to cover post-16. MHMI were at the same grade level as HMI (grade 6 within the civil service), but they would line manage their HMI teams.

The review also created a new division – the policy, planning and corporate services division – to lead the policy and planning functions of the inspectorate. The aim was to make this division the driving force of the organisation, even though no inspectors would work within it. A separate review of Estyn's service level agreements with the Welsh Assembly Government (WAG) led to the gradual shift of corporate functions to Estyn and this new division from the newly established WAG.

HMI INSPECTION OF POST-16 EDUCATION AND TRAINING

In 1992, the responsibility for inspecting post-16 provision was transferred from the inspectorate to the Further Education Funding Council for Wales (FEFCW) as a result of the Further and Higher Education Act 1992. The FEFCW chose OHMCI to inspect post-16 provision on their behalf, and two HMI transferred to FEFCW to manage the inspection arm of its work. This was helpful in establishing rapport for joint working in the years to come.

A new framework for the inspection of further education was negotiated between FEFCW and OHMCI. A key part of the new inspection arrangements was the requirement that further education (FE) colleges produce a self-assessment report on the quality of their own provision each year, based on the post-16 inspection framework. This requirement encouraged colleges to appoint quality managers with teams of staff who would analyse performance outcomes in order to identify successful courses and to improve weaker areas of provision. This strong focus on performance, self-assessment and inspection in post-16 would eventually have a strong impact on the new inspection arrangements for schools in the 2010 framework. While school inspections were outsourced from the inspectorate, it was the inspectorate's involvement in the direct inspection of post-16 education and training that kept the inspectorate flame burning.

The main model for inspecting FE colleges was a two-week structure with the first week focusing on standards and quality in curriculum areas and the second week focusing on the quality of leadership and management. In the first week, the large inspection teams were led by HMI, but included associate assessors: lecturers and managers from the FE sector who had been trained by HMI to undertake inspections alongside them. The findings from the first week informed the inspection of the educational effectiveness of the college (the effectiveness of its leadership and quality assurance systems) in the second week. For the second week, the inspection team was much smaller, usually four or five HMI plus a senior associate assessor, who was a senior leader from another college. Another, less frequent model for inspection involved a series of curriculum area assessments, undertaken over a period of months, followed by an overarching institutional assessment.

The inspectorate contained a few inspectors who worked solely in post-16, but inspectors from schools with experience of sixth-form teaching were also commonly deployed to FE inspection teams, and HMI working mainly in FE would also work in secondary schools. Over the years, the potential for deploying HMI across a range of sectors and settings has been an advantage to the inspectorate in Wales due to its relatively small size, the wide range of sectors covered and the need to maximise the use of HMI resources. Deploying inspectors across sectors has the advantage of giving HMI a broader understanding of the education system although its drawback is that HMI will inevitably lack some depth of experience in a few sectors.

The relatively small number of FE institutions in Wales also enabled Estyn to designate link inspectors for each individual college. The college link inspector would visit each college with a set agenda and would discuss aspects of the college's management and development with the principal and the quality manager while also looking at some curriculum area aspects in some depth.

The introduction of associate inspectors was an important innovation in the inspection of FE colleges during the 1990s. These were lecturers and curriculum area managers from FE colleges who joined inspection teams to work alongside HMI. The large size of FE colleges and the wide range of courses they provided meant that it was logistically untenable for HMI to cover the inspection of all the curriculum areas and courses within a college. Associate assessors brought their recent and relevant experience to bear as team members on the inspection and enabled the inspectorate to expand and deepen their coverage of the curriculum in colleges. Their training from HMI combined with a direct experience of inspection enabled them to hone skills in quality assurance that helped them to promote improvements in their own colleges.

The early 2000s saw the introduction of a risk-based approach to the inspection of FE colleges as well as of schools. Inspections were in three bands: short, standard and full. The risk banding related to a mixed profile of factors that included performance outcomes and the college's previous inspection report. The banding also dictated the size of the inspection team, with short and standard inspections focusing on a selection of curriculum areas whereas only the full inspections included them all. The risk-based approach reduced the size of teams on a significant number of inspections, but it still meant that there could be as many as forty associate/peer assessors on an FE inspection team as well as the HMI lead inspectors. This created significant logistical burdens in terms of the planning of inspections, especially as FE institutions often occupied several sites over a wide geographical area, a feature that became more common as colleges gradually merged to create ever larger institutions.

The quality assurance arrangements for post-16 inspections were direct, rigorous and challenging. Unlike in the schools sector, inspections were led by HMI teams, and judgements were monitored and challenged on all inspections. There was strong, analytical engagement with benchmarked performance measures and both the findings and grades awarded were moderated on site in a process that included the team and sector MHMI. Grades would be changed if the evidence was not sufficiently compelling or the findings did not match the criteria for the award of a specific inspection grade. There was a strong focus too on consistency in applying inspection protocols from one inspection to the next. Associate assessors from colleges saw this rigorous moderation and the strong focus on consistency of inspection judgements at first hand. This did much to create a generally high level of confidence in the inspection system across the post-16 sector.

The Learning and Skills Act 2000 restored to the inspectorate direct control over inspection in post-16 sectors after a period of working as an agent of the Further Education Funding Council for Wales. The Act created the Learning and Skills Council (LSC) in England and Education and Learning Wales, or ELWa, in Wales. ('ELWa' in Welsh means 'to benefit'.) ELWa combined in one body most of the previous responsibilities of the FEFCW, the four Training and Enterprise Councils (TECs) in Wales and the Council of Welsh TECs, together with the responsibilities previously held by local education authorities (LEAs) for adult and continuing education. It was responsible for funding, planning, securing and promoting post-16 education and training, except for higher education, and was the largest quango in Wales.

From 1997 onwards, Estyn was commissioned to undertake cyclical inspections in an increasing range of new sectors. Below is a list of the sectors together with the dates when formal inspection cycles were introduced between 1997 and 2009:

1997–8:	Pupil Referral Units
1998–9:	Work-based training providers
1999–2000:	New Deal providers
	Careers Companies
2000–1:	Best Value inspections of LEAs with the Audit Commission and Wales Audit Office
2003–4:	Youth justice/youth offending teams
	LEAs as part of the Wales Programme for Improvement
	Young People's Partnerships
2004–5:	Independent schools
	Workstep programmes
2008–9:	Offender learning with HMI Probation.

This increase in the range of sectors to inspect required a significant increase in the development of new inspection guidance documents, training for HMI, and substantial engagement with a new set of providers and agencies. It also required more flexibility in adapting existing inspection systems for sectors with different contexts and with a wide range of partners. In the justice system, for instance, the partnerships extended to include HM Inspectorate of Probation, HM Inspectorate of Prisons, HM Inspectorate of Constabulary, Care and Social Services Inspectorate Wales, Healthcare Commission, Ofsted and the Adult Learning Inspectorate.

HMI recruitment was at a standstill for most of the 1990s and, even after the 1999 recruitment drive for post-16 inspectors, the inspectorate was still relatively small, with around sixty inspectors to cover around fourteen separate sectors of education and training. To mitigate the effect of this on the work programme, more use was made of full-time secondments from education and training sectors and of part-time peer assessors with a strong track record on inspections.

From 1992 onwards, OHMCI/Estyn had been introducing innovative aspects of inspection practice in post-16 sectors where HMI continued to inspect directly. Provider nominees – usually the quality manager – were included as members of inspection teams, as were increasing numbers of peer assessors/inspectors from other providers. The HMI expectation that providers should produce pre-inspection self-assessment reports (SARs) expanded the capacity of post-16 providers to take control of their own quality improvement as well as quality assurance. This was at a time when the inspection of schools was more narrowly confined to the requirements of the privatised school inspection system. The innovative post-16 inspection approaches were to influence the next inspection cycle (2004–10) and would eventually become fully embedded within the 2010 inspection framework that was common to virtually all pre-16 and post-16 sectors.

CHALLENGES IN THE INSPECTION OF SCHOOLS AND CHANGES TO INSPECTION ARRANGEMENTS

The first common inspection framework was introduced in 2004, based on the same seven key questions used in 1992. Having a common framework made it easier for inspectors to work across sectors and facilitated more direct comparison of inspection outcomes between sectors. In 2004, Estyn also introduced a system of risk-assessment as the basis for allocating a full, standard or short inspection in schools, as had already occurred in post-16. The allocation of risk category was based on an analysis of previous inspection outcomes and of three years of performance data. High-risk schools received a full inspection, which included evaluating all the National Curriculum (NC) subjects or education and training programmes they offered. In a standard inspection, inspectors evaluated and reported on about half of the provision. In a short inspection, an even smaller sample of provision was inspected, including an evaluation of the planning, delivery and standards in key skills.

In 2004, based on consultation with education sectors and other stakeholders and an externally commissioned review of the previous cycle, some new features were added, including more focus on listening to and questioning learners about their well-being, and more checks on safeguarding (child protection and health and safety). A pre-inspection pupil questionnaire was introduced to go alongside the pre-existing parent questionnaire in order to give inspection teams more feedback on pupils' and parents' views.

In 2004, the inspectorate also began inviting associate or peer assessors/inspectors to join school inspections. These were serving head teachers and deputy head teachers from schools who were trained by Estyn as team inspectors. As in FE, this substantially increased the capacity of inspection teams and also enabled assessors to enhance evaluation practices in their own schools. The programme expanded over the years and, by 2020, there were nearly 400 peer inspectors in the primary sector (that is, in around one in three primary schools) and just under 200 in secondary schools (that is, in most secondary schools).

In 2005, a new Education Act (EA) was passed which maintained the privatised inspection model, but, after 2006, inspection became a devolved matter for the Welsh Assembly Government (WAG). The 2005 EA outlined the duties of the CI as reporting to the government and the public on the same aspects as in the Education Act 1992, but there was more emphasis on how far the education provided met the needs of the range of pupils, the quality of leadership and management, and a new focus on the contribution made by schools to the well-being of pupils.

The governance of Estyn also changed as a result of the 2005 EA. The Act gave WAG the power to set up a board to oversee Estyn's work. The CI constituted a board comprising three non-executive directors in addition to Estyn's own senior management team. The first three non-executive directors were from educational backgrounds, but, over the years, the board began to include non-executive directors from a wider range of backgrounds in the private and public sectors.

A valid criticism of the more intensive inspection of all schools after 1992 was that it placed undue stress on teachers. In the 1990s, schools were informed a year in advance of their impending inspection. According to the teacher and head teacher unions at the time, this led to a prolonged period of anxiety and stress for staff. The long notice period also allowed some LEAs to undertake 'mock' inspections of schools to prepare them for their 'proper' inspection. While some benefits might have accrued from these activities, they could also add to the pre-inspection stress on schools. In 1992, the inspectorate's view was that a long period of notice allowed schools to 'put their house in order'. By 2005, this view was changing and the inspectorate began to support shorter notice periods in order to reduce staff anxiety and to see schools with minimal 'window dressing'. Parents in particular were strongly supportive of inspections with less notice. The notification period was reduced substantially from 2005 onwards, and, by 2017, it was only fifteen working days.

As schools and LEAs experienced more and more inspections, so they began comparing experiences, and some inconsistencies were identified in the approaches of different teams. Certain RgIs were perceived to be more positive or negative than others, and some inspection reports with similar findings too often appeared to deliver a different set of inspection grades or judgements. Estyn attempted to address these concerns by monitoring inspections and customising training. Conducting a small number of HMI inspections each year, where there was no external bid, allowed comparisons between RgI-led and HMI-led inspections. However, the sample of inspections and reports that were directly monitored by HMI for quality asssurance purposes had reduced over time from the early 1990s to the early 2000s, by which time, monitoring had become very light touch. On principle, contractors were deemed to be responsible for their own quality assurance and for dealing with complaints as part of their contractual obligations. Only occasionally, as a result of an upheld complaint, would Estyn change a published report. Normally, reports would be published as received from contractors, without any pre-publication quality assurance by Estyn, and only after publication would a small sample of reports be monitored by Estyn in order to feed back a view on their work to RgIs. While there were provisions in the Education Act 1992 to remove RgIs from the register of inspectors, these were never used in practice as RgIs would either resign or accept restrictions on their work before the provisions were activated. The arm's-length approach to the quality monitoring of school inspection reports, unlike the hands-on approach in other sectors, meant that checks on the validity and reliability of the judgements and grades in reports were less consistent in the inspection of schools.

INSPECTION GRADE INFLATION AND PERFORMANCE OUTCOMES IN SCHOOLS

It was tenable for the CI in the *Annual Report 1996–1997* to talk about 'a significant improvement in standards' in schools and to say that 'in all four key stages there has been an increase of about 10 percentage points in the proportion of work where standards are satisfactory or better'.[4] This improvement in standards 'clearly reflected ... higher levels of achievement ... in pupils' performance ... in public examination results at GCSE and GCE'.[5] The emerging, generally positive trends from inspection and from examination outcomes were broadly similar – the education system in Wales was improving. According to the *Annual Report 2001–2002* 'the picture is a bright one. The quality of education and training is, in almost every way, better than it was last year.'[6]

The *Annual Report 2004–2005* was the first to consider the progress that schools had made since the last time that they were inspected.[7] Previous reports had looked at the year-on-year outcomes of inspection as a whole within each sector without taking this longitudinal approach based on individual school improvement over time. The *Annual Report 2004–2005* reported significant improvements made over time in terms of the inspection grades awarded. In the primary sector, it stated that '76% of lessons we inspected achieved the top two grades, compared with just over 46% five years ago, when we inspected many of the same schools that were in this year's sample'.[8] In the secondary sector, 'the amount of good work ... has increased by 16 percentage points from 47% to 63%' over the same five-year period.[9] The *Annual Report 2004–2005* is clear that this improvement in lesson grades was reflected in examination and test results: 'over the same period there have been considerable improvements in many of the examination and national assessment results in primary and secondary schools'.[10] Thus, the picture that was emerging in the 2004–2005 annual report was that all was well with the education system in Wales and that there were similar trends of improvement in both inspection findings and examination results.

However, despite the improved inspection picture, the level of improvement over the period was actually quite muted in terms of GCSE examination outcomes. Between 1999 and 2004, the proportion of pupils achieving the GCSE core subject indicator only rose from 34 per cent to 36 per cent, and the proportion gaining five or more GCSEs at grade C or above only rose from 48 per cent to 52 per cent. As the decade progressed, improvement in school performance measures became even more limited. For example, from 2003 to 2007, the proportion of pupils gaining the core subject indicator at the end of key stage 2 hardly rose at all (from 79 per cent to 80 per cent). In secondary schools in Wales, the proportion gaining five or more GCSEs at grade C or above only increased from 50 per cent to 54 per cent over the same period. This slow improvement in Wales also contrasted adversely with improvements in GCSE outcomes in England over the same period, where the proportion gaining five or more GCSEs at grade C or above rose from 52 per cent to 62 per cent.

The picture painted by school performance measures was that Wales was falling behind, the system was underperforming, and any improvements were rapidly running out of steam. Yet, the proportion of 'excellent' and 'good' standards awarded to lessons observed on inspections had jumped from 51 per cent to 80 per cent in primary schools and from 51 per cent to 72 per cent in secondary schools between 2001 and 2005. The inspection system and the systems for assessing pupil performance were communicating contradictory messages.

A similar narrative was also unfolding in post-16 inspections. In *Quality and Standards in Further Education in Wales 1993–1997*, produced by the inspectorate for FEFCW, the proportion of learners' work judged to be good or outstanding with no major shortcomings was 55 per cent.[11] However, within a decade, the picture had changed significantly. In the *Annual Report 2005–2006*, the proportion of good or very good work had risen to 81 per cent, and the report stated that 'this year, for the first time in the inspection cycle, none of the learning areas we inspected had shortcomings in important areas'.[12] By the following year, the proportion of good or very good work had risen even further to 90 per cent.[13]

However, this improvement was not all that it seemed. It coincided with ELWa's move from publishing data sets from the National Performance and Funding System (NPFS) to the use of data from the new Lifelong Learning Wales Record (LLWR) which meant that the census point for recording a learner's registration on a course leading to a qualification no longer reflected the date of their initial enrolment. This made it almost impossible for inspectors to consider the attrition rate on individual courses (how many learners had dropped out of their courses). In order to maximise their success rates, colleges would often formally 'enrol' the students remaining on a course only towards the end of it. Faced with the resulting inflation in the percentages of students achieving a successful outcome, it became impossible for inspectors to calibrate overall success rates confidently and robustly.

By comparison, trends in secondary school data on student performance did not offer a justification for inflating inspection judgements. Notwithstanding the reservations expressed in Chapter 7 of this volume about the general reliability of examination and test results, the accepted view was that there was a prima facie misalignment between the rate of annual improvement in inspection grades in schools and the rate of improvement in examination results. In an internal HMI analysis in the autumn of 2006, which considered inspection grade distributions in school inspections undertaken during the 2005–06 academic year, several inconsistencies were identified, notably between more modest grades for standards and inflated grades for leadership, management and support.[14] Twice as many grade 1s ('outstanding') were awarded for 'leadership and management' than for 'standards' in primary school inspections. Almost 100 per cent of schools were deemed 'outstanding' in the 'care, guidance and support' they offered to learners: 94 per cent in primary, 97 per cent in secondary and 94 per cent in special schools. To place so many schools in the grade 1 category when the scale of inspection judgements had five points seemed to make a nonsense of the five-point scale itself and undermined the very meaning of the word 'outstanding'. This inflation had become a common tendency among many independent inspection teams in their judgements on some of the seven key questions in the inspection framework although the distribution of grades for standards (key question 1) and teaching and assessment (key question 2) was far less skewed. However, in 2005–06, no primary school was judged to have less than satisfactory standards (grade 3) and 80 per cent were 'good' (grade 2) or 'outstanding' (grade 1). The analysis identified clear issues of consistency and reliability in grading practices across the board and their identification led to considerable internal debate. Eventually, it led to a programme of grade recalibration and retraining, the full impact of which was only felt after 2010 when a new inspection cycle and framework were established.

The misalignment between inspection judgements and data on learner performance was exacerbated in 2007 when the results of the Programme for International Student Assessment (PISA) survey were published for the first time for Wales.[15] The outcomes of PISA showed that 15-year-olds in Wales were not doing as well in reading, mathematics and science as pupils in other countries. In 2010, the mean score for Wales in the PISA survey outcomes in reading and mathematics were once again significantly lower than the average and below those of the other countries in the UK.[16] In reading, mathematics and science, Wales's mean score was actually getting worse.

These PISA outcomes gave weight to those within the inspectorate who had identified 'inspection grade inflation' as a growing issue. It led to soul-searching about the arm's-length quality assurance arrangements for contracted-out RgI inspections and whether these were fit for purpose. Consequently, Estyn began a root-and-branch review of its mission and structures. Strategic objectives were refocused on providing public accountability, informing national policy and promoting the spread of best practice. Two new appointments were made to the senior team, which would now comprise the CI and three strategic directors, who were all HMI. Six assistant directors were appointed, five mainly to manage inspection and one to manage corporate services. As of January 2010, the five assistant directors for inspection between them managed forty-nine HMI. They also managed twelve colleagues seconded to Estyn from education providers. Each HMI was allocated a lead role related to inspection, the curriculum or quality matters. The assistant director for corporate services managed forty-one permanent staff and six staff employed from agencies or contractors. From 2010 onwards, Estyn would return to inspecting schools directly and phase out the use of independent inspection contractors. A new lead officer for inspection policy and quality assurance was appointed and, although the inspectorate would continue to use RgIs for a reducing proportion of primary school and non-maintained nursery inspections, HMI would lead most inspections. (HMI would continue to lead all post-16 inspections as usual.) New guidance and a four-point grading scale were introduced and the 'quality threshold' moved from being below grade 3 (satisfactory) to being at grade 2 (good). The number of key questions was cut from seven to three and the number of graded judgements in reports was reduced to fifteen. The framework also required more resources to be allocated to post-inspection follow-up visits in order to support improvement in weaker schools.

Outsourcing inspection had had its benefits, as outlined earlier in this chapter, but it also had its disadvantages. The benefits included the enabling of an increased frequency of school inspection after 1992. The timing of inspections was no longer the luck of the draw. In the new system, every school knew that an inspection was coming at some point in the inspection cycle. There was greater transparency about the criteria that inspectors used to evaluate schools and to make judgements. Published reports, available on Estyn's website, led to greater public knowledge about standards and quality in individual schools. This allowed parents and others, including the media, to compare and contrast schools. And it fed an increasingly accountable culture across schools and the education and training landscape more generally. The new system also produced many more professionals with direct experience of inspection.

However, the new system had significant disadvantages too and these were exacerbated as time went on. The regulatory framework for managing the quality of the outsourced inspection system was weak. Inconsistencies between independent inspection teams in the way they managed inspections and came to their judgements and inspection grades slowly undermined schools' trust and confidence in the inspection outcomes. This became more and more acute as the accountability landscape in Wales placed increasing emphasis on comparisons between schools and leaders focused more and more on meeting accountability targets. The arm's-length nature of the quality assurance arrangements within the outsourced system were inadequate. Estyn's ability to rectify problems before the publication of a report was severely limited and schools could only attempt to address issues by making complaints after the inspection. As a result, complaints increased. Estyn had too few tools at its disposal to address these shortcomings, and some of the tools that were at their disposal, such as the capacity to remove accreditation from a RgI, were threatened, but not used. This also meant that Estyn was poorly placed to address directly the inspection grade inflation that gradually emerged while learner performance outcomes stagnated. Despite the positives, the negatives struck at the heart of the inspectorate's mission to report accurately on standards and quality in order to help to improve education in Wales.

One casualty of the new arrangements after 2010 was the reporting on standards in each of the subjects of the NC. With HMI now leading the majority of inspections, there simply were not enough specialist inspectors to inspect and report on all NC subjects in detail. The focus instead was on inspecting and reporting on standards in literacy (English/Welsh) and numeracy (ICT was a focus later too) and on a sample of subjects related to inspectors' subject-specific expertise.

In 2010, the inspectorate developed virtual inspection rooms (VIRs) where schools could upload their pre-inspection documents and where members of inspection teams could place their emerging findings as the inspection progressed. This allowed the live collation of inspection findings as each member of the team recorded their evidence and findings as they emerged. At the press of a button in the VIR, the reporting inspector (RI), who led the inspection, and managers and lead officers within Estyn, could see the emerging picture of the inspection in the VIR and could quickly monitor the work of the inspection team. The RI could also generate a draft of the inspection report through the VIR for the team to use as a draft report for their feedback to the senior leaders of the school at the end of the inspection. After the inspection, the report and its supporting evidence in the VIR faced a rigorous quality assurance process within Estyn and the text and judgements within the report could be amended if the evidence gathered did not clearly support the judgements made. Only after this process had been completed was the final report published.

Final inspection outcomes were uploaded to a database which the inspectorate could interrogate in multiple ways to generate a statistical dashboard to monitor and analyse the emerging, real-time inspection judgements in schools, sectors and local authorities across Wales. The tools were now available in real time to monitor and challenge inspection outcomes quickly, robustly and effectively before the publication of inspection reports.

The 2010 inspection framework set out new quality descriptors for each inspection judgement and offered more robust guidance to inspectors. This, together with the application by Estyn of rigorous quality assurance processes prior to publishing inspection reports, resulted in the recalibration of inspection judgements. The changes had an immediate impact in reversing 'inspection grade inflation'. For example, the proportion of primary and secondary schools with standards above the quality threshold fell significantly from 2010 onwards. The recalibration of judgements caused some initial turbulence in sectors, but this soon settled once the new criteria became established and inspection outcomes reflected a more consistent and realistic evaluation of standards.

In September 2011, the WAG introduced a banding system for secondary schools based on a range of performance measures. In

2014, this was replaced by a National School Categorisation System for all primary and secondary schools. This created a colour-coded league table of schools that was published annually, ostensibly to identify the level of support each school required. Schools were placed on a four-point scale from green (little or no support) through yellow and amber to red (intensive support). This had the effect of creating a parallel grading system alongside school inspections which added considerably to the tensions and stigma for schools as the 'colour' of their categorisation was made public and discussed in the press. At times, inspection outcomes would not reflect the school's 'category' as they were based on different processes and criteria, and this could be confusing for both parents and politicians. The reports on education from the Organisation for Economic Co-operation and Development (OECD) in 2014 and 2017 were critical of the cluttered accountability landscape in Wales.[17] In 2014, the OECD said that external school evaluations in Wales were 'over-elaborated and subject to duplication'. By 2017, they continued to say that there was 'scope to bring greater coherence and synergy' between Estyn inspection and the consortia's system of categorisation. Schools were becoming overburdened and this was affecting leaders' behaviours as they focused more and more on feeding accountability systems.

In 2017, inspection arrangements were once again reviewed and updated, and a new inspection framework produced in response to a formal review which included consultation with stakeholders, as usual. The review suggested that lesson observations by inspectors had become too formulaic and that inspectors were spending too long talking to leaders and managers and reading documentation rather than engaging directly with learners. It was also felt that there was too much emphasis on examination results, at the expense of looking at the progress learners had made from their initial starting-points. Finally, the review suggested that inspection reports did not fully recognise the unique context of each school.

The result was more emphasis on inspectors taking 'learning walks' to look at an aspect of provision across classes and holding fewer meetings with managers. Teachers were encouraged to discuss pupils' work and to show evidence of their work with pupils in discussions with inspectors in their classrooms. The inspection cycle was lengthened from six to seven years, but inspections continued to be held at any point in a cycle in order to reduce the scope for institutions to predict when inspections might take place.

The 2017 common inspection framework placed an increased emphasis on pupils' attitudes and the promotion of positive learning behaviours. The framework reflected the Welsh Government's (WG) Well-being of Future Generations Act (2015) and made more explicit reference to the United Nations Convention on the Rights of the Child. The framework was slimmed down further to improve its focus on key aspects of standards, learning, teaching and leadership.

The new guidance also urged inspectors to approach inspection with a 'positive mindset', in response to criticism from the field that inspection could be a negative experience for teachers, managers and leaders. The guidance tried to counteract some of the 'myths' associated with inspections, such as the idea that inspectors had already made up their minds about schools before they arrived. This led to the withdrawal of a previous requirement for schools to produce a pre-inspection self-evaluation report and for inspectors to produce a pre-inspection commentary on the school. These were both felt to emphasise unduly the outcomes of pre-inspection activity, which might be construed as coming to a preconceived view about the school and potentially skewing the judgements of inspectors during an inspection. The notice period for the inspection was reduced from six weeks to fifteen working days in order to reduce the pre-inspection stress on practitioners. Peer inspectors continued to be full members of all inspection teams. The aim was for inspections to do more to reflect joint ownership of the outcomes with practitioners and for inspections to be done 'with' providers rather than 'to' them.

THE INSPECTION OF WELSH AND BILINGUALISM

While the number of Welsh speakers in the population as a whole has declined over the course of the last century, from 977,366 in the 1911 census to 787,500 in the 2011 census, the engagement of young people in Welsh-medium/bilingual education has increased significantly, especially since 2000. For example, the proportion of primary-age children in classes where Welsh was the main medium of education increased from 18.8 per cent in 2000–1 to around 23.9 per cent in 2018–19. Over the same period, the proportion of secondary-age children in classes where Welsh was the main medium of education increased from 18.1 per cent to 22.3 per cent in 2009–10.[18]

A great deal of political and legislative work has been associated with the development of the Welsh language since 1992. The Welsh Language Act 1993 established that in the course of public business and the administration of justice, so far as was reasonably practicable, the Welsh and English languages were to be treated on the basis of equality. Full official recognition for Welsh as a subject in the curriculum came after 1988, with the implementation of the Education Reform Act in Wales. The Curriculum Council for Wales (CCW) published *The Whole Curriculum 5–16 in Wales* in 1991. Among other things, this paper set out the concept of the Cwricwlwm Cymreig, or the Welsh dimension to the curriculum. The CCW published an advisory paper on the Welsh dimension of the curriculum (*Developing a Cwricwlwm Cymreig*) in 1993. From 1995, the Welsh dimension became a statutory common requirement for every NC subject in Wales to give pupils opportunities, where appropriate, to develop and apply knowledge and understanding of the cultural, economic, historical and linguistic characteristics of Wales.

The WAG put in place a fully fledged Welsh language strategy in 2002: *Dyfodol Dwyieithog: A Bilingual Future*. This strategy was informed by HMI advice in a published report on standards in Welsh as a first and second language across all education sectors and by advice given by HMI in National Assembly for Wales Committee sessions held to call for evidence. The strategy led to the publication of a national action plan, *Iaith Pawb*, in February 2003. This set out a target that by 2011 the proportion of people in Wales able to speak Welsh would increase by five percentage points from the figure which emerged from the 2001 census where 21 per cent claimed to be able to use Welsh to some degree. However, rather than the five percentage point increase in Welsh speakers envisaged in *Iaith Pawb*, there was actually a two percentage point decrease by the 2011 census (from 21 per cent of the population to 19 per cent). This was unexpected, given the increasing proportion of young people attending schools where Welsh was the main medium of education.

In September 2016, the WG published *Taking Wales Forward*

2016–2021. As part of a wider programme, this outlined the government's ambitions for the Welsh language, which culminated with the publication of *Cymraeg 2050: A million Welsh speakers*. The WG's current target is to increase the proportion of each school year group receiving Welsh-medium education to 30 per cent by 2031, and then to 40 per cent by 2050. These are challenging targets, but it is the current view of the inspectorate that pupils only become fully bilingual in Welsh-medium schools where more pupils achieve a high standard of fluency in both Welsh and English.

Since the beginning of the twentieth century, the inspectorate in Wales has generally offered strong support and advocacy for the Welsh language, although this was not always the case in the past, as is indicated in Chapters 1 and 2 of this volume. However, since the early twentieth century, HMI support has continued to reflect an increasingly strong drive to promote the Welsh language. By means of their regular engagements with curriculum, assessment and examination bodies, HMI have been able to keep closely involved with and to influence the rapidly changing curriculum and assessment landscape, particularly with regard to those aspects of the curriculum, such as Welsh as a subject and the *Cwricwlwm Cymreig*, which affect Wales specifically.

The inspection framework and guidance handbook in 1994 focused clearly on the specific requirements in Wales in relation to these aspects of the curriculum. On its first page, it stated that:

> Schools in Wales are required to provide a curriculum which reflects the languages, culture and heritage of Wales. This includes the teaching of Welsh First or Second language and/or using the language as a medium of instruction in other areas of the curriculum. In history, geography, art and music, statutory orders for attainment targets and programmes of study specific to Wales are in force which schools in Wales are required to implement. These requirements have implications for staffing, resources, organisation and the ethos of the schools which inspection must take into account.[19]

The guidance to inspectors featured further comments that focused explicitly on the Welsh dimension of schools. For example, when awarding a judgement of 'excellent', inspectors were advised that 'A school exhibits high standards in pupils' spiritual, moral, social and cultural development when pupils have extensive knowledge of the culture and heritage of Wales.'[20] In the guidance focusing on the inspection of NC subjects, the advice asked inspectors to consider 'the extent to which the school has developed a Welsh dimension (*Cwricwlwm Cymreig*)'.[21] The inspection guidance also contained a separate technical paper on how to inspect the *Cwricwlwm Cymreig*, including the role of extracurricular activities, such as eisteddfodau and Urdd events, in fostering an appreciation of Welsh language, heritage and culture. Inspectors from England wishing to undertake inspections in Wales had to undertake training delivered by HMI in Wales to ensure that they had a full understanding of the inspection requirements specific to Wales. In practice, this meant that much of the time was spent explaining the differences between NC subject requirements in England and in Wales, and the ways in which schools in Wales were different in terms of their Welsh culture and heritage from those in England.

Even when risk-based inspections no longer focused on all the curriculum subjects, there was always a requirement in inspections to report on standards in literacy and numeracy and in Welsh (first and second language). The inspection framework would also continue to require inspectors to consider the Welsh dimension of the curriculum when coming to a judgement about the quality of the school's curriculum overall.

The first mention of 'bilingualism' in an *Annual Report* after 1992 came in the *Annual Report 1999–2000* and there was a separate section on 'dual literacy' in the following year's *Annual Report 2000–2001*. This emphasis on Welsh and bilingualism reflected the inspectorate's support for a bilingual Wales as the devolution settlement began to take shape within Wales. In the cycle of inspections introduced from 2004, separate guidance was published for the inspection of standards of bilingualism in all sectors of education and training. Consequently, reporting on bilingualism became a stronger and more evidence-based feature of all annual reports and reports on individual providers from then on. In the annual reports published during the 2004–10 cycle, one of the key challenges for the education and training system in Wales was ensuring that providers met the needs of bilingual learners. Although standards in Welsh and in English were often good in Welsh-medium schools and classes, standards in Welsh as a second language in English-medium schools were too often unsatisfactory. The *Annual Report 2007–2008* stated that 'Teaching in Welsh second language [in secondary schools] is much worse than in other subjects.' The report lamented that 'schools and other providers ... do not have enough teachers who are able to teach Welsh' and, even when trainees were undertaking their initial teacher training course in Welsh, they 'do not go on to teach Welsh'.[22]

Overall, in the view of the inspectorate, there was a lack of national coherence in planning for continuity in the provision for Welsh across the different sectors in the education and training system and this was holding back the development of a bilingual Wales. The message to policy makers was repeated in many annual reports:

> It is important that any new strategy for Welsh-medium education gives strong direction to providers, establishes clear targets at a national level, and helps to move providers beyond the language of encouragement towards a clearer view of learner entitlement to Welsh-medium education and training.[23]

The focus on standards in bilingualism in both Welsh-medium and English-medium settings continued to be a key component of successive inspection frameworks in 2004, 2010 and 2017. For example, in the 2017 guidance for primary school inspections, inspectors were directed to evaluate the extent and quality of the school's provision for the development of Welsh language skills in formal teaching activities and in informal situations. They were required to consider how well the school taught pupils about the advantages of learning Welsh and becoming bilingual. There was a particular emphasis on inspecting how schools develop pupils' oral Welsh skills in support of the WG's agenda to create a million Welsh speakers by 2050. This was the inspectorate reflecting and reinforcing WG policy direction in support of the Welsh language and the positive benefits of bilingualism.

CONCLUSION

For much of the first two decades after 1992, the inspectorate in Wales had a dual-track system. On the one hand, the inspectorate set up and regulated an outsourced school inspection system whereby the direct inspection of schools was largely undertaken by independent inspectors, not HMI. On the other hand, HMI continued to inspect post-16 provision and, over the period from 1992 until 2010, the reach of HMI extended into new sectors, often in collaboration with other agencies. Significant new approaches to inspection practice and quality assurance were developed in post-16 sector inspections which were later adopted in the inspection of schools.

While the system of outsourcing the inspection of schools had its benefits, as outlined above, it also had disadvantages that undermined the consistency and reliability of inspection judgements. From 2010, Estyn took direct control of all school inspections once more with HMI leading most inspections and contracting directly with independent inspectors for the rest. Quality assurance arrangements were strengthened considerably.

Developments in the twenty-first century have seen the inspectorate taking an increasingly collaborative approach with schools/ providers. The inspectorate has also been more active in supporting WG policies in undertaking joint work with key stakeholders, notably in relation to the new Curriculum for Wales and in creating a national resource for self-evaluation in schools. The period culminated with work being undertaken following the publication of a review of the inspectorate in 2018 by Professor Graham Donaldson (*A Learning Inspectorate*).[24] Commissioned by Estyn, with support from the Minister for Education, the report set out a future strategy for the inspectorate in promoting reforms to the education system in Wales. The thrust and implications of the Donaldson report on Estyn and its future role within the education and training landscape in Wales are discussed in this volume's final chapter on *The Future*.

ENDNOTES

1. Kenneth Baker, *The Turbulent Years: My Life in Politics* (London: Faber & Faber, 1993), p. 168.

2. Michael Ponton, *Building on achievements and shaping the future: a management and organisational review of Estyn* (unpublished report, 1999).
3. Ponton, *Building on achievements and shaping the future: a management and organisational review of Estyn*, p. 7.
4. OHMCI, *The Annual Report of Her Majesty's Chief Inspector of Schools in Wales 1996–1997* (HMSO: London, 1998), p. i.
5. OHMCI, *The Annual Report of Her Majesty's Chief Inspector of Schools in Wales 1996–1997*, p. i.
6. Estyn, *The Annual Report of Her Majesty's Chief Inspector of Education and Training in Wales 2001–2002* (Cardiff: Estyn, 2003), p. i.
7. Estyn, *The Annual Report of Her Majesty's Chief Inspector of Education and Training in Wales 2004–2005* (Cardiff: Estyn, 2006).
8. Estyn, *The Annual Report of Her Majesty's Chief Inspector of Education and Training in Wales 2004–2005*, p. 1.
9. Estyn, *The Annual Report of Her Majesty's Chief Inspector of Education and Training in Wales 2004–2005*, p. 2.
10. Estyn, *The Annual Report of Her Majesty's Chief Inspector of Education and Training in Wales 2004–2005*, p. 1.
11. FEFCW, *Quality and Standards in Further Education in Wales 1993–1997* (Cardiff: FEFCW, 1997), p. 9.
12. Estyn, *The Annual Report of the Chief Inspector for Education and Training in Wales 2005–2006* (Cardiff: Estyn, 2007), p. 26.
13. Estyn, *The Annual Report of the Chief Inspector for Education and Training in Wales 2006–2007* (Cardiff: Estyn, 2008), p. 46.
14. Paper presented at HMI cross-directorate day, September 2006 (in private collection of Ann Keane), p. 2.
15. H. Vappula, R. Ager, R. Wheater, L. Sturman and J. Bradshaw, *Achievement of 15-year-olds in Wales: PISA 2006 National Report* (Slough: National Foundation for Educational Research, 2007).
16. J. Bradshaw, R. Ager, B. Burge, R. Wheater, *Achievement of 15-year-olds in Wales: PISA 2009 National Report* (Slough: National Foundation for Educational Research, 2010).
17. OECD, *Improving Schools in Wales: An OECD Perspective* (Paris: OECD, 2014); and OECD, *The Welsh Education Reform Journey: A Rapid Policy Assessment* (Paris: OECD, 2017), pp. 40 and 43.
18. *https://statswales.gov.wales/Catalogue/Education-and-Skills/ Schools-and-Teachers/Schools-Census/Pupil-Level-Annual-School-Census/ Welsh-Language/pupils-by-localauthorityregion-welshmediumtype* (accessed on 10 October 2021).
19. OHMCI, *Inspection framework and guidance handbook* (Cardiff: OHMCI, 1994), p. 1.
20. OHMCI, *Inspection framework and guidance handbook*, p. 37.
21. OHMCI, *Inspection framework and guidance handbook*, p. 62.
22. Estyn, *The Annual Report of Her Majesty's Chief Inspector of Education and Training in Wales 2007–2008* (Cardiff: Estyn, 2009), p. 11.

23. Estyn, *The Annual Report of Her Majesty's Chief Inspector of Education and Training in Wales 2008–2009* (Cardiff: Estyn, 2010), p. 20.
24. Graham Donaldson, *A Learning Inspectorate: Independent Review of Estyn* (Cardiff: Estyn, 2018).

Chapter 6

WOMEN IN THE INSPECTORATE IN WALES

Sian Rhiannon Williams

INTRODUCTION

Women inspectors (WI) have been largely absent from both the history of education in Wales and Welsh women's history. This chapter begins to redress this omission and aims to assess their status and contribution against the background of developments within the inspectorate and in society in Wales and England more widely. It is based mainly on primary archival material and relevant secondary sources, but for the most recent period, evidence was gathered directly from retired members of Her Majesty's Inspectorate (HMI) via questionnaires, correspondence and interviews.[1] It is organised in four broadly chronological sections which examine changes in the Welsh inspectorate in relation to women, their roles and responsibilities and the gender issues which affected them. There is a strong biographical element to the chapter, particularly in relation to the women recruited in the earlier period. A focus on the interaction between the women's professional and personal lives and knowledge of their social networks informs our understanding both of gender issues and of the Welsh inspectorate itself at a formative time in its history.

It should be noted at the outset that in respect of the organisation and management of the inspectorate, the position of women working in Wales before the Second World War differed from that of their male colleagues. While men were attached to the Welsh Division (1882–1907) and, from 1907, the Welsh Department, women were officially considered to be 'lent by England' even when they worked exclusively in Wales. From 1905, when a separate women inspectorate was established, until 1934–44 when a process known as 'Aggregation' amalgamated the women inspectorate with the main body of the inspectorate, the women of the Welsh Department belonged officially to a corpus of staff under the direction of a chief woman inspector (CWI), based in England. They were 'subject [to her] general disciplinary and supervisory control' and answerable both to her and to the chief inspector in Wales (CI) who should 'act in close association with the Chief Woman Inspector' and who 'control[led] the organisation of their work'.[2]

During this period, the WI in Wales submitted their reports first to the CWI, who then passed them to the CI in Wales and relevant district inspectors (DIs). The CI sought the approval of the CWI for appointments and other changes affecting the women's work. It appears from the documentation that relations between the two were cordial and no evidence of friction has come to light, though it might be assumed that serving both mistress and master would have caused some tension for the WI themselves, a situation which men did not have to contend with. After Aggregation, the inspectorate was one body and the women were officially incorporated into the Welsh Department, though for all practical purposes they had been considered part of the Welsh inspectorate previously. Despite the separation of authority, it is clear that the women appointed specifically to work in Wales shared the values of the Welsh Department and contributed fully to its aims, even though they were also bound to the CWI's agenda.

WOMEN ENTER THE MALE PRESERVE

Increased access to secondary and university education from the late 1880s led to a growing number of well-educated women in Wales, yet there were few higher professional posts available to them. Women had gradually become more visible as members of school boards, governing bodies and management committees by the late nineteenth century, and the Cardiff school board appointed its own women 'inspectresses', a development supported by male HMI, such as C. T. Whitmell, who urged other local boards to do likewise. But despite calls for female school inspectors by both educationists who were responding to the inclusion of domestic subjects in the curriculum, and by advocates of professional posts for women, the Welsh Division of the inspectorate was composed entirely of men, although it occasionally 'borrowed' women from England. The description of the Board of Education's inspectorate in 1906 as 'a peculiar preserve of the male kind' applied equally to both England and Wales.[3]

The first women had been appointed in England to inspect needlework (1883) and laundry work and cookery (1890), initially on a temporary basis. Their numbers increased in the 1890s and, by 1904, there were six women designated as junior inspectors. They were under the control of male HMI and were not allowed to attain the HMI grade. Some were sent to inspect periodically in Wales. In 1899, a request to the Board of Education from several school boards in south Wales to appoint 'a lady inspector of schools' resulted in one of the best known (and most controversial) of the early women inspectors being transferred to Cardiff. She was Katherine (Kitty) Bathurst (1862–1933), the holder of one of the first non-domestic women's posts. The *Western Mail* commented that she was, 'likely to prove a useful acquisition to the inspectorial staff of south Wales'.[4] Indeed she was, for during her time in Cardiff she initiated the introduction of the kindergarten system, encouraged improvements in the teaching of physical training (PT) and promoted the well-being of pupils in special schools. She also acted 'as a kind of shop steward' for other 'sub-inspectors' and confronted the authorities regarding what she believed was an unreasonable workload, called for an increase in women inspectors' salaries to £200 p.a. and automatic promotion.[5] Although she made a valuable contribution to education locally, the Cardiff Cymrodorion Society complained that 'the only lady inspector of schools was lacking in necessary knowledge of the Welsh context', and in January 1900 resolved to ask the Board of Education to 'appoint a lady who is intimate with Wales and who has a knowledge of Welsh'.[6] Their request was not granted, even after Miss Bathurst's departure a year later, and women from England, such as Miss C. Callis, continued on temporary loan.

General dissatisfaction regarding the position of women inspectors resulted in the creation of the women inspectorate of eleven women led by CWI Maude Lawrence, daughter of the

Governor-General of India. Their remit was broadened somewhat and the women were given the designation HMI, but were not in the direct line of promotion. Although this denoted a certain status for women within the service, as Goodman and Harrop explain, the new establishment was formed in the context of social Darwinist discourses which underlay the consolidation of a differentiated curriculum based on social class and gender. The women inspectorate thus reflected the social mores of the time. It has also been argued that segregating women in their own sphere ensured that they were no longer perceived as a challenge to the general work of male inspectors.

Soon moves were afoot to establish a separate Welsh Department too. Owen [known popularly as 'O. M.'] Edwards, appointed CI in 1907, depended upon Miss Lawrence's cooperation in deploying her staff to assist with several aspects of inspection in Wales. In 1908, the first staff listing for the independent Welsh Department, describes Miss H. Sillitoe (b.1865) as being 'employed in Wales'. She was based in Bodfari, north-east Wales, until 1911, and inspected and reported 'upon Domestic Subjects, Centres and Classes for Public Elementary school children, together with training schools for domestic subjects and (when time permitted) these subjects in other day and Evening schools'.[7] Appointed in 1905, it is unclear whether she worked exclusively in Wales. Her workload suggests that most of her time would have been occupied locally, but in describing his inspection visit to a dressmaking class in 1910 Abel Jones stated that 'there were no women inspectors in those days in Wales and mere men had to do what they could'.[8] It is Menai Jane Rowlands (1873–1951) who is acknowledged in contemporary sources as Wales's first woman inspector. It is unclear too whether Miss Sillitoe, who was educated at a Catholic school in Staffordshire, spoke Welsh. However, she had undertaken some of her training (in domestic subjects) at Henblas and Bangor. During these years, Maude Lawrence herself and others assisted in the inspection of training colleges in Wales, both women's and mixed, 'especially in regard to Domestic Arrangements'.[9] Later, Miss R. L. Monkhouse helped Owen Edwards with training college inspections.

According to Lawton and Gordon, the male inspectors dubbed the new WI 'the washtub women', though, as Mullins and Prately have shown, this derogatory epithet was far from accurate.[10] Over half the forty-five or so WI in 1912 were university graduates, while the others were specialists in domestic subjects. Many were dedicated to promoting social improvement through the education of women and girls. The way in which WI were limited and defined by their work in relation to domestic subjects was a source of tension during the early twentieth century, a time when women in education were campaigning for equal pay and more equitable promotion prospects. Their arguments for equality were based upon notions of professionalism, not merely upon the general belief that women had superior knowledge of the 'needs of girls'. Space does not allow for a discussion of the position of these women as the Board's representatives in relation to the complex issues of gender and schooling and the relationship between the 'academic' and the 'technical' in the secondary education of girls, but the early WI in Wales encouraged rather than opposed an increasingly differentiated curriculum in the first half of the twentieth century.

The first two women to be appointed specifically to the inspectorate of the Welsh Department were, first and foremost, graduates in languages and the humanities, although their inspectorial responsibilities were firmly in the field of domestic subjects and girls' education. Menai Rowlands, of Bangor, appointed in 1911, was a former pupil of the Dr Williams High School for Girls at Dolgellau and a BA Honours (Wales) graduate in English and history. She had taught at the Girls' County School, Caernarfon and had examined locally in history and geography. She was (together with her father and sister Anna, headmistress of Ruthin Girls' County School) a member of the Court of Governors of the University College (UC) of North Wales. Her qualifications, as listed in 1914, included a 'Housewife's Diploma (1st Class)' from the Edinburgh School of Cookery and Domestic Economy, which, presumably she had gained as a condition of employment.[11]

Mary Elizabeth Ellis (1881–1974), appointed in December 1913, commenced her duties once she had completed a compulsory three-month course in domestic economy. Born in Dolgellau, she was also a former pupil of the Dr Williams School and had studied at both Aberystwyth and Bangor University Colleges, graduating in Welsh in 1904 and later, in Latin and English. She then taught at secondary girls' schools in Manchester and Bristol and also lectured in English at the *École Normale Superieure*, Sevres, near Paris, a college for women teachers. It might be assumed that her wide experience outside Wales, together with her Welsh credentials, were looked upon positively by both the women inspectorate and the Welsh Department. Hers was a sufficiently important and unusual appointment to merit a mention in local newspapers.

Both women fitted the profile of the first generation of those who had benefited from the expansion of university education in Wales, and their religious and cultural background was in keeping with that of the inspectorate as it developed under Owen Edwards. It is probable that both were known to Edwards through family connections and the social networks of Welsh Methodism and Liberal politics. Given that public advertising for HMI did not start until 1929, and that direct recruitment 'was not exceptional' even in 1930, it is possible that their names had been recommended to the Board.[12] In addition to their knowledge of Wales, the appointees' ability to speak and write through the medium of Welsh was a prime consideration. The Code now stipulated that infants should be taught through the medium of Welsh in Welsh-speaking areas and inspectors were encouraged to communicate in Welsh in schools. Both women would be able to inspect Welsh-medium provision and provide materials for schools in Welsh, thus improving the effectiveness of their remit.

The amount of work accomplished by Menai Rowlands in her first few years as an inspector was considerable. At the end of her first year, she regretted that she had not been able to undertake more visits due to the time she had dedicated to technical work and the ten full inspections undertaken during the summer. Even so, she had succeeded in visiting 146 centres and schools and had held forty-five 'conferences and interviews' with local education authorities (LEAs) or their official representatives regarding the inclusion of domestic subjects in the curriculum and the provision of suitable facilities and trained staff. The following year the statistics were 189 and forty-four respectively.[13] Although some LEAs were slow to make progress, it is clear that Miss Rowlands was beginning to make an impact on her remit, but was also overworked. In the summer of 1913 Owen Edwards appealed for funding for a new appointment to relieve her, noting that this was 'a pressing difficulty'.[14]

Interestingly, Maude Lawrence's suggestion was that the new appointee should also be able 'to assist to a certain extent in the ordinary inspection of Primary Schools', and 'so to employ a woman rather than a man when the next Elementary vacancy arose in Wales'.[15] However, because the staff of the Technical Department in England were unable to assist in the meantime, it was agreed that money should be allocated for a new WI post in Wales without waiting for a vacancy to occur. Responding to Miss Lawrence on receipt of Miss Rowlands's report for 1912–13 Owen Edwards paid tribute to the latter's work;

> These notes give an excellent summary of the great work Miss Rowlands has done for us. It is a matter of great relief to me that Miss Ellis will soon be in the field, I have long felt we were driving Miss Rowlands too much.[16]

Menai Rowlands acted as a mentor to Mary Ellis and they made twenty-nine (of 193) visits relating to the teaching of domestic subjects together in 1913–14.

The war years caused disruption to the women's work but also expanded its scope. They were responsible for promoting the War Savings scheme (whereby pupils were encouraged to help the war effort by subscribing to Savings Certificates). This and the Food Economy Campaign, which included organising the translation of propaganda pamphlets for schools into Welsh, took up much of their time. It appears that the women's role, and Miss Rowlands's in particular, developed during the war years. In 1919, for example, she inspected English and 'Accommodation and Premises' in addition to homecraft at Howells School, Denbigh, though this might have been due to a lack of male personnel at the time. In her study of professional women in Wales, Beth Jenkins has shown that the war marked an important phase in women's entry into the professional sector in Wales, yet argues that it did not change dominant attitudes towards traditional gender roles fundamentally.[17]

This is reflected in the inspection service where pay and promotion prospects remained the same. Despite the fact that all WI were now appointed to the rank of HMI, their scale of pay was half that of male HMI. In 1913, it commenced at £200 per annum, rising annually by £15 to a maximum of £400, whereas the men's starting salary was £400 per annum, rising annually by £20 to £800. This was considerably less than salaries paid to some 'Lady Organisers' of education in the London area and was equal to the salaries of the lowest grade of male inspectors, the junior inspectors. The differential was also wider than in teaching in most LEAs at the time. WI might, exceptionally, be advanced to a higher salary of £500 per annum but it was emphasised that 'the number of posts on this scale is strictly limited'.[18] After the war, scales were revised, and women senior /staff inspectors (WSI) could earn up to £550 per annum but the Treasury refused to increase the basic salary for women. In 1920, both Menai Rowlands and Mary Ellis earned £400, then the maximum for ordinary WI.[19] Interestingly, in 1924 Miss Ellis seriously considered applying for the headship of her former school at Dolgellau, and, although there were factors other than pay involved in the decision, it is significant that the salary and status of a headmistress were still attractive to her.

Discrepancies in pay meant differences in superannuation, so women's pensions were worth less than men's, thus negatively affecting their standard of living in retirement. The argument that the male 'breadwinner' had to 'keep' his wife and children persisted well into the twentieth century, a view that ignored the fact that many single women also had dependants to support. Issues such as the segregation of the workforce, the lack of promotion and the effect of the marriage bar for women in the civil service were discussed in the wake of the McDonnell Commission in 1914, but women's position hardly changed following a Reorganisation Report after the war. Despite the passing of the Sex Disqualification (Removal) Act, which coincided with the promotion of the first of five women to the grade of WSI for the first time in England in 1919, many inequalities remained.

The *Western Mail* declared in 1920 that 'Miss Menai Rowlands B.A., like Miss Mary Ellis ... has shown that women can be very effective as inspectors of schools and have done much useful and unobtrusive work ...'.[20] In that year the inspectorate in Wales consisted of twenty-seven men and the two women (still described as 'lent from England') (7 per cent) compared with 269 men and fifty-four women in England (20 per cent). A note in a letter regarding staffing addressed to the Welsh Department's permanent secretary, A. T. Davies, in 1920, read, 'It must be noted that nothing has been stated as to Women HMIs; according to the English standard, Wales is entitled to another two.'[21] However, no additional women were recruited, and the Welsh Department continued to depend on assistance from England for the inspection of women's training colleges and also for Physical Training (PT) (which was under the direction of the M (Medical) Branch of the Board). This practice continued even after the expansion that eventually took place.

WOMEN OF THE WELSH DEPARTMENT DURING THE INTER-WAR YEARS

In the new circumstances of the 1920s, very little changed for Wales's WI until 1927 when, in the wake of a general reorganisation of the inspectorate (after 1924), Wales at last received its aforementioned numerical entitlement. Two new appointees doubled the number of women. The four WI were allocated to discrete districts and Menai Rowlands was promoted to Women Senior Inspector grade, an important symbolic breakthrough. In England, too, the number of senior posts for women increased at this time.

Both new WI were appointed as HMI and were Welsh speakers and Nonconformists. Angharad White (1881–1974) of Pontarddulais, was an arts graduate of University College Cardiff and a former secondary school assistant mistress. Mary Davies (1890–1938), the daughter of a minister of religion from Harlech and graduate of University College Bangor, had formerly worked for the Board as a primary school inspector in London. She had been senior mistress at Barmouth County School (where she had made a stand for equal pay) before returning to Bangor to study for her MA on the teaching of English in Welsh schools. The women were to be responsible for 'the inspection of Domestic Subjects in schools of all types ... in their allocated districts' and were to 'cooperate with HMIs (men) in matters affecting the education of women, girls and younger children, and, as far as time permits, in the inspection of evening schools and classes'. In addition to her district work, Miss Rowlands was to be responsible for 'the coordination of educational questions affecting women, girls and younger children', while the divisional inspector to whom she was answerable, would 'work in close association with the CWI ... on all matters affecting the work of the Women Inspectorate'.[22]

The strengthening of the corpus of women in Wales coincided with two other developments in the inspectorate at this time. One was the establishment of a system of 'joint and unified inspection' between the Board of Education and the Central Welsh Board (CWB). The other was the publication, in 1927, of the report of the Departmental Committee which had been set up to investigate the place of the Welsh language in the schools of Wales (see Chapters 2 and 3). It might be presumed that the former led to an increased involvement with secondary schools for the WI but based on current evidence it seems that the impact on their work was minimal. One instance of note in relation to the question of cooperation with the CWB is the employment of Miss A. M. Davies, a well-established inspector of PT for that body, who became an occasional inspector for the Welsh Department between 1922 and 1926. As she was the sister of A. T. Davies, who had taken on the duties of CI at the time, her appointment led to accusations of nepotism and overspending by his opponents. One defence which he used to justify her employment was Miss Davies's knowledge of the needs of Welsh schools, in contrast to that of the M Branch inspectors.

Although their main responsibility was domestic subjects and girls' education, the WI's work also concerned the teaching and use of Welsh in schools. By 1929, Mary Davies's duties included assisting the special adviser for Welsh on the 'special problems connected with the education of girls in Welsh' and undertaking observations of St David's Day in schools, while Mary Ellis assisted with music.[23] Of particular relevance was the women's involvement (far more so than that of the men) with the 'under fives' and infants provision where Welsh was most commonly used as a medium of teaching, and also their role in organising and presenting at summer schools and conferences for teachers. In this context they cooperated with like-minded educationalists such as Ellen Evans, principal of Glamorgan Training College, Barry, a member of the Departmental Committee, and her lecturer in Welsh, Cassie Davies, who later joined the inspectorate (see below).

The women were also involved in the wider educational and cultural life of Wales and supported several movements, especially those concerned with the well-being of future generations. Menai Rowlands and Mary Ellis were prominent figures in the Welsh School of Social Service from 1919 and active in the Welsh League of Nations Union (WLNU) throughout the inter-war years. The WLNU promoted international education in schools. In early 1924, Mary Ellis visited schools and colleges in America, observation work which coincided with her role in the WLNU deputation that presented the Welsh Women's Peace Memorial to the women of America in New York and to the US President in Washington. Miss Wark, the CWI at the time, initially forbade her from taking part in the Washington presentation, which she probably deemed to be a political act, but later capitulated.[24] Both Menai Rowlands and Mary Davies were present at the opening of Coleg Harlech in 1927, while Angharad White adjudicated at *Urdd Gobaith Cymru* events in the 1930s. The women's support for such national initiatives is indicative of their political leanings and their prominence in Welsh life.

Questions relating to the position of women in the inspectorate came under close scrutiny again in 1930–31 through the deliberations of the Royal Commission on the Civil Service, known as the Tomlin Commission. The evidence presented by the representatives of the women inspectors (based in England) argued that theirs was a subordinate role, particularly in the primary sector, where the majority were based. Inequalities highlighted included a lack of opportunity to work directly with LEAs or to utilise their administrative abilities and to be included in meetings, conferences and policy making. It is difficult to ascertain whether their views fairly represented those of the Welsh WI, but it might be that some of the differences were less pronounced in Wales. Both Menai Rowlands and Mary Ellis held interviews and 'conferences' with LEA directors of education and their representatives on matters relating to domestic subjects, while Mary Davies is likely to have contributed her expertise to the deliberations of the Departmental Committee on Welsh, although she was not among the six formal HMI witnesses, all of whom were men. Miss Ellis (with seven male colleagues) gave evidence to the Departmental Committee on Rural Education in

Wales in 1927–30. Its report (1930) emphasised the importance of domestic science for girls in agricultural districts. In this sense, it can be said that the WI were contributing to education policy.

In their evidence to Tomlin, some representatives favoured uniting the male and female inspectorates, while others preferred, as a first step, to increase the number of WI and extend their responsibilities. The views of the Welsh WI are unknown, but, although their professional interests and work activities were broader than their official remit, they were, like all other WI, in a subordinate position in several respects. In the event, the Aggregation of the male and female inspectorates occurred in 1934; the position of CWI disappeared four years later and led to the cessation of the woman inspectorate as a separate body in 1944. All posts were, in principle, to be equally open to both sexes, but given the gendered nature of the curriculum and specialisation, it was realised that would be unlikely to work in practice and that 'securing reasonable proportions of men and women' would, instead, be the aim when recruiting new staff.[25]

Despite the promise of greater equality in roles and responsibilities, Aggregation changed little in relation to other firmly entrenched inequalities. Calls by women for equal pay in education and the civil service increased in the inter-war years, but, although the differential had narrowed somewhat by the early 1930s, women's pay scales were well below that of men. A male HMI could earn from £500 per annum to a maximum of £900 and a woman from £300 to £500. Miss Rowlands's maximum, even though she was a WSI with a starting salary of £550, was £650 per annum, far lower than the £1,000 maximum for male senior inspectors (SIs) (in England).[26]

Similarly, the marriage bar in the professions and civil service, another contested issue at the time, remained unchanged. Women inspectors' conditions of employment stated: 'Retirement is compulsory on marriage at any age.'[27] As in the case of teachers, not all WI agreed with the employment of married women in their profession, but, in a survey undertaken as evidence to Tomlin in 1930, 75 per cent of the sixty who responded were in favour of abolishing the bar. It cannot be assumed that there were no personal dilemmas regarding marriage and relationships. For instance, it is reasonable to assume that Mary Ellis, who, at the age of sixty-one, wed the peace campaigner Gwilym Davies, had delayed her marriage almost until retirement age. Mary Davies's relationship with the academic, journalist and litterateur W. J. Gruffydd between 1926 and her death in 1938, was extra-marital in his case. He considered himself as a husband to her, but she could neither marry nor live openly with him without forfeiting her career. Despite her expertise in Welsh, in 1930 she contemplated applying for a post in East Anglia to escape Wales, but was persuaded otherwise.[28]

Gruffydd, an admirer of Owen Edwards (later his biographer), was a member of the Departmental Committee on Welsh of 1925–27. His letters to Mary Davies, over 500 of which survive (though hers to him were destroyed) provide brief glimpses of the life of a WI. In addition to travelling long distances regularly to schools, meetings and conferences, from 1933 onwards Mary spent each July in Oxford at the Welsh Department's annual conference for teachers. She confessed she sometimes felt lonely, while he often expressed concern that she was over-working. She was able to travel abroad for holidays, but in December 1937 he advised her to inform the Board that she could 'no longer carry on in this way' (*na ellwch fynd ymlaen fel hyn*).[29] She soon became seriously ill and died some months later. His tribute to her in *Y Llenor*, the journal he edited, praised her character and contribution as a person of importance in Welsh education who had been held in high regard in councils and committees. Her early death was described by one of her male colleagues as 'a serious loss to Wales'.[30]

Gruffydd's tribute to Mary Davies revealed that she had felt restricted by her official status as an inspector because she was unable 'to fight on the front lines' (*ymladd yn y rhengau blaenaf*) to promote the causes in which she believed.[31] Her successor, appointed in September 1938, was Cathrin Jane Davies, known as Cassie, who also felt initially that the inspectorate might prove restrictive. As mentioned above, she had previously lectured at Glamorgan Training College, which had been at the forefront of developments in relation to the teaching of Welsh. A powerful advocate of Welsh-medium teaching and of the promotion of Welsh cultural identity in schools, she was the product of Tregaron County School and University College Aberystwyth. At the time of her appointment, she was already well-known in Welsh cultural circles. In her published memoir she states that she was encouraged to apply for the post by friends and acquaintances, and did so despite doubting her expertise for the role and worries about leading 'a wandering life' (*bywyd crwydrol*).[32] Crucially for her, an active member of *Plaid Genedlaethol Cymru* (the Welsh National Party), she would not be free to take part in political campaigns. It was the nationalist Saunders Lewis who convinced her that as an inspector of schools she could still be useful to Wales. It therefore became her mission to ensure that the education system fulfilled the role of upholding the nation and Welsh as an official language. She was initially employed as an assistant inspector (AI) and, as such, was officially subordinate to a higher authority. Her assertion that she was given the freedom to plough her own furrow somewhat undermines the view that women AIs were unable to act on their own initiative. During the next twenty years, Cassie Davies became a prime driver of policy on Welsh in schools within the inspectorate.

A few changes had taken place prior to Cassie Davies's appointment. Miss M. Parry of Conway (b.1898), a first-class honours graduate in French with over ten years' teaching experience in both elementary and secondary schools, was appointed in 1933 when Menai Rowlands retired, an event which merited a mention in the *Western Mail*. By 1937, her responsibilities included some districts previously covered by Mary Davies, presumably because the latter's remit now included teacher training colleges (although specialists from England still provided assistance). From 1935, Wales also had its own inspector for girls' PT, working in all districts. Although still attached to the M Branch (until 1944), Annie Rogers was described as 'an integral part of the Welsh inspectorate'.[33] The daughter of a newsagent and bookseller from Ynysybwl, she had attended the Chelsea College of Physical Training and had worked as an LEA organiser in Yorkshire and south Wales. Her appointment can be seen as further evidence that the Welsh Department was eager to appoint bilingual inspectors who were familiar with the Welsh context. Another pre-war appointment (April 1938) was Mary Elizabeth Stanley Jones (1895–1956), daughter of a minister of religion from Caernarfon. Like Miss Parry, she was a first-class honours graduate with secondary school teaching experience. She was also the first scientist (a botanist) amongst the women. The women were therefore highly qualified, often more so than the men under whose direction they worked.

Hunt and Goodman and Harrop have argued that rather than improve women's position within the inspectorate in England and Wales, Aggregation had a detrimental effect. They point to a reduction in numbers: fifty women in 1940 from high point of sixty-nine in the 1920s, while the number of men rose; and fewer women in senior posts as segregation was abolished, seeming to confirm women's lower status in the service. While it cannot be said that the number and proportion of women had fallen in Wales, it was still the case that women were not promoted equally and were mainly concentrated in traditional spheres of work. In 1941, six women (including Miss Rogers) constituted 21 per cent of the inspectorate (six/twenty-eight) and three of the six had attained HMI grade. However, 82 per cent of the men were HMI, all fifteen District Inspectors (DI) were men and men held all the coordinating roles and 'special duties'. While the three women AIs assisted the DIs with general work, all women inspected 'girls' subjects'. The work of the three female HMI was concerned exclusively with either domestic subjects or girls' PT.[34]

POST-WAR CHANGES: TOWARDS EQUALITY?

In order to respond to the widening range of duties in the wake of the 1944 Education Act, an expansion took place in the inspectorates of both Wales and England. Seventeen new staff were appointed in Wales during 1946, six of whom were women. They included Gwyneth Evans (1903–92) another minister's daughter who later became a much respected figure among women in Wales as the first President of *Merched y Wawr* (1967), and Mary C. Thomas (1915–2013) (see below). In all, twelve women were appointed between 1946 and 1950 (nine before 1948). According to one official study, the Rayner Report of 1982, the full complement in Wales (men and women) increased from forty-seven in 1947 to fifty-four in 1950, so some turnover must have been involved. But the increase from six women (if Miss Rogers is included) in 1942 to seventeen, ten years later, was significant. That year, 1952, when almost a third of the Welsh inspectorate was female, constitutes a numerical high point for women (see Table 1). The AI grade had been abolished in the wake of Aggregation and Cassie Davies was promoted to HMI status in 1945. This brought her a higher salary and special responsibility for Pembrokeshire where she enjoyed 'considerable independence' (*cryn annibyniaeth*).[35] Later, as staff inspector (SI), she shared special responsibility for Welsh with a male colleague, and became fully responsible for primary schools, with the freedom to visit any school in Wales.

The marriage bar in the home civil service was officially lifted in October 1946. During the war the bar had been relaxed in some 'special circumstances' and some married women were retained 'as exceptions' afterwards.[36] Mary Ellis became Wales's first married woman inspector when she was given special permission to marry in January 1942 and to remain in post for another year. Yet, despite the change in official policy, married women were often considered to be problematic to employ and were once described post-1947 as 'a perfect nuisance'.[37]

The lack of information on women's resignations makes it hard to ascertain the impact of the marriage bar and its abolition on the inspectorate in Wales, but the example of Mary Thomas, later Mrs Llywelfryn Davies, provides a glimpse of what was lost to the inspectorate because of negative attitudes towards married women. The former graduate of University College Aberystwyth, described as a 'dynamic and inspirational teacher of Welsh' and someone who 'pushed the boundaries', was appointed in January 1946 at the comparatively young age of thirty. According to a family tribute, 'Her world was soon turned upside down by a marriage proposal ... this meant that she would have to resign her post.' She resigned and married in 1952, a decision which her family suggests was one she felt compelled to make, despite the bar having been removed by then.[38]

In 1969, only one female inspector, Mrs M. K. McCausland (home economics), appointed in 1960, was married, while a list of eighteen retired women inspectors dating from 1987 shows a further three married women, Mrs E. Emerson and Mrs K. P. Godfrey, appointed and retired in 1947–59 and 1973–83 respectively, and Mrs Jean E. Davies (née Hughes, appointed 1967) who was married in post during the 1970s.[39] However, three of the four women

HMIs appointed in 1984 were married, an indication of changing attitudes.

It also took many years before women's salary scales achieved parity with those of men. Equal pay had been hard fought for for half a century before it was finally in place. From 1954, staged increases were awarded annually. By 1958, female SI earned up to £2,257.00 p.a. while the top rate for male SI was £2,650.00, with over a £100 differential at the starting rate. Male and female inspectors (not SI) started on £1,475.00 and £1,469.00 p.a. respectively, but with a widening differential at the top of the scale. Indeed, women SI at the top of their scale earned only seven pounds more each year than men at the top of the ordinary scale.[40] Rates of pay crept closer until a common national scale was eventually achieved in 1961. However, women were not among the higher earners in the following decades. When Annie Rogers and Cassie Davies retired in 1953 and 1958 respectively, they were replaced by male SI. This pattern of promoting men to senior posts continued, with one exception, until the 1990s.

Overall, Cassie Davies's memoir draws a positive picture of the life of a woman inspector. She felt she was part of a team, with several like-minded people and others who were not so much '*pobl y pethe*'.[41] Interestingly, not once does she mention her female colleagues by name and, unsurprisingly perhaps, neither does she mention her inspectorial responsibility for domestic subjects, although these were part of her remit. Aspects of her work which she particularly enjoyed included visiting schools, organising teachers' conferences and summer schools, promoting local studies activities, attending committees and international conferences. Less enjoyable tasks were writing reports, inspecting buildings and creating or translating pamphlets on various aspects of educational practice. The experience she disliked most was having to uproot herself at comparatively short notice, leaving plans unfinished, and having to find new lodgings away from an established circle of friends. During her twenty years of service, she was moved six times. This was one aspect of an inspector's life which was used as an argument against the abolition of the marriage bar, though having to relocate with a family was also difficult for men.

The number and proportion of women in the service in Wales fell significantly between 1952 and 1982, though with some fluctuations. (See Table 1.) In 1967–8, the question of the comparatively small number of women recruited to the inspectorate was discussed by the Select Committee on Education and Science. Although no specific mention was made of Wales, witnesses raised issues such as the lack of encouragement for women to apply compared with men and the small number of professional women who were free to take up a position which involved constant travel and periods away from home. However, it was anticipated that the situation would improve. No evidence has been found which indicates that the inspectorate in Wales faced a problem in recruiting well-qualified women to the limited number of posts available. The respect which the inspectorate commanded would have made it an attractive proposition to those (mainly unmarried) women who were in a position to apply, despite some disadvantages compared to other professional jobs.

In addition to their minority status, the scope of the women's remit remained circumscribed. A snapshot of inspectors' responsibilities in 1969, when eleven women constituted a relatively high 23 per cent of the Welsh inspectorate, shows that they were concentrated in the traditionally feminised spheres of home economics, the younger age phases (nursery in particular) and 'special treatment education' (now called 'additional learning needs') and were largely excluded from 'special duties' in other fields.[42] With the exception of Miss E. M. (Betty) Davies (appointed in 1956) and her two colleagues in home economics, and Miss W. M. Hopkins-Jones (appointed in 1950) who was responsible for girls' physical education (PE) and associated subjects and activities, very few women were given 'special duties' in the higher, further and secondary education sectors (and none in adult education). Furthermore, representatives of the inspectorate on various educational boards and councils were all men, although Betty Davies later became the only female member of the Standing Reference Committee, which included the CI and all SI. According to an informant, this was probably due to her long service and rich experience, though tokenism might also have played a part. In 1969, she was awarded the OBE for her services to education, but it could be argued that her official rank did not reflect her professional status and local influence.

Table 1: Gender composition of the Welsh inspectorate 1952–82

Year	CI (M)	Women Staff Inspectors		Inspectors		% Women Inspectors	Total in post		Women as
		W	% W to M	M	W		M	W	% of corps
1952	1	2	2/7 (28.5)	27	15	15/42 (35.7)	33	17	17/50 (31.25)
1958	1	0	0/7	22	14–12 (2 deleted)	12/34 (35.2)	30	12	12/42 (28.5)
1960	1	0	0/7	26	11	11/37 (29.7)	34	11	11/45 (24.4)
1963	1	0	0/8	28	9	9/37 (24.3)	37	9	9/46 (19.5)
1965	1	0	0/8	33	9	9/42 (21.4)	42	9	9/51 (17.5)
1969	1	0	0/8	27	10–11 (1 added)	11/38 (28.9)	36	11	11/47 (23.4)
1970	1	0	—	—	—	—	41	9	9/50 (18.0)
1972	1	0	0/9	29	7–8 (1 added)	8/37 (21.6)	38	8	8/47 (17.0)
		1*							
1979	1	0	0/8	38	8–4 (4 deleted)	4/42 (9.5)	47	4	4/51 (7.8)
1982	1	0	0/7	38	5	5/43 (11.6)	46	5	5/51 (9.8)

Source: TNA Ed 270/70, Ministry of Education Establishment and Seniority Lists: List 25, Part II (Inspectorate) (1952–69) (1972; 1979; 1982); information via questionnaire (1970)

NB: The figures are as corrected by the chief inspectors at the time, and reflect actual numbers in post, rather than the official complement/establishment

*Data missing 1973–8. One woman staff inspector during this period (Miss E. C. Edwards)

The range of subjects inspected and work undertaken by women gradually expanded during the 1970s and 1980s, and the appointment of Sheila Browne as the first woman Senior CI in England in 1974 was in keeping with the era of second wave feminism. In Wales, Miss E. C. (Betty) Edwards (appointed in 1961), whose expertise was in English, was promoted to SI with responsibility for special education in the early 1970s. Both she and Betty Davies are remembered as strong, yet amiable characters by one former CI. Given their prominence in the primary sector, the women inspectors played a leading role in this period in promoting the principles of two major reports on primary education, Plowden and Gittins (1967). Miss Mary Anthony, appointed in that year, was particularly involved with these efforts and became a sharp critic of schools which did not share this transformative vision. In this respect, it cannot be claimed that the inspectorate was entirely neutral with regard to teaching methods and approaches to learning, and it seems that this was particularly the case in the primary sector where women were dominant. In fact, those who specialised in early years education enjoyed more autonomy than many male HMI since they were free to enter schools throughout Wales.

This view of the women's influence is confirmed by one interviewee, appointed to the primary sector in 1972, who described how she sought to share her personal philosophy of education with teachers and develop their practice. This informant provides one woman HMI's perspective on life, work and gender issues in the Welsh inspectorate during the 1970s and 1980s.[43] Invited to apply for the post by the then CI, she did so with the aim of moving nearer home in order to care for a family member, despite a consequent reduction in salary. Suitably attired for the role according to the dress code of the time in 'a neat suit, normally dark in colour – no slacks', she travelled extensively undertaking both pastoral and inspectorial visits, teaching on training courses and attending monthly meetings in Cardiff (150 miles from her home) and other meetings in London. She expressed the view that neither the extent of her caring responsibilities as a single woman nor the challenges of long-distance driving in all weathers or late at night were always appreciated by those in authority in Cardiff, whereas some meetings were organised at men's convenience, for instance, to coincide with rugby games. Although relations were mostly good natured, she felt that some men's attitude towards female colleagues could be patronising and that they considered the primary sector inferior to others. She was not alone in holding this view; however, alternative evidence gathered emphasises the respect which men and women had for each other's expertise. Her testimony also reveals the importance of cross-border links between women via sectors and specialisms. She emphasised her professional contacts with colleagues in England and how senior women there, especially those who, like herself, were trained in Fröebel methods, became her role models.

In 1970, one former CI in England described the inspectorate as 'the Brotherhood', a term which conjures up images of a secret male society with its own rituals and one which, significantly, went unquestioned in relation to gender by Lawton and Gordon in 1987.[44] During the course of this research the Welsh term '*y chwiorydd*' ('the sisters' or 'the sisterhood') was used in relation to female colleagues in Wales in the 1970s and 1980s. This collective term for women was (and is) specific to Welsh Nonconformist chapels. In the context of traditional chapel culture, it implied a separate or parallel role and circumscribed (though not unimportant) field of work. The use of the term is telling as it suggests that an ethos of 'separate spheres' continued to some extent, even into the final quarter of the century. An increase in female appointments occurred in the 1980s, an indication of changes to come. By 1992, twelve women comprised 21 per cent of the new OHMCI Wales. There had been no female SI since Betty Edwards's retirement in 1978, but this was rectified in the mid-1990s by which time two women, Mrs Iola Thomas and Ms Susan Lewis, had been promoted. The latter became Wales's first female CI in 1997.

INTO THE TWENTY-FIRST CENTURY: PERSONAL PERSPECTIVES ON GENDER

The final section is based on responses received from nine former full-time women inspectors.[45] All were born between 1943 and 1951, joined the inspectorate in Wales between 1983 and 2002 and left their posts or retired between 2001 and 2017. All had family commitments either as parents, including as divorced or separated single parents, or caring responsibilities for infirm or elderly relatives. All had previously held senior posts either in teaching, lecturing or LEA advisory services and almost all had experience of working outside Wales, mainly, but not exclusively, in England.

One of the nine was initially appointed on a temporary basis as an additional inspector; the others started as permanent ordinary grade HMI. The majority stated that their reason for applying was to be able to contribute their skills to help improve education or to serve the public. A few mentioned personal career advancement or the inspectorate being 'the natural next step'. This could be interpreted as a matter of achieving a relatively higher status post, rather than one which offered better remuneration, since several had taken a reduction in salary to work for the inspectorate. Their expertise ranged across subjects and phases and included further education (FE) and initial teacher education (ITE). Most experienced changes in their responsibilities during their employment due to reorganisation, curricular developments or movements between teams. Although several became leaders of particular initiatives, most considered promotion to be a remote possibility for them. This would also have been true for many male colleagues given the limited number of higher level posts available.

Several of those appointed in the late 1990s and early 2000s came from more varied cultural and educational backgrounds than many previous appointees. These more recent appointees all commented positively on relationships with male colleagues. Their overwhelming response was that work relations were 'professional' and 'friendly'; men were 'chums' and 'good company', and gender 'never came into it'. This was confirmed by the responses of two male respondents, both former CI, who stated that women were not treated differently from men. A few women felt that the men could sometimes be 'over-protective', but one welcomed the way in which her male colleagues took care to 'look after' her when away on inspections, 'though not in a condescending way'. Some reported 'banter' and 'ribbing about making the tea', and considered this harmless. According to one respondent, 'The women in the Welsh inspectorate were not the kind to put up with any slight, discrimination etc. relating to them being female (anyway) had it happened at all.'

Those who had worked in the FE sector had often been the only women in an otherwise all-male team, but stated that, despite this, they had managed to 'hold their own'. They also said that they had needed to show that they were 'tough' and 'knew their stuff', for example with ex-military personnel in catering contexts. One felt that the fact that she was a woman 'had something to do with' her regularly being given responsibility for inspecting 'care, support and guidance'. This reference to the concept of 'social maternalism', which assumes that women are natural carers by virtue of their sex, suggests some continuation of gender appropriated roles, though far less consciously and systematically than before. But the prevailing view was that women were 'accepted as equals and their views sought and respected'.

Respondents reported that as representatives of HMI they were also received with respect in schools, and 'never felt any discrimination or animosity' but neither did they feel any 'particular advantages to being a woman'. Occasionally, male head teachers expressed surprise at seeing a woman arrive, especially when they were responsible for subjects which had previously been male dominated.

Disadvantages of the work for women were mainly linked to the difficulties of managing a domestic as well as a professional workload and the necessity of having to move home at intervals with little or no consideration given to family concerns. It was acknowledged that the latter could also be very difficult for men, as was the travelling. Driving long distances at night, staying at hotels and eating alone were also viewed as negative aspects which were not necessarily gender related, but several women found these challenging due to prevailing social attitudes and possible risks. A reversal in the late 1990s of a long-standing policy of home working was felt to have made life more difficult for women in particular, and the relief of later returning to more flexible arrangements was mentioned by several respondents.

Responses relating to changes in the status or role of women during the respondents' time in the inspectorate included the appointment of 'the first female staff inspector for many years'. Other comments noted that 'women HMI were becoming more obviously prominent' and that an increasing number of women were being appointed to roles 'that did not specifically require a female inspector'. The outcome of the 1999–2000 reorganisation was described by one respondent as part of 'a move to make the inspectorate in Wales a less paternalistic ... organisation' which had led to 'a more balanced gender structure at all promoted levels, so not just more women but more with additional responsibilities'. There were women among the new 'Head of Division' post-holders, and Mrs Ann Keane's appointment as the second female CI in 2010 is indicative of the changes which had occurred by the beginning of the second decade of the twenty-first century. As one respondent wrote, 'Having two women of five Chief Inspectors since 1982 gave a powerful message.'

CONCLUSION

The most recent testimony of former WIs shows how women's roles within the inspectorate had expanded by the end of the century and reflects the view that these changes placed women on a more equal footing with men in what previously had been a male-dominated institution. This chapter has shown that the transition had been slow and uneven.

A series of reforms from the mid-1930s, and particularly post-1945, gradually removed the most obvious barriers to equality such as the pay differential, the marriage bar and, officially at least, gender-specific appointments. Yet, it cannot be said that women had truly 'broken through' the 'glass ceiling' which continued within the inspectorate until the full impact of the social and cultural changes of the late twentieth century started to be felt from the mid-1990s onwards.

Further research is needed to ascertain whether Wales's WIs, like many women teachers and head teachers, were active in campaigning for these improvements. As noted, members of the inspectorate were prevented from taking an openly political stance in public, though it is also probable that there would have been an element of acquiescence to the norm within a high-status profession. However, at least three of the women appointed in the pre-war period were supporters of feminist causes and believed in women's agency in society and politics, so it can be assumed that they would have supported those who campaigned for change. The women who came after them were also strongly independent women and the likelihood is that they also would have taken a similar stance, even if they did not or could not speak out.

For much of the twentieth century, WIs in Wales were in a minority, were undervalued professionally and enjoyed only limited opportunity to reach their potential. For most, their roles remained restricted by gendered conceptions of duty and expertise and the gendered nature of schools and the curriculum. Yet they held a relatively elevated position within Welsh education and took advantage of the opportunities this offered. As in the case of other groups of professional women of the period whose understanding of professionalism encompassed both equality and difference, their position was a complex one. For example, their support early on for a differentiated curriculum for girls cannot be judged by present day understandings of gender equality. Similarly, they did not always challenge head-on the boundaries set by contemporary gender norms. Nevertheless, they were strong characters; energetic, independent women who were often exceptionally able academically, knowledgeable in their fields and respected for their wisdom in committees. They worked tremendously hard, often under taxing conditions. The systematic teaching of domestic science/home economics and developments in girls' PE, in nursery and primary education, Welsh-medium and Welsh language teaching and in special education owe much to the women within the inspectorate. They were among the most influential people in education in Wales in their time, and their contribution deserves to be better known.

ENDNOTES

1. Eighteen former women inspectors were sent a questionnaire by e-mail or post in November 2018. Between December 2018 and March 2019 eight questionnaires were returned and two further women were interviewed (one face to face and one by telephone). Two former male CIs responded to a separate questionnaire in January 2019. Several of the participants contributed further information via e-mail or in writing.
2. Welsh Department, *Education in Wales Directory 1929*, p. 6; *Royal Commission on the Civil Service 1929–31*, Minutes of Evidence, Statement submitted by Permanent Secretary to Board of Education, p. 543, para. 47.

3. *The Schoolmaster*, 24 February 1906, quoted in J. Goodman and S. Harrop, '"The peculiar preserve of the male kind": women and the education inspectorate, 1893 to the Second World War', in J. Goodman and S. Harrop (eds), *Women, Educational Policy-Making and Administration in England: Authoritative women since 1880* (London: Routledge, 2000), pp. 137–55.
4. *Western Mail*, 21 January 1899.
5. P. Gordon, 'Katherine Bathurst: A Controversial Woman Inspector', *History of Education Bulletin*, 17/3 (1988), 193–207. See also C. A. Mullins, '"Washtub Women": A Study of female school inspectors from the 1890s to the 1920s' (unpublished MEd thesis, University of Liverpool, 1999); S. Robertson, 'Katherine Bathurst (1862–1933)', in C. Richards and S. Robertson (eds), *A Scrutiny of Inspectors: Her Majesty's Inspectors in England and Wales* (Association of Retired and Former HMI, 2019).
6. *Western Mail*, 19 January 1900; *South Wales Daily News*, 20 January 1900.
7. Board of Education Welsh Department, *List 6 Wales: The Inspectors of the Welsh Department of the Board of Education as allocated in relation to the LEAs' areas in Wales* (London, 1908).
8. Abel J. Jones, *I was Privileged* (Cardiff: Abbrevia, 1943), p. 62.
9. *List 6*, 1908, p. 4.
10. D. Lawton and P. Gordon, *HMI* (London: Routledge, Kegan and Paul, 1987), p. 92; Mullins, 'Washtub Women'; B. Prately, 'Washtub Women', in Richards and Robertson, *A Scrutiny*, pp. 91–4.
11. The National Archive (TNA) ED 270/32, *List 36 Board of Education Inspectors' Qualifications, 1914–39*.
12. Lawton and Gordon, *HMI*, p. 119.
13. TNA ED 92/10, Wales (with Mon) Domestic Subjects in Public Elementary Schools, Annual Reports 1911–12; 1912–13.
14. TNA ED 23/407 and ED 23/146, Owen Edwards (OE) to Secretary, 19 June 1913.
15. TNA ED 23/407, Maude Lawrence (ML) to OE, 1 July 1913.
16. TNA ED 92/10, OE to ML, 10 December 1913.
17. Beth Jenkins, 'Women's Professional Employment in Wales, 1880–1930' (unpublished PhD thesis, Cardiff University, 2017).
18. National Library of Wales (NLW) BC1/8/13, *HM Inspectors (Women) Board of Education, Office Rules 25, 1913. Conditions of Employment etc. of Woman inspectors*.
19. TNA ED 23/152A, Welsh Department Cost of Staff.
20. *Western Mail*, 22 September 1920, p. 4.
21. TNA ED 23/152A, Note added to letter from 126, Ruabon Road, Wrexham to A. T. Davies. Correspondent unknown, 15 May 1920.
22. Board of Education Welsh Department, *List 6: The Inspectors of the Welsh Department of the Board of Education 1927* (London, 1927), pp. 9–11.
23. TNA ED 22/179/393, Inspectorate Memoranda: Arrangements for allocation of special subjects or departments of work among inspectors, 1929.

24. Diary of Annie Hughes Griffiths: NLW T. I. Ellis and Mari Ellis Papers. Digitised on WCIA website: *https://www.wcia.org.uk/wcia-news/wcia-history/womenspeacepetition/* and *https://www.flickr.com/photos/129767871@N03/albums/72157680212085978* (accessed 22 June 2020).
25. TNA ED 23/671, 1937–43: Permanent Secretary's letter to Miss E. M. Whyte, 17 September 1937.
26. *Royal Commission on the Civil Service*, 25 and 26 March, 1930, p. 503; p. 546.
27. NLW BC1/8/13, *HM Inspectors (Women) Conditions of Employment*.
28. R. Chapman, *W. J. Gruffydd* (Cardiff: University of Wales Press, 1993), p. 143.
29. Chapman, *Gruffydd*, p. 157. WJG to MD, 1 December 1937.
30. Jones, *I was Privileged*, p. 84.
31. *Y Llenor*, XVII/2, 1938, p. 75.
32. C. Davies, *Hwb i'r Galon* (Abertawe: John Penry, 1973), pp. 86–7.
33. TNA ED 23/717, RGL to Mr Sugen, 30 November 1944.
34. TNA ED 270/68, *List 6: The Inspectors of the Welsh Department of the Board of Education, 1941*.
35. Davies, *Hwb*, p. 109.
36. TNA ED 23/847, Women Inspectors after Marriage, 1945–6.
37. TNA T 275/137, quoted in 'Women in the UK Civil Service', *https://www.civilservant.org.uk/women-history.html* (accessed 3 April 2019).
38. Lynn Davies (2014, updated 2016), Mary Llywelfryn Davies, 1915–2013, *https://osaannual.wordpress.com/2014/06/01/mary-llywelfryn-davies-1915-2013/* (accessed 26 March 2019).
39. *HMI of Schools in E and W: Register of retired members May 1987* (Association of HMI, 1987).
40. TNA ED 270/70, *Ministry of Education Establishment List 25. Part II. Board of Education (Welsh Department) List of HM Inspectors 1958*.
41. Davies, *Hwb*, p. 135. 'Pobl y pethe' refers to people involved in Welsh literary and cultural life.
42. TNA ED 270/72, *Board of Education (WD) List of HMI, 1969*.
43. Interview with retired woman inspector, 4 December 2018.
44. Lawton and Gordon, *HMI*, p. 115; p. 119.
45. See note 1.

Chapter 7

DEVOLUTION, EDUCATION POLICY AND INSPECTION IN WALES: A POLICY ANALYSIS

David Egan

INTRODUCTION

In 1997, the Welsh electorate narrowly voted in favour of political devolution being granted to Wales, thereby creating a National Assembly for Wales (hereinafter Assembly) with powers over named policy areas including education. Initially the Assembly and its Welsh Assembly Government (later renamed the Welsh Government) exercised these powers over all aspects of education in Wales other than school inspections and teachers' pay and conditions, which were not to become devolved until 2006 and 2018 respectively.

Prior to devolution, Wales had been governed by Westminster legislation which almost completely made little distinction between Wales and England. Whilst the establishment of the Welsh Office (WO) in 1964 and the existence of an independent inspectorate had contributed to what one historian has called 'creeping devolution' of education policy in the period before 1999, the arrival of political devolution created the first national system of education in Wales 'significantly demarcated in a way previously impossible'.[1] For the first time in its long history, the inspectorate in Wales would henceforth be operating in an environment where its work could directly influence education policy and eventually education legislation solely focused on Wales.

This chapter differs from others in this volume in that it does not focus primarily on providing a historical account of the work of Estyn during the period since devolution, something which is considered in detail in Chapter 5. Rather, it attempts a policy analysis of the role of the inspectorate in relation to education developments during the first two decades of devolved government. It draws upon Estyn documentation – in the main the annual reports of the chief inspector (CI) throughout the period – and a range of academic interpretations. Whilst this evidence provides a robust enough basis for their objective analysis, like all accounts of contemporary historical events, the interpretation offered here inevitably also reflects the subjective experience of the author, who during this period was extensively involved at various times as a practitioner, researcher, Welsh Assembly Government (WAG) policy adviser and registered inspector of schools in the Welsh education system.

OVERVIEW

As indicated in Chapter 8, over the first two decades of devolved government in Wales education policy relating to schools in Wales can be seen to have passed through three broad periods. The first, from the birth of the Assembly through to the end of the first decade of devolution, was associated with the positioning of Wales as a 'learning country' where 'clear red water'[2] existed between the policies followed by a Labour Party-led government in Cardiff and its equivalent in London.

The second period, traversing the first years of the second decade of devolved government, saw a significant change in policy trajectory. This was strongly influenced by what was interpreted as being evidence of unfavourable comparisons between the educational attainment of pupils in Wales compared to their UK and international counterparts. It led to the adoption of more market-driven, neo-liberal policies that had become commonplace in many countries, including England, and characterised by the Finnish academic, Pasi Sahlberg, as constituting a 'Global Education Reform Movement' (GERM).[3] Some of the dominant features of this policy paradigm are high levels of accountability, the reliance on a narrow range of attainment data as indicators of educational progress and the introduction of national strategies (often called 'frameworks' or 'tool-kits') designed to direct teacher pedagogy.

The third, and current, period has seen a gradual move away from many – but not all – of these education policies and their replacement by a wide-ranging and ambitious 'education reform movement'.

INSPECTION AND 'THE LEARNING COUNTRY'

Since 1964 and the creation of the WO, the devolution of administrative powers had led to the growth in the number of civil servants focused on education policy in Wales. Their ability to develop discrete policies for Wales or to shape those formulated in Whitehall to meet the needs of the country were circumscribed. The fact that there were only approximately seventy civil servants in the WO focusing on education policy and administration in Wales compared to some 2,500 in the Department of Education in Whitehall, illustrates that capacity was limited.[4]

With the coming of devolution of government in 1999, the limitations of policy-making capacity in Wales became very apparent. Over the period of the first two Assemblies up to 2007, however, there was a radical change. The policy community expanded to include a range of representative and advocacy policy-influencers, including, in education, the teacher and head teacher unions and fforwm, representing post-16.

However, by comparison with England or even Scotland, Wales still lacked a strong research-based policy capacity within its universities that was specifically focused on Wales and, other than the Institute of Welsh Affairs, there were no specialist education policy 'think-tanks'. In 2006, the WAG incorporated the former quasi-independent bodies ELWa (Education and Lifelong Learning Wales), which controlled post-16 tertiary education and training, and ACCAC (the specialist curriculum and assessment organisation). It was also the case that devolution did not lead to an increase in democratic policy making and advocacy in education that reached beyond the policy 'elites' to embrace civil society and the wider electorate.[5] Given these circumstances, the only major independent organisation outside government that had extensive expertise in education was Estyn. It might be expected, therefore, that the Assembly, the WAG and its civil service would rely heavily on its advice, even more so than was the case in the period before devolution.

The evidence base on which such advice could be offered had expanded considerably through the 'privatisation' of the inspection system in 1992. By 1998, for example, 350 primary, 44 secondary and 13 special schools were being inspected in a single year as well 6 pupil referral units.[6] As described in Chapter 5, HMI now led very few school inspections, although they still inspected directly in other sectors such as post-16 provision, local authority (LA) education services and initial teacher education (ITE). HMI also trained school inspectors for the new outsourced inspection system and monitored their work. And they analysed and interpreted the outcomes of school inspections in published reports and records of graded judgements. This meant that Estyn was well placed to provide the evidence and advice increasingly required by civil service officials, Assembly Members and Ministers. This was in addition to its work on policy remits commissioned by the government, the preparation of an ever-expanding annual report, responding to increased media interest, and a range of other functions as well as its quality assurance and inspection work.

Whilst some of this activity was probably more visible than had been the case before devolution, much of it took place 'behind the scenes' in the corridors of Cathays Park and Tŷ Hywel in Cardiff Bay as well as out in the field. This almost hidden role of Estyn reflected the traditions of independent advice offered without 'fear or favour' that the inspectorate was well known for, and which reflected the wider values of the civil service. This might explain why in the key policy documents produced by the government during this period, there was limited direct reference to Estyn and the role it performed.

An example of this is *The Learning Country* of 2001, which represented a seminal expression of the policy direction that was to be followed in the first decade of devolution and up to that point the most complete vision ever produced on the configuration of a distinctive education system in Wales. The single mention of Estyn in the document noted the Education Minister's request that Estyn produce a compendium of 'best practice' for the use of practitioners.[7]

In its successor document *The Learning Country: Vision into Action* of 2006, there was not a single reference to Estyn despite the fact that each section of the document began with an introduction headed 'What does our analysis and research tell us?'[8] Towards the end of this first period of devolved education policy, the WAG produced in 2008 a major policy document, *The School Effectiveness Framework*, which had been influenced by the work of academic researchers in the field of school improvement and effectiveness and head teachers of highly successful schools in Wales. This was also virtually silent on Estyn in relation to its evidence base, with the only reference to it being in a section on 'improvement and accountability' where its role in holding schools to account was acknowledged.[9]

While it might indeed be that, in the tradition of offering independent advice, Estyn was an 'unseen hand', the inspectorate was clearly a rich source of evidence about education standards and provision in Wales for politicians in a newly devolved Welsh Assembly Government. An analysis of the annual reports of the CI during this period suggests that the main features of the evidence from Estyn were as follows:

- Continuing progress was being made within the Welsh education system. At the start of the period, it reported that 'overall, education standards are still rising every year'[10] and by the end of the five-year cycle of inspections in 2004 there was 'much to celebrate with standards improving'.[11] Exceptions to this general picture were the standards of 11–14-year-olds, the relatively high performance of girls compared to boys, and examination performance at the age of 15, which were seen to be falling behind the levels in other UK nations.
- Within this overall positive picture, significant variability existed between schools with similar pupil intakes and within schools between classes and departments. Some of this variability clearly resulted from socio-economic inequality and it was recognised that this was not easy to overcome and that schools could not alone tackle the issues involved. This was particularly identified as being an issue in a small number of low-performing secondary schools where attendance, enthusiasm for learning and

engagement were all identified as challenges and the importance of engaging parents, raising expectations and offering a more relevant curriculum was seen as being crucial in addressing this situation. It was also reported that many of these schools took a narrow view of what constituted success for pupils by the age of 15, with the 2002 report recommending 'a broader view of their work that goes beyond what is easily measured, such as examination results' and noting that too often secondary schools had a narrow view of learning, valuing traditional education approaches and eschewing vocational training.[12]

- Beginning in the 2003 report and continuing through the annual reports for this period, the importance of what is called 'community schooling' and the need for joint working between schools, other parts of the education service, and other multi-agency services such as family support and health, were highlighted in relation to some of the challenges faced by the most vulnerable pupils and the schools most affected by socio-economic disadvantage.

- The reports repeatedly emphasised the importance of leadership and management in bringing about improvements. Generally, senior leadership of schools was painted in a positive light, although variation between schools was again noted and middle leadership was portrayed as being less strong. Far less emphasis was placed on issues relating to the quality of teaching, possibly because by the end of the inspection cycle in 2004 it was reported as having improved a great deal over a five-year period.[13]

It is interesting, therefore, that Estyn during this period highlighted issues such as low levels of achievement by disadvantaged learners, an over-concentration on examination performance and the need for stronger engagement of families and communities in education, all of which would have had increasing focus placed upon them throughout the post-devolution period. The extent to which these findings publicly influenced WAG policy during this period appears to be limited, however, perhaps because Estyn also continued to report year-on-year improvements in the standards being achieved in schools and the quality of teaching and leadership.

Chapter 5 outlines how, within Estyn, questions were being raised at this time about the consistency and reliability of the judgements in some school inspection reports being produced by independent, contracted-out inspectors and the trend of 'grade-inflation' in judgements on some key aspects of standards and provision. This discussion would eventually lead to a review of inspection arrangements and consultation with education and training sectors on the introduction of new guidance on inspection methods and a return to HMI-led inspections in 2010. Interim measures to address concerns were also taken in training sessions with independent inspectors, from 2006 onwards, based on the findings from Estyn quality monitoring.

In general, the extent to which distinctive policies were developed in this initial period of devolution has attracted different interpretations. The policies most often associated with 'clear red water' distinctiveness included the introduction of the Foundation Phase (FP) for the early years, the Welsh Baccalaureate and a broader 14–19 curriculum and qualifications framework, the ending of national testing at ages 7, 11 and 14 in 2005, and the rejection of 'league-table' type comparisons between schools and the support for LEA-provided comprehensive schooling. Estyn both directly and indirectly influenced the framing and development of these policies.

It has, however, been argued that many of these policies (the FP, for example) were only variants of approaches being developed in England and that in other instances the WAG, rather than following England in introducing new policies in some areas, decided that it would maintain the status quo, as had often been the stance adopted by the WO prior to devolution.[14] School organisation and governance might be viewed as a typical case in point. Wales rejected various types of specialist school and academy models of school organisation governed outside local authority control. Such instances led to one observer describing talk of 'distinctive policies' as 'meaningless blather' providing a smoke screen for not adopting policies that had been successful within the English education system, although it was unclear what those policies might actually be and why they should have been taken up in Wales.[15]

The reality of the situation was probably best expressed by the Education Minister, Jane Davidson, who argued that: 'We share key strategic goals with our colleagues in England – but we often need to take a different route to achieve them.'[16] What this reflected, in the view of Wales's most eminent historian of education, was 'different social principles, which amounts to a statement about the nature of Welsh society'.[17] What these judgements do not suggest, however, is any major policy divergence initially between the Labour-led governments in Cardiff and Westminster. When Westminster moved on, politicians and policy makers in Wales were reluctant to move away from the status quo in Welsh schools or to take Wales in radically new directions in education policy. In time, some of the political decisions taken in Wales, to suspend end-of-key-stage tests from 2002 along with the annual publication of league tables of school performance, and to eschew any replacement of comprehensive schools, were to take Wales on a different route from England.

In those early years of devolution, while the WAG responded to some of the evidence and recommendations offered by Estyn in reports commissioned in the annual Ministerial remit, there was already an increasing appetite to look to findings from experience in other countries and to advice from academics. Early on, Estyn continued to point to ongoing progress in the Welsh education system, while offering more nuanced reporting on the impact of policies to reduce disadvantage and on the need to consider new and alternative models of schooling. Its influence was mixed. While there were many occasions when Estyn offered recommendations that did influence policy and its implementation, Estyn advice did not always chime with the policy direction or thinking in government. Estyn argued for the retention and expansion of community-focused schools, for example, but this was an initiative whose grant was withdrawn not long after Estyn published a supportive report. Estyn offered a blueprint for expanding bilingualism in education in its report to the Children, Education and Lifelong Learning Committee in 2002 in support of the review of the Welsh language that led to that Committee's report on *Iaith Pawb* but few of its recommendations were taken forward at the time.

Although an HMI was seconded to WAG to lead the implementation of the Foundation Phase, the initiative itself was based on international models. Over time it became more common for Ministers to look beyond Wales for inspiration and in the mid-2000s a new, and internationally respected, director-general for the education department was appointed from Australia. Many eminent education professors from outside Wales were taken on as advisers, some linked to the Blair Labour government policy unit or, later on, to successful initiatives in England such as the London Challenge.

AN ACCOUNTABILITY-DRIVEN SYSTEM

As the first decade of devolved responsibility over education came to an end, a significant change took place in the ethos and direction of education policy in Wales. The publication of the Organisation for Economic Co-operation and Development (OECD) Programme for International Student Assessment (PISA) test results for Wales in 2007 and 2010 revealed a disappointing comparison with outcomes for other UK nations. There followed an introduction of much stronger forms of accountability and more direct control over the education system by a new Minister for Education and Skills, Leighton Andrews. He launched a twenty-point action plan in 2011[18] and a WG publication on *Improving Schools* in 2012.[19] In policy terms it led to the reintroduction of national testing for key age groups in literacy and numeracy; a centrally driven *Literacy and Numeracy Framework*[20] designed to influence classroom practice; and greater system accountability, including a strengthened role for the regional education consortia that Andrews had created, leading to a national system of school banding (later called categorisation) based on performance. Regional consortia were established in the four regions of Wales to take over delivery of the service for school improvement from the local authorities (LAs). In the earlier period, Estyn, whilst reporting that overall, year-on-year improvements in education standards were being achieved, had also pointed regularly to variations that existed between schools, within schools, between phases of education, gender and socio-economic groups. As indicated above, Estyn, through its monitoring of the work undertaken by private inspection teams, had identified and was addressing concerns about this evidence base. Increasingly from 2007, the annual reports of the CI began to present a more balanced interpretation of standards within the system, and this became further accentuated following the introduction of a new inspection cycle in 2010 that saw HMI again leading the inspections of schools and working to a recalibrated set of expectations in a new common inspection framework.

A more measured approach was now apparent in Estyn's judgements on standards. Whilst some aspects were seen to be improving, it was stressed that overall, very few schools were rated as outstanding and that the variabilities and inconsistencies in standards were notable. Whereas reports from the first period of devolution had judged the quality of schools' self-evaluation to be a strength, now it was reported as a weak feature in about 20 per cent of primary and 25 per cent of secondary schools. Whilst caution was stressed about drawing comparisons from available data on educational performance across the UK nations, it was nevertheless pointed out that in relation to pupil achievement in secondary schools, including examination outcomes at the age of 15, it appeared that Wales lagged behind the other nations. Wales's disappointing performance in the OECD PISA tests were pointed to as further evidence of this pattern of relatively low performance.

The work of LAs, which had previously generally been presented in a favourable light, was also now found wanting in many respects. Those which had been inspected in 2009 were judged to be 'good' but by 2012 it was being reported that the majority that had been visited required 'follow-up' inspections caused by 'issues of structural complexity and failures of capacity, capability and scrutiny'.[21] ITE institutions, which had also been consistently inspected by HMI, were also now found to have many weaknesses, leading to the commissioning by WG of an independent review of the sector.[22]

Some features of the education system which had been highlighted in annual reports during the first period of devolution continued to feature during this second period. The relatively low achievement of more disadvantaged and vulnerable pupils remained a persistent theme as did the need for leaders to take a whole-school approach in responding to these challenges. Emphasis continued to be placed on the importance of 'community schooling' as a response to this situation and it was noted that, despite almost a decade of proposing policy developments in this area, still not enough was being done in the areas of Wales that most needed such schools.

A newer feature in inspection reports after 2010 was the more holistic reporting on standards of pupil well-being, although these were in essence the sum of many aspects of school life (attendance, behaviour, safeguarding practice and pastoral support, etc.) and the relationship between this aspect of a child's experience and their levels of achievement was not fully considered until the inspection framework was revised in 2017.

Whilst the reports continued to reflect on the importance of school leadership and the need to develop leaders 'in a more sophisticated way',[23] there was also an increasing emphasis on the quality of teaching and learning.

The second set of PISA test results for 15-year-olds in Wales fuelled the Education Minister's perception that Wales had a 'complacent' education system that fell 'short of being consistently good and was not delivering the outcomes our learners deserve'.[24] For him, PISA was a 'wake-up' call to the education system in Wales and the media reflected his view that standards in Wales were not improving as well as in other countries.[25] One academic commentator has depicted this as a 'misrecognition' of Wales which sometimes shaded into one of 'derision' for its choice of a different educational path that had led to a 'failing' system.[26] Given that this popular consensus provided the backdrop to a major shift in government policies towards the high-stakes testing and accountability approaches adopted by some countries across the globe, including governments in England, the question inevitably arises as to whether this was in fact justified. The detailed quantitative analysis of the data sets that would be needed to arrive at a firm answer to this question has not yet been undertaken. Estyn in 2010 had concluded that end-of-key-stage teacher assessment outcomes, which have seen an even greater increase in levels of pupil achievement since then, were unreliable.[27] The reliability of the national tests introduced after 2011 is often called into question by schools and others in the education system. Examination outcomes at age of 15 are more reliable and, particularly in the case of our most disadvantaged pupils, suggest that Wales trails behind the other UK nations. Even here, however, the increasingly divergent nature of these systems across the UK calls into question the continuing validity of comparisons that can be made.

PISA is held up as the 'gold standard' of validity and reliability in the testing of specific aspects of cognitive ability, yet it too is open to challenge in terms of its technical features and particularly in the way that its lack of cultural sensitivity can lead to misleading conclusions.[28] In the case of Wales, for example, it takes no account of Wales's ambition to develop a bilingual education system where many 15-year-olds who sit the PISA tests participate in Welsh-medium education but come from homes where English is the spoken language. This appears to have had a significant impact upon the outcomes of Wales in the PISA tests, as did the significant impact which socio-economic disadvantage continued to have on educational achievement in Wales.[29]

Some of the academic researchers who have undertaken the most rigorous analysis of the data used to support the notion of 'a crisis in Welsh education' have questioned the reliability of the evidence used to suggest the comparative 'underperformance' of Welsh schools. They argue that whilst Wales may trail behind other nations in some key indicators, the extent of this has been considerably overstated. They also point to evidence drawn from the *Millennium Cohort Study* which indicates that whereas, by the age of seven, Wales's children are behind those of the other UK nations in literacy levels, their mathematics achievement is similar, and they are ahead on pattern construction and, in the case of our most disadvantaged children, in relation to their well-being.[30]

In relation to Estyn evidence, with the return in 2010 to an HMI-led inspection system it would be a reasonable hypothesis to suggest that much greater consistency was achieved by having fewer, full-time inspectors under the leadership of HMI and more rigorous quality assurance processes in place than existed previously. It was the case, however, that some of the weaknesses identified after 2010 had already been pointed out in earlier annual reports from the outset of devolution, including unfavourable comparisons with similar socio-economic areas of the UK and other nations. And it is possible that what has been called the 'PISA panic' which took place in Wales in 2010 exaggerated a response that led to the introduction of too heavy a burden of new layers of accountability.

What of the impact of this major change in policy direction from the start of the second decade of devolution? It has undoubtedly been hugely significant. In his report on curriculum and assessment arrangements in Wales, Graham Donaldson noted that at its most extreme the 'mission of primary schools was almost reduced to the teaching of literacy and numeracy and of secondary schools to preparation for qualifications'.[31] His report, therefore, sought to address what he perceived as the 'hollowing out' of the curriculum in schools that had resulted from the introduction of the Literacy and Numeracy Frameworks, national tests and school categorisation.

In advising on how Wales might use the powers it had gained in 2018 to develop its own terms and conditions of employment for teachers, Professor Mick Waters has observed that teacher and head teacher workload had become a major issue for the Welsh education system as it attempted to respond to ever increasing accountability.[32] The deleterious impact of this accountability-driven ethos on staff and pupil well-being was identified by Estyn in annual reports some time before being highlighted by a major study published in 2018 by one of the subject committees of the Assembly.[33] Recruitment to secondary ITE courses, which had been a problem for many years, has grown ever more challenging over the last decade and the numbers applying for primary ITE courses has declined.[34] Retention of teachers within the profession has also become an issue, many disillusioned by workload issues and the stifling of innovation in learning and teaching resulting from centrally driven strategies and a focus on examination outcomes above all else.[35]

Reflecting in 2007 on the first period of devolution in education, two eminent observers opined that perhaps the most profound impact of devolution might be 'the ways in which the Welsh understand themselves' rather than a reliance on 'the easily measurable, technocratic outcomes which currently preoccupy so much educational debate'.[36] The policy direction followed over the next five or six years was to frustrate these hopes.

SYSTEM REFORM AND THE INSPECTORATE

Following the appointment of a new Education Minister in June 2013, a gradual move away from this accountability-driven period in Welsh education policy began. This change in direction was implicit in *Qualified for Life* published by the WG in 2014 but was increasingly explicitly articulated as part of a new policy narrative.[37] It was influenced by engagement with international evidence on successful system-wide reform of education, through engagement with OECD[38] and other sources, of the type that had influenced the development of the *School Effectiveness Framework*[39] in 2008 but had been abandoned after 2010. This embraced a focus on developing capacity within the teaching profession in areas such as leadership, professional development and teacher pedagogy, the need for which Estyn had consistently emphasised. International evidence was used as 'policy learning' and adapted to the specific and unique context to be found within the Welsh education system, rather than the 'policy borrowing' approach that had led to the replication of accountability-based approaches to school improvement, which had not transferred well to the post-devolution consensus in Welsh education.[40]

From 2014, the WG began to undertake a range of key policy initiatives which in time became part of a wider reform programme. The commissioning of the former chief inspector of education in Scotland, Graham Donaldson, to review curriculum and assessment arrangements in Wales marked the first stage on this journey. This provided a first opportunity to undertake a root and branch review of the National Curriculum of 1988 that Wales had inherited at the point of devolution and, thereafter, tinkered with through the introduction of the FP, the Welsh Baccalaureate and changes to assessment procedures.[41] Graham Donaldson was assisted in his work by head teachers and two HMI seconded from Estyn. His radical report, published in 2015, was fully accepted by WG, received positively within the teaching profession and led to an innovative approach to curriculum design and planning involving teachers alongside other educational professionals as members of 'pioneer' groups.

This work led to the publication of the final version of the new curriculum in January 2020, ready for phased introduction from September 2022.[42] Estyn HMI were involved heavily in this development process and, when it is finally in place, the monitoring of the new curriculum will become an important aspect of the work of the inspectorate in Wales.

Another major area for reform was ITE. Evidence from Estyn in the period up to 2015 had identified a range of weaknesses in the sector and this led the WG to commission two independent reviews. The second of these, led by Professor John Furlong, proposed a new model for ITE in Wales based on strengthened arrangements between universities and groups of lead partnership schools and a research-informed approach to 'clinical-practice' of a type that had been effectively used within medical education.[43] Estyn was fully involved in the process, led by the Education Workforce Council, of accrediting the new programmes that commenced in September 2019.

Estyn has also played a full part in a raft of reforms that are designed to transform professional learning for teachers in Wales, including the introduction of new professional standards for teaching and leadership,[44] the development of a National Approach to Professional Learning,[45] the creation of national networks to promote teacher pedagogy, a *National Strategy for Education Research and Enquiry* and the setting up of a *National Academy for Educational Leadership*,[46] something which implicitly Estyn had always pointed to the need for and which a former Estyn CI skilfully worked to bring into being.

The important role which Estyn is required to play in this ambitious reform programme is clearly expressed within the WG's 2017 publication *Education in Wales: Our National Mission* setting out its action plan for the period up to 2021.[47] Estyn is described as a 'key partner' within the reform process as a part of the second (middle) tier of the architecture of the Welsh education system, which 'facilitate and support the sharing of best practice and collaboration'. This is the most explicit expression of the role envisioned for Estyn contained in any strategic policy document produced by WG since devolution.

Estyn's own key publications during the most recent period, particularly the annual reports of the CI, are generally in tune with the messages and language of the reform agenda and this repositioning of its role within the process. Whilst the impact of poverty on educational attainment continued to be recognised, it was stressed that socio-economic deprivation need not always limit student achievement, with some of the strongest providers inspected by Estyn being found in such communities. These schools – particularly those in the primary phase – had built their success on close engagement with their families and communities. Such an approach had long been championed by Estyn as the key to sustainable success in attempting to overcome the impact of disadvantage on pupil achievement.[48] Improvements in the work of LAs in monitoring their schools were noted and the role of the new regional education consortia recognised in this respect, although they were felt to be at an early stage of development and needed to improve their work if the concept of a 'self-improving' educational system was to have salience. In alignment with one of the key features of the education reform programme, increasing focus has been given by Estyn to the quality of teaching and leadership in its reports. In 2016, HMCI's annual report again identified the quality of teaching as 'one of the weakest aspects of provision', with insufficient attention being paid in schools to key aspects of effective teaching including engagement with educational research and thinking 'critically about pedagogy'. The long-term changes that HMCI judged necessary, in areas such as the curriculum, ITE, professional learning and school self-evaluation, have become central elements of the current education reform programme.[49] And Estyn is to continue to play its part in co-constructing and evaluating the success of that programme.

ENDNOTES

1. Gareth Elwyn Jones, 'Education and Nationhood in Wales: An Historiographical Analysis', *Journal of Educational Administration and History*, 38/3 (2006), 263–77.
2. Rhodri Morgan, 'Clear Red Water', speech to the National Centre for Public Policy, Swansea (Swansea: National Centre for Public Policy, 2002).
3. Pasi Sahlberg, *Finnish Lessons: What can the world learn from educational change in Finland?* (New York: Teachers College Press, 2011), pp. 99–106.
4. Russell Deacon, *The Governance of Wales* (Cardiff: Welsh Academic Press, 2002), p. 111.
5. Gareth Rees, 'Democratic Devolution and Education Policy in Wales: The Emergence of a National System', *Contemporary Wales*, 17 (2004), 28–43.
6. OHMCI Wales, *Annual Report of the Chief Inspector of Education and Training for Wales 1997–1998* (Cardiff: OHMCI, 1999).
7. Welsh Assembly Government (WAG), *The Learning Country* (Cardiff: WAG, 2001), p. 35.

8. WAG, *Vision into Action, The Learning Country 2: delivering the promise* (Cardiff: WAG, 2006).
9. WAG, *The School Effectiveness Framework* (Cardiff: WAG, 2008), p. 19.
10. Estyn, *Annual Report 1999–2000* (Cardiff: Estyn, 2001), p. 28.
11. Estyn, *Annual Report 2003–2004* (Cardiff: Estyn, 2005), p. 39.
12. Estyn, *Annual Report 2002–2003* (Cardiff: Estyn, 2004), p. 27.
13. Estyn, *Annual Report 2003–2004*, p. 14.
14. David Egan and Roy James, 'Education', in John Osmond and J. Barry Jones (eds), *Birth of Welsh Democracy: The First Term of the National Assembly for Wales* (Cardiff: Institute for Welsh Affairs and Wales Governance Centre, 2003), pp. 99–114.
15. David Reynolds, *Times Educational Supplement*, 5 October 2001.
16. WAG, *The Learning Country* (2001), p. 2.
17. Gareth Elwyn Jones and Gordon Wynne Roderick, *A History of Education in Wales* (Cardiff: University of Wales Press, 2003), p. 225.
18. Leighton Andrews, 'Teaching makes a difference', 2 February 2011, speech given at Reardon Smith Lecture Theatre, National Museum of Wales, Cardiff.
19. Welsh Government (WG), *Improving Schools* (Cardiff: WG, 2012).
20. WG, *National Literacy and Numeracy Framework* (Cardiff: WG, 2013).
21. Estyn, *Annual Report 2011–2012* (Cardiff: Estyn, 2013), p. 37.
22. Ralph Tabberer, *A Review of Initial Teacher Education in Wales* (Cardiff: WG, 2013).
23. Estyn, *Annual Report 2012-2013* (Cardiff: Estyn, 2014), p. 19.
24. Leighton Andrews, *Ministering to Education* (Cardigan: Parthian, 2014).
25. Gareth Evans, *A Class Apart: Learning the Lessons of Education in Post-Devolution Wales* (Cardiff: Welsh Academic Press, 2015), pp. 160–8.
26. Sally Power, 'The politics of education and the misrepresentation of Wales', *Oxford Review of Education*, 42/3 (2016), 285–98.
27. Estyn, *Annual Report 2009–2010* (Cardiff: Estyn, 2011), Section 4, p. 4.
28. Bob Lingard, Wayne Martino and Goli Rezai-Rashti, 'Testing regimes, accountabilities and education policy', *Journal of Education Policy*, 28/5 (2013), 539–56; Geraint Johnes, 'Medium Efficiency: Comparing Inputs and Outputs by Language of Instruction in Secondary Schools in Wales', *Wales Journal of Education*, 22/2 (2020), 52–66; Lizzie Swaffield, 'Never Waste a Crisis: Understanding the Welsh Policy Response to PISA in the Context of the Globally Structured Reform Agenda', *Wales Journal of Education*, 19/1 (2017), 178–87.
29. David Egan, 'Educational Equity in Wales', *Wales Journal of Education*, 18/1 (2016), 21–44; David Egan, 'Shifting Paradigms: Can Education Compensate for Society?' in Susanne Gannon, Robert Hattam and Wayne Sawyer (eds), *Resisting Educational Inequality: Reframing policy and practice in schools serving vulnerable communities* (London: Routledge, 2018).
30. Gareth Rees and Chris Taylor, 'Is There a Crisis in Welsh Education?', *Transactions of the Honourable Society of Cymmrodorion* (2014), 97–113.

31. Graham Donaldson, *Successful Futures: Independent Review of Curriculum and Assessment Arrangements in Wales* (Cardiff: WG, 2015), p. 10.
32. WG, *Teaching: A valued profession – working towards a Career, Conditions and Pay Framework for School Teachers in Wales. The report of the independent review* (Cardiff: WG, 2018), pp. 18–19.
33. National Assembly for Wales (NAfW) Children and Young People and Education Committee, *Mind over matter: A report on the step change needed in emotional and mental health support for children and young people in Wales* (Cardiff: NAfW, 2018).
34. Rebecca Allen and Sam Sims, *The Teacher Gap* (Abingdon: Routledge, 2018).
35. Allen and Sims, *The Teacher Gap* and Welsh Government, 2018.
36. Gareth Rees and Sally Power, 'Educational Research and the Restructuring of the State: The Impacts of Parliamentary Devolution in Wales', *European Educational Research Journal*, 6/1 (2007), 87–100.
37. WG, *Qualified for Life: an education improvement plan for 3 to 19 year olds in Wales* (Cardiff: WG, 2014).
38. OECD, *Improving Schools in Wales: An OECD Perspective* (Paris: OECD, 2014).
39. WAG, *The School Effectiveness Framework* (Cardiff: WAG, 2008).
40. David Raff, 'Policy borrowing or policy learning? How (not) to improve education systems', *CES Briefing*, 57, 1/4 (2011).
41. Donaldson, *Successful Futures*.
42. WG, Curriculum and Assessment Bill 2020.
43. John Furlong, *Teaching Tomorrow's Teachers: Options for the future of initial teacher education in Wales* (Cardiff: WG, 2015).
44. WG, *Professional Standards for Teaching and Leadership* (Cardiff: WG, 2017).
45. WG, *The National Approach to Professional Learning (NAPL)* (Cardiff: WG, 2018).
46. National Academy for Educational Leadership (NAEL), *Inspiring Leaders: Enriching Lives* (Swansea: NAEL, 2019).
47. WG, *Education in Wales: Our National Mission* (Cardiff: WG, 2017).
48. Estyn, *Annual Report 2016–2017* (Cardiff: Estyn, 2018); Estyn, *Excellent Schools: A vision for schools in Wales in the 21st Century* (Cardiff: Estyn, 2002); Estyn, *Transforming Schools: A Discussion Paper* (Cardiff: Estyn, 2007).
49. Estyn, *Annual Report 2015–2016* (Cardiff: Estyn, 2017), p. 5.

Chapter 8

INSPECTION IN WALES AND INTERNATIONALLY: SOME COMPARISONS

Russell Grigg and Ann Keane

INTRODUCTION

This chapter identifies some of the features and trends in Wales's education inspectorate and explores some parallels with developments in other inspectorates, mainly in Europe. It contextualises the changes to inspection policy in Wales by exploring inspection policy responses in other countries, particularly those within the Organisation for Economic and Co-operation and Development (OECD) countries choosing to be part of the Programme for International Student Assessment (PISA).

Previous chapters have described how the Wales inspectorate developed over time. In 1839, a single England and Wales inspectorate was established and HMI were organised in regions that combined responsibilities for districts in both countries. By 1882, Wales had its own division within the inspectorate and a further degree of autonomy was granted in 1907 when the Welsh Department was established within the Board of Education. Westminster legislation for inspection would continue to create parallel duties for both Wales and England inspectorates during the twentieth century although the Welsh Office assumed administrative responsibilities for education in 1970. In 1992, two separate offices were set up: the Office of Her Majesty's Chief Inspector (OHMCI) Wales – accountable to the Secretary of State for Wales – and OHMCI England. The legislation laid the same duties upon the respective HMCI but there was some further bifurcation in practice between the inspectorates. The close relationship between both countries which had previously involved annual joint conferences and regular subject specialist meetings as well as regular joint inspectors' courses (IC) fell into abeyance. There would be fewer joint inspections of British armed services schools overseas. However, the Wales inspectorate would still work with what became Ofsted on some inspections of independent special schools and colleges (if students from both countries were on roll) and join teams from the UK Prisons and Probation inspectorates to inspect offender learning in Wales. Parallel legislation on inspection for both education inspectorates would continue up until the 2005 Education Act, after which Ofsted took on substantial further responsibilities, including the inspection of children's services, while Estyn did not. Ofsted was the subject of further legislation that changed the pattern of their school inspections after 2005 but Estyn's school inspections continued – and still continue – to be subject to the provisions of the 2005 Act. However, some of its subsidiary regulations have been amended by the Welsh Government (WG) and Estyn has been affected by new statutory requirements in National Assembly for Wales (NAfW) Measures and Acts since 2007.

The separation between the Wales and England education inspectorates after 1992 represented a significant loss of a long-established community for professional dialogue and training. It was therefore timely that the Standing International Conference of Inspectorates (SICI) was established in 1995 to offer membership of a new professional community with a much larger number of member-countries. SICI has expanded over time to represent thirty-eight bodies that inspect and evaluate education across Europe. It has offered, and continues to offer, a programme of conferences, projects, peer reviews and a forum for sharing experiences and discussing policy, both in education and inspection. Some of the key issues affecting the inspectorate in Wales have also been issues in other countries and in approaching challenge, Estyn has benefited from its long-standing membership of SICI. Representatives from Estyn have attended its conferences, visited schools and joined inspections in various European countries, and been visited by inspectors from other countries. HMI from Wales have made many presentations at SICI conference workshops and it is rare for them to be absent from conferences.

This chapter will compare how the Wales inspectorate has approached some key issues that it has in common with other inspectorates, how Wales has been influenced by others, as well as the extent to which it has itself set an example in relation to the functions of an inspectorate: by promoting peer involvement in inspection; encouraging school self-evaluation (SSE); informing education policy; inspecting well-being; and reporting on accountability. The chapter begins with an overview of the functions of an inspectorate.

THE FUNCTIONS OF AN INSPECTORATE

European inspectorates elsewhere would recognise the view of an inspectorate's core functions as represented in the three objectives that have appeared regularly in Estyn's annual plans:

- providing public accountability to service users on the quality and standards of education and training provision in Wales;
- informing the development of national policy by the Welsh Government; and
- building capacity for improvement of the delivery of the education and training system in Wales.[1]

However, there is considerable variation in practice between the objectives of different inspection systems across the UK and beyond. Each inspection system is the product of those historical and political processes that preceded their current institutional configuration. Many of the older European inspectorates have been strengthened over the last twenty years as a result of policy decisions by their political masters to intervene more directly in order to hold schools to account. Responses to PISA account for much of the turbulence in the recent period. It was because of PISA that, in some countries, central inspectorates were strengthened or reintroduced, such as happened in Sweden in 2003 and in Denmark in 2006. In other instances, new inspectorates were established for the first time due to PISA, such as those in Norway (2006), in the Austrian provinces and German states (from 2003). Although the older inspectorates, such as those established in the early 1800s in the Netherlands,

France, England and Wales, have evolved more gradually over a longer period, none of the European inspectorates has escaped completely the shining light or shadow cast by PISA. The variety of ways in which inspectorates have responded, in Wales and other countries, is explored in further detail in the last section of this chapter.

The neo-liberal sharpening of the tools in accountability toolkits had already had an impact on some inspectorates before PISA. From 1992 onwards, inspection in Wales and England had been outsourced to private contractors with the aim of inspecting schools and publishing reports more regularly, as is described in Chapter 5. For the first time, HMI published guidance on inspection in which the criteria for making judgements and grading schools on a five-point scale were made explicit. As Chapter 7 has indicated, after the devolution of powers to a Welsh Assembly in 1999, the first decade of the twenty-first century was devoted to reiterating a trust-based 'Learning Country' education policy for Wales whereby tests and league tables were abandoned. Towards the end of the decade, a new Minister introduced new accountability mechanisms in Wales in the form of an annual banding of schools (later called 'categorisation') on the basis of performance and national tests in literacy and numeracy for pupils.[2] More recently, there has been a significant shift in the paradigm for the whole business of accountability, including inspection, and many influential thinkers have questioned whether it is necessary to have external accountability at all when so much academic theory of change holds that internal accountability is what drives improvement in schools. Graham Donaldson has outlined in his review of Estyn how high-stakes accountability systems – that is, systems which involve publishing graded judgements on schools – can lead to significant, negative unintended consequences, so that 'undue attention may be given to those pupils whose marginal improvement will affect performance figures'.[3]

The literature on self-improvement is divided on the question of whether an independent inspectorate is even necessary. Steve Marshall, the highly respected educationalist who was brought from Australia to Wales in the mid-2000s to lead the then Welsh Assembly Government's Department for Children, Education and Lifelong Learning and to create and promote the *School Effectiveness Framework* (SEF), was not a strong supporter of school inspection as a mechanism for school improvement although he worked with the inspectorate to mobilise its support to introduce the SEF. According to Professor Michael Fullan, who joined the SEF programme team as an adviser at Marshall's invitation (on the basis of the success of his strategies for improvement in Ontario schools): 'Successful large-scale change doesn't require punitive forms of accountability.'[4] SEF was launched in 2008 as a strategy to promote tri-level collaboration across government, local authorities and schools within a school effectiveness framework that was intended to promote system leadership and professional learning in a high performance culture. Chapter 7 acknowledges that there was scant reference to Estyn in the SEF strategy.

The early twenty-first century was a period in which inspectorates across Europe were seeking to explore and redefine the scope and functions of inspection in order to maximise their value to the political and education systems they served. SICI's *Bratislava Memorandum on Inspection and Innovation* was agreed in 2013 as a result of deliberations at SICI conferences between inspectors who were themselves caught in the battle between politicians who wanted inspection to drive more accountability and academics and practitioners in education who were shifting to a very different paradigm for school improvement in which school evaluation would not involve inspection. The memorandum represented the range of views about what were and should be the priorities of inspectorates across Europe and tried to reconcile some of the main opposing positions: the view of inspectors as 'direct enforcers of policy' or compliance-checking regulators who take a 'tick-box' approach that rewards orthodoxy; as compared to a view of inspectors as 'helping to stimulate well-founded innovation' and 'strengthening the catalytic and capacity-building contributions of inspection'.[5] These seeming conflicts of role have existed throughout the history of inspection. Inspection was once used to measure schools' compliance with the restrictive Lowe Code of the mid-Victorian era and several HMI were critical of the Code and expressed a commitment to a wider ambition for education than the narrow vision which it embodied. Equally, since the introduction of a National Curriculum in Wales and England, HMI have (until 2010 in Wales) exercised a governance role in reporting on schools' compliance with its delivery while also reporting on wider aspects of provision and standards. Although inspectorates throughout their history have fulfilled the role of 'watchdogs' in reporting on compliance, they have also exercised a reforming role in attempting to change inspection and education policy for the better. It would be fair to say that their impact on education and on policy has perhaps been more incremental than revelatory. Some of the significant innovations that inspectorates have introduced and challenges they have faced in Wales and elsewhere over recent years are discussed below.

PEER INVOLVEMENT IN INSPECTION

It has perhaps not been fully acknowledged that inspectorates, including in Wales, have for a long period been addressing the problems associated with inspection experienced as something 'done to' rather than 'done with' schools and other providers. The challenge of creating an inclusive inspection system that would be of benefit both internally to the provider and externally to fulfil an accountability role was met in part in Wales by including staff from other providers (peers) and a nominee from the provider being inspected as members of inspection teams. Donaldson notes that:

> Estyn reflects, and has in some aspects pioneered, much of current thinking internationally about effective inspection. For example, the involvement of peer and lay inspectors, the introduction of a nominee from the school to participate in an inspection ... were all bold moves to open up inspection and encourage schools to engage more constructively with the process.[6]

As Chapter 5 outlines, peers (associate assessors) were introduced into inspections of further education (FE) colleges in Wales in the 1990s. At this stage few other countries were using teachers as inspectors although Spanish secondary teachers in the 1990s 'could take part in inspection activities'.[7] In Wales, from 2004, serving head teachers and deputies were introduced into school inspection teams, following the success of peer inspectors in FE. One aim was to give them an experience of inspecting schools other than their own, after training by HMI, so as to enable a more robust internal scrutiny of quality in their own institution. Increasing numbers of school and college heads and heads of department were trained annually with the aim of sharing inspectorial expertise across the system so that emerging system leaders would be armed not only with data analysis skills but with a better understanding of different kinds of classroom practice and the quality of learning in them. A PricewaterhouseCoopers (PWC) evaluation of Estyn's new common inspection arrangements in 2006 found that both inspectors and providers deemed the use of peers on inspection as 'already a familiar and valued feature in further education' and 'beneficial' though still relatively new in schools.[8] In 2014 Ofsted began making systematic use of head teachers as inspectors. A recent study of the implications and impact of this policy in England concluded that 'Their sense of commitment to the duality of their professional lives, as headteacher and inspector, resonates with the concept of a systemic leadership orientation.'[9] The practice of using peers as inspectors has also been adopted in Northern Ireland, Scotland and Ireland and, according to Gray, 'the increased use of serving practitioners' has been a theme of the period in several countries and states, including Italy, Romania, Latvia, Lower Saxony and Bavaria.[10] The strategy meets several objectives: it can help to reduce what has previously been characterised as the 'adversarial relationship' between provider staff and inspectors; it can facilitate the practices of inspection within schools as part of their own internal self-evaluation; and peer inspectors also bring valuable current experience to an inspection team, always an advantage when full-time inspectors are sometimes criticised for not having enough 'recent and relevant' experience. In Wales, by now, few schools remain that do not have at least one peer inspector on their staff and many secondary schools have several.

The benefit of using nominees from the provider being inspected as members of inspection teams has been widely recognised by inspectors, providers and stakeholders in Wales. Their use was welcomed across all sectors from 2004 as part of the new common inspection framework arrangements. However, there was little reference to the use of nominees in other countries' inspection systems at the time and, when presenting a case for their wider adoption in inspection at SICI conferences, HMI from Wales were often met with considerable scepticism. Objections to the practice tended to focus on the risk of 'inspector capture' on one hand or, on the other hand, the challenge of managing critical findings during team meetings on inspections when a nominee from the school was present. Nevertheless, all the providers interviewed as part of the 2006 evaluation considered the introduction of the nominee role as either *helpful* or *very helpful*. Providers explained that nominees could clear up misconceptions; they could be a link to the provider's staff to explain issues and to inform post-inspection discussions about responses to the team's recommendations; and they made the whole process 'more transparent'.[11]

SCHOOL SELF-EVALUATION (SSE)

Like the introduction of peers and nominees to inspection teams, the purpose of SSE is to build capacity in a self-improving system. During the 1990s, inspectorates across Europe began to include SSE as part of their approach, including Spain (1991), Finland (1993), the Netherlands (1998) and England (1999). However, progress was slow despite support from the OECD and European Parliament and Council.[12] The Wales inspectorate introduced a requirement for self-evaluation reports (SERs) as part of pre-inspection preparation and internal quality assurance in further education from the mid-1990s and in schools from 2004. Although the production of SERs was initially seen by providers merely as a part of their pre-inspection preparation, gradually, systematic self-evaluation become a part of providers' annual cycles of quality assurance and forward planning to generate development plans. PWC in their 2006 evaluation of Estyn's 2004 inspection cycle concluded that SSE in Wales put a focus on and drove improvement:

> Self-evaluation is an established part of the development planning cycle and a key management tool for improvement at all levels ... There was strong agreement across providers, stakeholders and inspectors in all sectors that the self-evaluation process was beneficial both to the inspection itself and to providers.[13]

In Finland, by 1999, centralised school inspection was abolished and replaced by a model of self-evaluation supported by local municipalities. Support for SSE grew quickly in the 2000s: Portugal (2002), Spain and Estonia (2006) and Poland (2009) made SSE mandatory. Nonetheless, more detailed guidance was found to be necessary given the lack of skills and experience among staff in schools.[14] In Wales, because self-evaluation reports were used to raise questions during inspection, there developed a tendency among some providers to use them to paint too rosy a picture. Nevertheless, Estyn, like the other UK inspectorates, has promoted SSE heavily and is currently collaborating with the Welsh Government on new arrangements for SSE in the context of the wide-ranging education reforms focused around the co-construction of the Curriculum for Wales.

INFORMING EDUCATION POLICY

As indicated in Chapter 4, the Rayner report (1982) gave priority to the HMI function of information gathering for government and offering independent advice. 'Speaking truth to power' has always been seen as a duty of civil servants and the independence given to HMI as officers of the Crown (appointed by the Queen in Privy Council) offers them a role in the network of 'checks and balances' that underpin the governance of the education system. It has always been a convention that HMI may not challenge government policy publicly but may criticise the outworking of policy on the grounds that the state requires consistent implementation of its laws and regulations and therefore needs to know where they are working and where they are not. The seeming independence offered to HMI in this way is not, in practice, as straightforward as it seems. Published survey and inspection reports have long been sources of information both for policy makers and the wider public but, as Chapter 7 has explained, much of the advice that the inspectorate offers to Ministers is protected, even when taking account of the provisions of the Freedom of Information Act, as part of the process of policy making.

There are published reports by inspectors across Europe, including in France, the Netherlands and the UK which have been critical of the implementation of government policy and some have been critical of government policy itself, albeit indirectly. The Wales and England inspectorate's right to publish its views independently of government was established in the nineteenth century although it has been common for government officials in Wales to read and make suggestions on survey and annual reports before they are published. It is exceptional for the inspectorate to be requested not to publish.

The extent to which inspectorates can challenge government policy publicly is generally limited but it varies according to the position of an inspectorate within the state infrastructure. It is governments, ultimately, that have the power to change legislation and inspection policy, accountable as they are to the electorate. Inspectorates are more a part of the governance of education than they are totally autonomous and fearless public reporters. But inspectors across the generations claim to have spoken without fear or favour in confidential discussions about education policy with politicians. It is the case that policy makers often do take account of the findings of inspectorates by adapting or even introducing policy to address the failings that inspectorates reveal. But it is also the case that some inspectorates have more direct influence than others. Some are closer to the policy-making process than others. In the recent past, inspectorates in Ireland, Scotland and Portugal have routinely integrated inspectors directly into the detail of the policy-making process and the business of drafting legislation and statutory guidance. By comparison, the inspectorate in Wales has been independent of government since 1992, in terms of its status as a non-Ministerial department of the civil service, its physical location and its stand-alone management structure. However, HMI have been members of official networks in which policy and its implementation are under review and matters relating to policy thinking and planning are regularly discussed in the termly meetings between Ministers and the CI. Confidential requests from Ministers for advice on matters of policy are not unusual and some Ministers have been pleased to make full use of the inspectorate in this respect.

Published recommendations for government in the Wales inspectorate's survey reports relate to streamlining the implementation of policy rather than challenging the policy itself. There are sensitivities and ideologies at work and it is also the case that new Ministers in particular wish to own agency in the policy direction they take. In the final analysis, inspectorates are expected to promote as well as inform government priorities.

In Wales, power was devolved to a new National Assembly for Wales (NAfW) and its Welsh Assembly Government (WAG) in 1999, two years after the UK Labour Government was elected and before its Policy Unit and the mantra of 'education, education, education' had had time to begin changing the face of schools and inspection in Wales. It was an era in which university academics enjoyed greater direct influence on education policy initiatives. In Wales, as in England and elsewhere in Europe, academics who had previously studied and written about school improvement and managing change became the new generation of policy influencers. This was the case in the UK Labour government after 1997 and some of the gurus of the Blair Policy Unit enjoyed an afterlife in Wales long after Labour had lost power in England.

INSPECTING WELL-BEING

The growth in recognising children's rights across Europe can be traced back to the 1970s. They were crystallised in the United Nations Convention on the Rights of the Child (1989) which the Welsh Government adopted early on. It was the first government among UK nations to appoint a Children's Commissioner in 2001 to advocate for children's rights. The inspectorate in Wales has long been concerned with reporting on the welfare of children and the 2005 Education Act required HMI in Wales to inspect and report on the well-being of pupils. Within the meaning of the Act, the reference was to two main aspects of well-being: the health and safety of students (although Estyn does not have the same legal duties as the Health and Safety Executive); and child protection (later expanded into 'safeguarding', which includes vulnerable adults). By now the well-being of children and young people is generally understood also to include the quality of their lives, as indicated by objective data (rates of attainment and school attendance and/ or exclusion) and subjective measures (how content they are about their education and their welfare in school). The inspectorate in

Wales also operates within the context of legislation such as the Social Services and Well-being (Wales) Act 2014 and the Well-being of Future Generations (Wales) Act 2015, which both established personal rights and national goals that expand the range of definitions of 'well-being' significantly.

Well-being has become a common feature of inspection frameworks across Europe, although it is interpreted in different ways. For example, the Dutch inspectorate reports annually on how well schools are doing in promoting a safe environment. Schools are also required to monitor annually their pupils' perceptions of safety, while governing bodies are required to ensure the 'social, psychological and physical safety' of pupils.[15] Inspectorates across Europe have had to ensure that their expectations of education providers and their own procedures and practices are in keeping with legislative and policy changes in relation to well-being.

Like Ofsted, Her Majesty's Inspectorate of Education in Scotland and the inspectorate of the Department of Education in Northern Ireland, Estyn has strengthened its focus on well-being in its revisions of inspection frameworks, most notably in 2010 and 2017, and through the issuing of supplementary guidance on inspecting safeguarding (2010, 2015, 2017), healthy living (2017) and reducing the impact of poverty on attainment and well-being (2019). As part of its annual remit from the Welsh Government, Estyn has also undertaken surveys on a range of well-being issues such as substance misuse (2007) and action on bullying (2014). These publications highlight examples of good practice and offer an evaluation of children and young people's well-being to inform policy makers. And the picture of children's well-being in schools is a generally positive one, particularly at primary level where practices are often more consistent than in secondary schools.[16] Estyn and the Welsh Government acknowledge that while there have been improvements in some aspects of children's health, there remain significant causes for concern. These include the impact of income poverty on more than one in four children and the significant variations in educational attainment between socio-economic groups.[17]

Estyn has also reported on teacher well-being. In the early 2000s, it reported on the deployment of para-professional and other support for teachers, issues relating to teachers' workload and the impact of the government's National Agreement on pay and working conditions for teachers in England and Wales. Staff well-being is particularly important for policy makers, partly because of the challenges of recruiting and retaining an education workforce of high quality. As noted in earlier chapters, there have been long-standing concerns that the process and outcomes of inspection have contributed towards increased levels of teacher stress. These concerns are neither new nor confined to Wales. For example, comparative studies of inspectorates in Austria, the Czech Republic, England, Ireland, the Netherlands, Sweden and Switzerland report that unintended negative side-effects of inspection have the potential to undo positive effects.[18] These include the pressure to align provision with perceptions of what inspectors want to see. However, over many years, Estyn, along with other inspectorates, have worked hard to explode the myths about the expectations of inspectors, to encourage innovation, to include teachers and leaders in the inspection process and to slim down inspection frameworks.[19]

ACCOUNTABILITY

Throughout Europe, part of the rationale for the inspection of education providers is to hold them accountable for the quality and outcomes of their publicly funded services. Early on, in most of the oldest inspectorates, such as those in Prussia, the Netherlands and England and Wales, such financial accountability meant that state funding was linked to school efficiency. In more recent times, policy agendas have been driven by a commitment to promoting more equitable educational systems although value for money indicators of efficiency and effectiveness have remained staples of many inspection frameworks.

European inspectorates vary in how they hold schools and colleges accountable, the nature of that accountability and the follow-up action they pursue. Austria and Switzerland represent *low-stakes* systems which rely on non-punitive means of persuasion and support to motivate school improvement, whereas in Sweden, schools face sanctions and even financial penalties as potential consequences of poor inspections reports; in Montenegro, head teachers can be dismissed if their school is rated unsatisfactory.[20]

Some inspectorates, such as Bulgaria and Norway, do not grade education providers although many inspectorates use some form of numerical or alphabetic scale.[21] In some cases, such as France, teachers are graded on the basis of their individual lessons and this can have an impact on their career development.

In general, there has been a trend across Europe towards risk-based inspections where low-performing schools receive greater focus than those judged to be good or better. In Sweden, for example, prior to inspection ('supervision'), school results are scrutinised along with a survey completed by individual schools and the responsible authority. Schools considered to be functioning well receive a basic supervision visit. If there are uncertainties, a 'widened supervision' is arranged, and where there are clear problems, this leads to a 'deepened supervision'. Around one in four schools in Sweden are monitored more closely.[22] In Estyn's case, a model of risk-based inspections of varying length was established in the 1990s but replaced in 2010 by a model whereby a short core inspection for all providers was followed by a proportionate form of monitoring in 'follow-up' visits where necessary, on a model that was initiated in Scotland.

Since the 1980s, accountability has gradually taken on a different form in many countries with the application of market-style regulatory methods to public services, such as 'results-based accountability' and 'total quality management'. Such accountability is often cast in a negative light as creating unhealthy competition that can undermine collaborative improvement projects. It has been argued that it is another form of accountability, one which emphasises participation and networking, that has the best prospect of fostering a socially cohesive self-improving educational system.[23]

One definition of accountability is a relationship between two parties in which one is answerable for their actions to another but in so doing carries a sense of ownership or personal responsibility.[24] This suggests a more positive interpretation of accountability as offering opportunities to demonstrate progress and achievement. The challenge for policy makers lies in striking that balance between accountability and autonomy which best benefits students.

In the Welsh policy context, accountability has had a recent history that is different from that of the other UK nations. Since devolution in 1999, some commentators have suggested that accountability within the educational system in Wales can be analysed in three distinct phases.[25] In the early years, the Welsh Assembly Government adopted an 'experimental' approach which was characterised by 'high trust' rather than 'mistrust'[26] in the profession and this led, for example, to the abandonment of Standardised Assessment Tests and school league tables in the early 2000s. There is some empirical research to support the view that such a move was 'disastrous' in dragging down not only Wales but the UK's overall performance as judged by PISA.[27] The poor results in 2009 prompted a policy shift as Wales entered a second phase of accountability under Leighton Andrews, the Minister for Education who, in 2011, set out his stall in a much-publicised speech in which he described the educational system as complacent and signalled 'a new approach to accountability'.[28] In relation to Estyn, Andrews was critical of the 2004–10 inspection cycle for failing to follow up on weaker or mediocre schools and he considered the inspection framework 'not fit for purpose until very recently'. He argued that the use of data was 'critical to performance' and warned governing bodies that their schools would fail unless they engaged with performance data and set targets in improvement plans on the basis of data analysis.

The focus on data had, by 2011, already been strengthened in Estyn's 2010 inspection framework with standardised pre-inspection analysis of data on student outcomes and of the self-evaluation report from the provider a mandatory pre-cursor to the process of identifying the questions to be asked and the hypotheses to test during the actual inspection. Andrews supported a sharper edge for accountability mechanisms and introduced further accountability mechanisms in the form of national tests in reading and numeracy (for all 7–14-year-olds) and the 'banding' (later categorisation) of schools by the newly formed regional consortia. From 2011, schools – first secondary and then primary schools – were ranked in bands whose listings were published annually.

During this period, growing concerns were expressed about the lack of coherence within the educational system. Most notably, the OECD reported in 2014 that the relationship between accountability and improvement was unclear.[29] Trade unions expressed concern that the layers of accountability were becoming increasingly complex and sometimes generated contradictory outcomes. Two chief inspectors in several annual reports have been critical of the weight of expectations laid on the education providers by the plethora of layers of accountability. Such disquiet formed the backdrop to the third phase of policy 'movement' in which the Welsh government sought to restore good relations and confidence in the teaching profession.

Since 2014, discussions about the need to relax the demands of 'high-stakes accountability' have been aligned with the current programme of education reforms. There has been reflection, as part of the programme, on how schools should be held accountable and their performance measured without recourse to interpretations of data on student outcomes against a narrow set of measures which could limit the range of the curriculum and encourage 'teaching to the test'.

Globally, most systems of accountability in education are based not only on measures of student attainment but also on the extent to which providers comply with regulations or adhere to professional norms and standards.[30] One of the characteristics of the most successful educational systems can be identified as the coherence or alignment between the various aspects of provision: the educational objectives, governance and leadership, curriculum planning, pupil assessment and internal and external forms of evaluation. In Wales, as in other countries, there is a tension between external accountability and the professional, internal autonomy of SSE. In its Education Policy Outlook series, the OECD has noted in a range of jurisdictions that there needs to be better integration between evaluation and inspection.[31]

When accountability is cast as an outcome rather than a collaborative process, achieving the goals of supporting improvement in education becomes more challenging. Some inspectorates, such as that in the Netherlands, include opportunities for schools to propose their own quality indicators, to be inspected alongside those which are mandatory.[32] In other cases, such as New Zealand and Hong Kong, alternative models of peer review and self-evaluation are preferred, but, arguably, neither by themselves provides a robust enough picture of national and comparative performance. In Finland, the national sample-based assessments that take place are used to inform policy, not to classify schools as weak or otherwise, and teachers are not subjected to top-down control. The Finnish success story, in terms of performance in international tests, is largely attributed to the investment in teaching quality and trust in teachers' professionalism.[33] There is emerging evidence that the most effective inspection systems, in terms of contributing to sustainable school improvement, promote local multi-agency collaboration.[34] Such a polycentric view of inspection rests on the assumption that this approach can be successful once schools have reached a certain quality threshold. Trends across Europe involve engaging education providers more in 'horizontal' rather than 'vertical' forms of accountability.[35] This is seen as fostering 'professional accountability' in which teachers are answerable to their peers and head teachers.[36] Such models exist in jurisdictions such as Canada (Ontario), Finland, Japan and New Zealand, whose educational systems consistently perform at high levels. Similar developments in Wales, as indicated earlier in this chapter, have involved including teachers and managers in Estyn inspection teams and in the peer inspections organised by regional consortia to promote school improvement. However, the ownership of the formal inspection system still lies with Estyn and ultimately with a Welsh Government that has in the past depended upon the inspectorate for objective external school evaluation both to provide assurance and to inform policy.

It is difficult to establish definitively which approach to accountability leads to the most successful outcomes because so many factors affect the quality of education, some of which are outside the control of education providers themselves. And it will always be the case that the unintended consequences of accountability reforms often take some time to surface. The last chapter of this book considers the future locus of the inspectorate and of accountability in the context of current system reform.

ENDNOTES

1. Estyn, *Annual Plan 2019–2020* (Cardiff: Estyn, 2019), p. 3.
2. Welsh Assembly Government (WAG), *The Learning Country: A Paving Document* (Cardiff: WAG, 2001); WAG, *The Learning Country: Vision into Action* (Cardiff: WAG, 2006); Welsh Government (WG), *National school categorisation system* (Cardiff: WG, 2019).

3. Graham Donaldson, *A Learning Inspectorate* (Cardiff: Estyn, 2018), p. 23.
4. Michael Fullan, *Motion Leadership*, presentation at WAG workshop in Swansea, 12 May 2010.
5. SICI, *Memorandum on Inspection and Innovation (Bratislava Memorandum)*. Available at *www.sici-inspectorates.eu* (2013) (accessed 12 October 2020).
6. Donaldson, *A Learning Inspectorate*, p. 15.
7. Adrian Gray, *European School Inspection and Evaluation History and Principles* (Retford: SICI, 2019), p. 160.
8. PricewaterhouseCoopers, *Her Majesty's Inspectorate for Education and Training in Wales (Estyn) Evaluation of inspection arrangements* (Cardiff: PricewaterhouseCoopers, March 2006), pp. 4–9.
9. H. J. Moreton, M. Boylan and T. Simkins, 'Headteachers Who also Inspect: Practitioner Inspectors in England', in J. Baxter (ed.), *School Inspectors: Policy Implementers, Policy Shapers in National Policy Contexts* (Switzerland: Springer International Publishing, 2017), p. 155.
10. Gray, *European School Inspection and Evaluation History and Principles*, pp. 197–8.
11. PriceWaterhouseCoopers, *Evaluation of inspection arrangements*, p. 10.
12. Gray, *European School Inspection and Evaluation History and Principles*, pp. 169–70.
13. PriceWaterhouseCoopers, *Evaluation of inspection arrangements*, p. 7.
14. Gray, *European School Inspection and Evaluation History and Principles*, pp. 202–4.
15. Inspectorate of Education, *State of Education* (Utrecht: Inspectorate of Education, 2020).
16. Estyn, *Healthy and happy: school impact on pupils' health and wellbeing* (Cardiff: Estyn, 2019).
17. WG, *Well-being of Wales 2017–18: what do we know about children's well-being?* (Cardiff: WG, 2018).
18. Karen L. Jones, Peter Tymms, David Kemethofer, Joe O'Hara, Gerry McNamara, Stephan Huber, Eva Myrberg, Guri Skedsmo and David Greger, 'The unintended consequences of school inspection: the prevalence of inspection side-effects in Austria, the Czech Republic, England, Ireland, the Netherlands, Sweden, and Switzerland', *Oxford Review of Education*, 43/6 (2017), 805–22.
19. Estyn, *Inspection Clarified* (Cardiff: Estyn, 2016); Ofsted, *Summary and recommendations: teacher well-being research report* (Manchester: Ofsted, 2019).
20. D. Kemethofer, J. Gustafsson and H. Altrichter, 'Comparing effects of school inspections in Sweden and Austria', *Educ Asse Eval Acc*, 29 (2017), 319–37.
21. Information based on country profiles available at the Standing International Conference of Inspectorates. Available at *www.sici-inspectorates.eu/Members/Inspection-Profiles* (accessed 12 October 2020).

22. Jan-Eric Gustafsson, Rolf Lander and Eva Myrberg, 'Inspections of Swedish schools: A critical reflection on intended effects, causal mechanisms and methods', *Education Inquiry*, 5/4 (2014), 23862, DOI: 10.3402/edui.v5.23862.
23. Anne West, Paola Mattei and Jonathan Roberts, 'Accountability and Sanctions in English Schools', *British Journal of Educational Studies*, 59/1 (2011), 41–62.
24. Mark Brundrett and Christopher Rhodes, *Leadership for quality and accountability in education* (London and New York: Routledge, 2011).
25. Elizabeth Titley, Andrew James Davies and Stephen Atherton, '"[It] isn't designed to be assessed how we assess": rethinking assessment for qualification in the context of the implementation of the Curriculum for Wales', *The Curriculum Journal*, 31/2 (2020), 303–16.
26. Sally Power, 'The politics of education and the misrecognition of Wales', *Oxford Review of Education*, 42/3 (2016), 285–98.
27. Abbie Wightwick, 'Wales is flunking Pisa because it scrapped SAT tests, says schools inspector', *WalesOnline*, 7 December 2016. See S. Burgess, D. Wilson and J. Worth, 'A natural experiment in school accountability: The impact of school performance information on pupil progress', *Journal of Public Economics*, 106 (2013), 57–67.
28. Leighton Andrews, *Teaching makes a difference* (Speech at the Reardon Smith Lecture Theatre, Cardiff, 2 February 2011).
29. OECD, *Improving Schools in Wales: An OECD Perspective* (Paris: OECD, 2014), p. 29.
30. Jo Anne Anderson, *Accountability in Education* (Paris: UNESCO, 2005), p. 1.
31. OECD, *Education Policy Outlook 2019* (Paris: OECD, 2019).
32. The Educational Institute of Scotland, *Education Scotland Inspections* (Edinburgh: EIS, 2019); Education Inspectorate, *Inspection Framework Secondary Education* (Utrecht: Education Inspectorate, 2017).
33. Mari-Pauliina Vainikainen, Helena Thuneberg, Jukka Marjanen, Jarkko Hautamäki, Sirkku Kupiainen and Risto Hotulainen, 'How Do Finns Know? Educational Monitoring without Inspection and Standard Setting', in S. Blömeke, J.-E. Gustafsson (eds), *Standard Setting in Education: The Nordic Countries in an International Perspective* (Methodology of Educational Measurement and Assessment) (Cham, Switzerland: Springer, 2017), pp. 243–59.
34. Martin Brown, Gerry McNamara, Joe O'Hara and Paddy Shevlin, 'Polycentric inspection: A catalyst for sparking positive interactions in educational networks', *Research Methods and Evaluation*, 26/1 (2019), 76–97.
35. F. Brill, H. Grayson, L. Kuhn and S. O'Donnell, *What Impact Does Accountability Have On Curriculum, Standards and Engagement In Education? A Literature Review* (Slough: NFER, 2018).
36. Andreas Schleicher, *World Class: How to Build a 21st-Century School System* (Paris: OECD, 2018).

THE FUTURE

Ann Keane

Over the period of almost two centuries of their existence, HMI have assumed many roles. They have been gatherers of information, regulators, examiners, auditors, mediators, arbitrators, watchdogs, critics, functionaries, advisers and visionaries. The balance of their roles has varied over time and the role of 'watchdog', in the sense of monitoring standards in education, has been a constant strand in their work. However, the extent to which any HMI can be said to be a visionary raises issues about the constraints within which they work. Even that most visionary of chief inspectors (CI), Owen Edwards, did not succeed in his mission to normalise fully the use and teaching of Welsh and the Welsh dimension of the curriculum in schools, during his lifetime. Others, like Dan Isaac Davies[1] and Cassie Davies[2] also promoted a similar vision of a fully bilingual education system in Wales and the chapters of this book provide a measure of their success. But HMI have mostly been involved, not in promoting their personal vision for education but in informing and reporting on the vision of their political masters.

HMI were in the early days mainly advisers and overseers of schools, sent out to gather information for government on the efficiency of elementary schools. They became harsher critics with the publication of the 1847 *Blue Books* which, with their critique of the language, religion and morals of the Welsh, cast a long shadow over the subsequent history of education in Wales. The introduction of Payment by Results and the 1862 Code turned HMI into annual examiners and regulators who were feared by teachers and pupils alike, not least because Welsh, the language of the many monoglot pupils, did not feature at all in the Code until the 1890s and children were taught and tested in English. After the establishment of the Board of Education in 1899, followed by the local education authorities in 1902, while HMI were still expected to approve the curriculum of each school annually, their role on visits became more advisory in tone and visits were made every three years with responsibility for education standards shifting to the LEAs, with whom HMI were expected to liaise.

The balance between pastoral visits and full (or Formal) inspections (FI) varied over the course of the twentieth century, and rates of both pastoral and formal inspection reduced in intensity during wartime. Some schools escaped FIs for decades until the advent of the outsourced five-year inspection cycles in 1992. After that, HMI themselves gradually became more remote from the direct inspection of schools although they continued to inspect post-16 and other providers in Wales, to complete surveys of education provision, and to report on the implementation of government policy, thus furnishing politicians with evidence about the success of education policies and standards of provision. HMI reports on individual providers have been published since 1983, when they became available to parents and the public for the first time. This meant that criticism of education standards and, by extension, of education policy itself became more generally accessible.

Over the last two decades of the twentieth century, Secretaries of State and Ministers in Westminster developed more ambivalent views about the value of HMI and instigated several reviews of the inspectorate. While HMI escaped direct criticism in the Rayner report of 1982, after that, political opposition to the inspectorate grew. According to Kenneth Baker, Secretary of State (SoS) for Education in the late 1980s, HMI were the 'priesthood' of an 'agenda' that:

> was rooted in 'progressive' orthodoxies, in egalitarianism and in the comprehensive school system. It was devoutly anti-excellence, anti-selection, and anti-market.[3]

And Dominic Morris, who held the education brief at the Number 10 Policy Unit in the 1990s, claimed that:

> Although its [HMI] abolition was dressed up in the [Parent's] Charter, it was part of the long-running

ideological battle and Kenneth Clarke [then SoS] was up for it.[4]

But attitudes in the Welsh Office were more sympathetic and appreciative of the work of HMI and HMI Wales did not suffer the dismantling that happened to HMI England before the setting up of Ofsted. In Wales, post-1992, the same CI continued in post, as did most of his HMI, although school inspection was privatised in Wales on the same model as in England.

Over the past thirty years the inspectorate in Wales has shifted from being the regulator of an outsourced school inspection system to reclaiming the delivery of its core business of inspection and including school and college teachers and managers in the process. The period has been one of considerable turbulence. There was in the first decade of the twenty-first century a trend of grade inflation in school inspection reports despite the limited progress seemingly being made in the GCSE results of schools and the series of 'PISA shocks' they endured, PISA being the Programme of International Student Assessments, the tests set for 15-year-olds in countries that opt in to the scheme. In relation to 'grade inflation' or upward shifts in the distribution of judgements or grades in inspection cycles, it is the relative positions either of schools or post-16 providers on the scale of judgements within a cycle that is important. Making comparisons between outcomes from one inspection cycle to the next or across sectors is not always useful simply because the focus and emphasis of inspections change with each new iteration of guidance for inspectors, which must reflect the emergence of new regulations, policies and performance indicators that affect the education sectors themselves. To some extent, inspection will always be a moveable feast and the re-calibration of levels in scales of judgement is sometimes necessary. Nevertheless, to question the validity of the PISA methodology or of comparative GCSE outcomes, as Chapter 7 does, does not alter the fact that Estyn inspection judgements tend to confirm what PISA and GCSE outcomes tell us about standards in the main.

By the beginning of the 2020s, the pendulum has swung away from a system of formal external accountability towards a future in which the inspection system will have a stronger focus on validating self-evaluation by providers, abjuring summative judgements on standards in favour of expressing degrees of confidence in the school's own self-evaluation, in addition to promoting changes to the shape and culture of learning. Inspectors are preparing to move away from being the predominantly managerial watchdogs they have been in the past to becoming more supportive collaborators in a shared vision for system-wide reform.

The challenges that the education system in Wales faces as it strives for both excellence and equity remain considerable. The abiding weakness of Wales's education system remains the relatively low educational achievement of its most disadvantaged children, schools and communities. Schools alone cannot bring about a sustainable step-change to overcome the complex challenges that exist. The hope is that the current reform of the education system will develop new collaborative approaches, with an expectation that a range of providers from both education and other children's and public services will work together to engage in reform. To remain relevant to a vision of the future that has a focus on self-evaluation, professional learning, research-informed practice and the development of providers as learning organisations, the inspectorate is making changes to its own culture and practices in order to play a full part in enabling and promoting reform. Its independence should continue to be valued, but its activities will be expected to align closely with key areas of provider and system improvement. In this developing scenario, it will be important for inspectors to avoid the risk of focusing exclusively on schools' 'compliance' with the new Curriculum for Wales and to continue exercising their professional independence in evaluating standards and encouraging innovation.

As part of the ongoing reform process, in 2017 the then chief inspector, with the support of the Minister for Education, commissioned Professor Graham Donaldson to undertake an independent review of the inspectorate. Donaldson's report, published in June 2018, found that Estyn enjoyed 'high credibility for its independence and professionalism' but that the 'scope of the educational reform programme will place very significant additional demands' on Estyn and require a radical re-thinking of its role.[5] The acceptance by Estyn and Welsh Government of the main recommendations of this report has meant that the inspectorate in Wales is to begin a new period in its history.

The 2018 review was built on an earlier review of school curriculum and assessment arrangements in Wales (published in 2015), which was also led by Donaldson.[6] The inspectorate seconded two inspectors to work on the review. Subsequently, inspectors joined the 'pioneer school' working groups charged with shaping the areas of learning and experience and other elements in the new curriculum; inspectors also contributed to the work of producing online adaptive testing in literacy and numeracy for pupils. The focus, for all those engaged in this process of co-construction, was and remains on the four purposes of 'seeking to develop young people as: successful, capable learners; ethical, informed citizens; enterprising, creative contributors; and healthy, confident individuals'.[7]

During 2020–1 all formal inspection was suspended in order to make time for adjustment and radical re-imagining. The inspectorate had been intended, in this transitional year, to undertake engagement visits to every school in Wales in order to support curriculum development and plans for self-evaluation. However, due to the intervention of the COVID-19 pandemic, telephone calls to schools replaced in-person visits and served a dual purpose of monitoring and supporting how schools/providers and their students were coping with delivering blended and online learning to home-based learners; and enquiring about progress in developing new approaches to the planning of the Curriculum for Wales and its associated pedagogy. The direction of travel that was signposted in the 2018 review report has had to take account of unforeseen circumstances and it has been expanded to take account of new factors. However, the very fact that 'life as usual' has been interrupted has meant that practitioners, inspectors and policy makers have had to think afresh about how learning can be supported in different ways and there may be benefits beyond their response to the unexpected pressures of lockdowns.

In a July 2020 webinar on 'COVID-19: do we need to reimagine the purpose of school inspections?' thirty-five delegates from the inspectorates of education in twelve countries, including Wales, debated whether changes in the purpose and methods of inspection that were the results of the pandemic were likely to be temporary or permanent.[8] Some of the participants envisaged a return to normal after the pandemic while others expected a more permanent change in purpose, arguing that the crisis offered an opportunity to reconsider what is in the best interests of learners. The phrase 'building back better' was used to reflect the changes in evaluation methods that would be required in order to reflect the innovations in learning and teaching that followed the imposition of pandemic constraints. Delegates questioned whether the new conditions under which both practitioners and inspectors had adopted new ways of working required inspectorates to consider continuing to be more supportive and less judgemental. For Wales, this discussion reflected the changes in thinking that were already instrumental to the country's programme of education reform.

Also in 2020, the Organisation for Economic Co-operation and Development (OECD) published its most recent review of education policy in Wales.[9] The OECD report described the main role of Estyn as helping the transition from 'high-stakes' accountability to a system of internal accountability based on trust among capable professionals. (The stakes are described as high because inspection reports by external inspectors normally publish graded judgements on each school and doing so can inflict reputational damage.) The Welsh Government responded to the challenges in the OECD report by adding an appendix to its national mission document detailing the actions it would be taking.[10] Although the actions gave scant attention to Estyn's role, the scene was set for the subsequent publication for consultation of a *Framework for evaluation, improvement and accountability* which set out more clearly the vision for the future role of the inspectorate and other agencies.[11] The *Framework* developed further the thinking first outlined in the 2018 Donaldson report on Estyn. In this scenario, the accountability infrastructure of previous inspection cycles will give way to a lighter-touch system of more frequent visits to schools: two to every school during a six-year cycle. In their visits, inspectors will focus on validating school self-evaluation of the new curriculum, learner progression, and pupil well-being. The inspectorate will be able to flex the scope of the visits, with some likely to be similar to the pastoral visits familiar to twentieth-century inspectors and others feeding into thematic survey reports. Reports on schools will continue to be published to offer assurance to stakeholders and these reports will continue to identify 'strengths and areas for improvement', which, subsequently, schools will need to consider in their annual revisions of school development plans. The inspectorate's reports will still identify schools that give cause for concern and diagnostic inspections might follow, on the pattern indicated by Donaldson. However, there will be no publication of high stakes summative judgements in inspection reports. Neither should regional consortia publish the annual league tables of categories into which they have previously placed schools on the basis of their 'need for support'.

Accountability should become less high stakes than it has been although there will actually be an intensification of inspectors' engagement with schools. HMI visits to schools will be more frequent under the arrangements proposed by Donaldson: the role of district inspectors is to be revived to introduce closer links with schools in each area; inspectors will train more peer reviewers; thematic survey visits and reports will continue; improvement conferences will be organised; HMI attendance at education and training committees and meetings with civil service officials and Ministers will continue; and Estyn will continue inspecting other sectors including the regional consortia and local authority services. This expansion in the activities of the inspectorate has implications for a budget that has either been reduced or flat-lined over many years. Estyn's budget for the current year (£11.5m in 2020–1) is considerably lower than it was fifteen years ago (£15.4m in 2005–6) and its value in real terms has reduced further. The budget for 2021–2 is flat-lined at £11.5m. Donaldson was clear about the funding implications of implementing the recommendations in his 2018 report:

> Estyn's funding arrangements should be reviewed to allow longer-term planning of resources and to recognise more explicitly the resource implications of additional activities associated with the reform.[12]

During the 2021–2 academic year, Estyn is piloting a revised inspection framework that aligns with the principles expressed in the Welsh Government's *Framework for evaluation, improvement and accountability*, reflecting those aspects that Welsh Government identifies as important for schools to scrutinise and promote in their own self-evaluation: including vision and leadership; curriculum; learning and teaching; and well-being.[13] In a linked project, Estyn is currently engaging with schools, regional consortia, local authorities and the OECD to produce a national evaluation and improvement resource (NEIR) for schools, which will offer detailed guidance on and tools for effective self-evaluation.

It is as yet unclear to what extent Estyn will differentiate their inspection approaches across the full range of the other sectors in which they inspect (see Appendix I) as a result of changes to school inspection. It is possible that the use of a common inspection framework, first introduced in 2004, will give way to a more customised approach in future. If so, it will be one that is likely to benefit from the learning that is taking place as part of the inspectorate's current involvement in the wide-ranging reforms to school self-evaluation and inspection. Should one be introduced on a larger canvas, a lighter-touch approach to inspection would not be wholly novel. 'Inspection in inverse proportion to success' was a common mantra in the first decade of the twenty-first century during which Estyn deployed a range of approaches to risk-based inspection across the sectors it inspected according to whether they were deemed to pose high, medium or low risk levels.

There have been many changes of direction in inspection policy since the inception of the inspectorate in 1839 but accountability has always been a central consideration. Over most of almost two centuries of the inspectorate's existence, inspections have involved making judgements on the standards achieved, in schools, colleges and other public education services, normally on a four- or five-point scale whether it is in numbers, from grade 1 to grade 4 or 5, or in words, from 'outstanding' or 'excellent' to 'unsatisfactory' or 'inadequate'. Without such metrics, based on a scale of judgements, there can be no collation of data, no easy comparisons across providers, and no consistently reliable indicators of progress in quality from one inspection to the next. Annual reports cannot draw conclusions about progress across the board on the basis of comparable data from year to year. And, in a data-hungry age, when governments, parents and the public more generally demand more information and greater transparency, without a common scale of judgements, Estyn could become peripheral, unable to report with clarity on standards, their reports at risk of obfuscation. Other UK inspectorates have debated and confirmed the continuing use of a scale of judgements in inspection reports: Ofsted has recorded the arguments for and against a grading system and argued in its favour.[14]

The counter argument presses the advantages of a revised inspection system that has objectives beyond high-stakes accountability, although still providing assurance for stakeholders in reports that include an evaluation of strengths and areas for improvement in each provider inspected.[15] An important objective of the new system is to promote an ambitious vision for curriculum reform that cedes ownership of evaluation and improvement primarily to those who deliver and own the provision of education and in whose hands direct action is arguably best placed to make any improvements required.

ENDNOTES

1. Dan Isaac Davies, *1785, 1885, 1985! Neu, Tair Miliwn o Gymry Dwyieithawg mewn can mlynedd: Cyfres O Lythyrau* (Denbigh: T. Gee and Son, 1886). There are references to Dan Isaac Davies in Chapters 1 and 2.
2. Cassie Davies, *Hwb i'r Galon* (Swansea: Gwasg John Penry, 1973). There are references to Cassie Davies in Chapters 3 and 6.
3. Kenneth Baker, *The Turbulent Years: My Life in Politics* (London: Faber & Faber, 1993), p. 168.
4. Quoted in Daniel Callaghan, *Conservative Party Education Policies 1976–1997: The Influence of Politics and Personality* (Brighton: Sussex Academic Press, 2006), p. 134.
5. Graham Donaldson, *A Learning Inspectorate: Independent review of Estyn* (Cardiff: Welsh Government, 2018), p. 63.
6. Graham Donaldson, *Successful Futures* (Cardiff: Welsh Government, 2015).
7. Donaldson, *A Learning Inspectorate*, p. 7.
8. M. Ehren, C. Chapman and C. Montecinos, *COVID-19: do we need to reimagine the purpose of school inspections?* (International Congress for School Effectiveness and Improvement internal paper, 2020).
9. OECD, *Achieving the new curriculum for Wales* (Cardiff: Welsh Government, 2020).
10. Welsh Government. *Education in Wales: Our national mission, update October 2020* (Cardiff: Welsh Government, 2020).

11. Welsh Government, *School improvement guidance: framework for evaluation, improvement and accountability* (Cardiff: Welsh Government, 2021).
12. Donaldson, *A Learning Inspectorate*, p. 72.
13. Welsh Government, *School improvement guidance: framework*, pp. 13–14.
14. Ofsted, *Retaining the current grading system in education: Some arguments and evidence* (London: Ofsted, 2019).
15. See Estyn, *Guidance for inspectors: What we inspect: Maintained schools and PRUs – for inspections from 2022* (Cardiff: Estyn, 2021). Under the revised arrangements, inspectors will report on schools and pupil referral units under the following headings: learning; well-being and attitudes to learning; teaching and learning experiences; care, support and guidance; and leadership and management. Inspectors will offer an overview of strengths and areas for improvement and include recommendations but will not use a scale of judgements.

Appendix I

THE STATUTORY BASIS OF THE INSPECTORATE

Her Majesty's Chief Inspector (HMCI) is appointed by the Queen in Privy Council. HMCI's general duties, as set out in the Government of Wales Act 1998, include keeping the First Minister informed about:

- the quality of activities within HMCI's remit and (where appropriate) the standards achieved by those for whose benefit such activities are carried out;
- improvements in the quality of such activities and in any such standards;
- the extent to which such activities are being carried out as learner-focused activities; and
- the efficient and effective use of resources in carrying out such activities and services.

If requested to do so by the First Minister, HMCI must provide the First Minister with information or advice on such matters relating to activities within HMCI's remit as are specified in the requests. HMCI may at any time provide advice to the First Minister on any matter connected with activities within his or her remit, including advice relating to a particular establishment, institution or agency. HMCI is to have other functions in connection with activities within his or her remit as may be assigned by the First Minister. HMCI must ensure that:

- his or her functions are performed efficiently and effectively; and
- so far as is practicable, those functions are performed in a way that responds to:

- the needs of people for whose benefit activities within HMCI's remit are carried out
- the views expressed by other relevant people about such activities.[1]

Further duties and powers are set out in legislation. The 2005 Education Act (EA) sets out HMCI's general duty to keep the government and the public informed about:

(a) the quality of the education provided by schools in Wales,
(b) how far that education meets the needs of the range of pupils at those schools,
(c) the educational standards achieved in those schools,
(d) the quality of the leadership in and management of those schools, including whether the financial resources made available to those schools are managed efficiently,
(e) the spiritual, moral, social and cultural development of pupils at those schools, and
(f) the contribution made by those schools to the well-being of those pupils,
(g) actions taken at maintained schools to promote healthy eating and drinking.[2]

Section 75 of the 2000 Learning and Skills Act (LSA) confers powers and duties upon HMCI in relation to post-16 education and training provision that are similar to those for schools under the 2005 EA. In addition, sections 38 and 39 of the 1997 EA, sections 25 and 26 of the 2000 LSA and section 51 of the 2004 Children Act provide various powers and duties related to the inspection of local government education services inspections, some of which are undertaken in collaboration with other regulators.

In fulfilment of these duties and of those laid down in other legislation, including legislation laid down by the National Assembly for Wales, HMCI is responsible for inspecting and reporting on the following sectors:

- non-school settings for children under five
- primary schools

- secondary schools
- maintained all-age schools
- maintained special schools
- independent special schools
- independent mainstream schools
- independent specialist colleges
- pupil referral units
- local government education services
- further education
- work-based learning
- adult learning
- teacher education
- Welsh for adults
- careers
- learning in the justice sector.[3]

ENDNOTES

1. Estyn, *Corporate Governance Framework* (Cardiff: Estyn, 2019), pp. 3–4.
2. UK Parliament Acts/E/EA-EG/Education Act 2005 (2005 c. 18), Chapter 3 School Inspectors and School Inspections: Wales.
3. Estyn, *The Annual Report of Her Majesty's Chief Inspector of Education and Training in Wales 2018–2019* (Cardiff: Estyn, 2019), pp. 3–4.

Appendix II

LIST OF SENIOR OR CHIEF INSPECTORS IN WALES

Pre-1882	Inspectors worked in districts, with many HMI in Wales also covering parts of England.
1882–96	William Williams (Divisional Inspector of a newly created Welsh Division in the England and Wales inspectorate).
1896–1907	Albert G. Legard (Divisional Inspector for Elementary Schools in Wales).
1907–20	Owen Edwards (first HMCI of education in Wales in a newly established Welsh Department).
1920–5	Alfred T. Davies took over the duties of HMCI in Whitehall but delegated all inspectorial duties to two divisional inspectors: G. Prys Williams and William J. Williams.
1925–8	No HMCI in Welsh Department but Percy Watkins as permanent secretary continued the previous arrangement.
1928–33	G. Prys Williams
1933–44	William J. Williams
1945–52	William Thomas
1952–72	Wynne Ll. Lloyd
1972–82	Eryl O. Davies
1982–90	Illtyd R. Lloyd
1990–7	Roy L. James

1997–2008	Susan Lewis
2008–10	William Maxwell
2010–15	Ann Keane
2015–21	Meilyr Rowlands
2021	Claire Morgan
2022	Owen Evans

Appendix III

LIST OF KEY MILESTONES

1839	Creation of the Committee of Council for Education and Her Majesty's Inspectorate for England and Wales.
1840	Instructions to Inspectors setting out the functions of HMI.
1847	Report of the Commissioners of Inquiry into the State of Education in Wales.
1861	Report of the Commissioners of Inquiry into the State of Popular Education in England and Wales (with Wales covered in specimen mining districts only).
1862	Revised Code (Lowe) and introduction of Payment by Results.
1870	Elementary Education Act (Forster).
1881	Report of the Departmental Committee on Intermediate and Higher Education in Wales (Aberdare report).
1882	The Welsh Division placed under the charge of senior inspector William Williams.
1888	Report of the Commissioners on the Elementary Education Acts, England and Wales (Cross report).
1889	Welsh Intermediate and Technical Education Act enabled establishment of intermediate (secondary) schools.
1896	Central Welsh Board created to administer and inspect intermediate schools.
1899	Board of Education Act.
1902	Education Act (Balfour) abolished school boards and created local education authorities.

1905 Chief woman inspector post created for England and Wales.

1907 Welsh Department established in the Board of Education, with its own chief inspector (Owen Edwards), permanent secretary (Alfred T. Davies) and body of HMI; new Codes introduced for schools in Wales.

1911 Menai Rowlands appointed as the first woman inspector to serve exclusively in the Wales inspectorate.

1918 Education Act (Fisher).

1920 Report of the Departmental Committee to Inquire into the Organisation of Secondary Education in Wales (Bruce report).

1924 Circular 153 and the reorganisation of the Wales inspectorate.

1925 Joint arrangements for inspecting intermediate schools established between HMI and Central Welsh Board.

1927 Menai Rowlands appointed as staff inspector: the first woman to hold a senior position in the Wales inspectorate; also in 1927, the number of women inspectors doubled from two to four.

1927 Publication of the Departmental report on *Welsh in Education and Life*.

1928 Welsh Department opened an office in Cardiff.

1934 Aggregation: process of integrating Women inspectors into the mainstream structure of inspectorate begun; the Woman Inspectorate ceased to exist as a separate body in 1944.

1942 Mary Ellis became the first woman inspector to marry in post (by special permission) although the civil service marriage bar was not removed until 1946.

1944 Education Act (Butler).

1946–8 Central Welsh Board replaced by Welsh Joint Education Board.

1956	Roseveare report on the functions and organisation of the inspectorate in England and Wales.
1961	Equal pay for men and women HMI.
1965	Circular 10/65 on the reorganisation of secondary schools and introduction of comprehensive schools.
1968	Fulton Committee report on the (Home) civil service.
1968	Report of the Central Advisory Council for Education (Wales) on primary education in Wales (Gittins report).
1970	Responsibility for schools transferred from the Department of Education and Science to the Welsh Office.
1976	Prime Minister James Callaghan's Ruskin College speech.
1978	Responsibility for further education transferred to the Welsh Office.
1982	Rayner report on the review of the inspectorates in England and Wales.
1983	HMI reports on individual education providers made public for the first time.
1988	Education Reform Act ushered in the National Curriculum with separate Subject Orders for Wales and including a cross-curricular Welsh dimension.
1992	Education (Schools) Act introduced new outsourced school inspection system and established the Office of Her Majesty's Inspectorate (Wales), a non-Ministerial department of the civil service.
1992	Education (Further and Higher Education) Act established new Wales funding councils.
1995	Standing International Conference of Inspectorates established.
1996	Education Act set out arrangements for inspection of schools in Wales and England.

1997　First female chief inspector appointed for Wales (Susan Lewis).

1998　Government of Wales Act set out the general duties of HMCI (Wales).

1999　Devolution of power to the National Assembly for Wales.

1999　Review leading to the reorganisation of Wales inspectorate, renamed 'Estyn'.

2000　Learning and Skills Act set out arrangements that still apply (at date of this publication) in Wales for the inspection of post-16 education and training.

2001　First iteration of devolved education policy published in *The Learning Country*. Further policy documents in the same series appeared in 2006 and 2008.

2004　Children Act set out arrangements for the inspection of local government education services.

2005　Education Act set out arrangements that still apply (at date of this publication) in Wales for the inspection of schools.

2006　Government of Wales Act (power to legislate on inspection was devolved to the National Assembly for Wales after 2006).

2008　*The School Effectiveness Framework* (Welsh Assembly Government policy document).

2013　The Hill review on the future delivery of education services in Wales led to the establishment of regional consortia in 2015 to deliver school improvement services.

2014　*Qualified for Life: An education improvement plan for 3 to 19 year olds in Wales* (Welsh Government policy document).

2015　Well-being of Future Generations (Wales) Act.

2015　Publication of Professor Graham Donaldson's review of school curriculum and assessment arrangements in Wales, *Successful Futures*.

2017 *Education in Wales: Our national mission Action plan 2017–21* (Welsh Government policy document).

2018 Donaldson's review of Estyn published: *A Learning Inspectorate.*

2020 Curriculum and Assessment (Wales) Act.

SELECT BIBLIOGRAPHY

The bibliography does not list all the sources consulted but the chapter endnotes reference all sources quoted in the text.

Archive sources
National Library of Wales at Aberystwyth.
The National Archive at Kew.
The Welsh Government Library at Cardiff.
Estyn (Her Majesty's Inspectorate of Education and Training in Wales).

Newspapers
Western Mail

Official reports of the Board of Education
Board of Education, *Circular 532* (1907).
Board of Education Welsh Department, *Code of Regulations for Public Elementary Schools in Wales (including Monmouthshire)* (London: HMSO, 1908).
Board of Education Welsh Department, *Regulations for Secondary Schools in Wales (including Monmouthshire)* (London: HMSO, 1908).
Board of Education Welsh Department, *List 6 Wales: The Inspectors of the Welsh Department of the Board of Education as allocated in relation to the LEAs' Areas in Wales (including Monmouthshire)* (London, 1908).
Board of Education, *Report of the Board of Education for the Year 1910–11* (London: HMSO, 1912).
Board of Education, *Report of the Board of Education under the Welsh Intermediate Education Act 1889, for the Year 1926* (London: HMSO, 1927).
Board of Education, *Report of the Board of Education for the Year 1904–1905 on the administration of schools under the Wales Intermediate Education Act 1889* (London: HMSO, 1906).

Board of Education, *Report of the Board of Education under the Welsh Intermediate Education Act 1889, for the Year 1909* (London: HMSO, 1910).

Board of Education, *Report of the Board of Education for the Year 1909–1910 under the Welsh Intermediate Act 1889* (London: HMSO, 1911).

Board of Education, *Report of the Board of Education for the Year 1917 under the Welsh Intermediate Act 1889* (London: HMSO, 1918).

Board of Education, *Report of the Departmental Committee on Education in Wales, 1919–1920* (London: HMSO, 1920).

Board of Education, *Education in Wales: Report of the Board of Education under the Welsh Intermediate Act 1889, for the year 1925* (London: HMSO, 1926).

Board of Education, *Report of the Departmental Committee Appointed by the President of the Board of Education to Inquire into the Position of the Welsh Language and to advise as to Its Promotion in the Educational System of Wales* (London: HMSO, 1927).

Board of Education, *Educational Pamphlet 114: The Organisation of Sixth Forms in Secondary Schools* (London: HMSO, 1938).

Board of Education Welsh Department, *List 6: List of the Inspectorate and Inspection Arrangements in Wales (including Monmouthshire)* (1941).

Official publications – England

Department of Education and Science (DES), *HMI Today and Tomorrow* (London: HMSO, 1970).

National Audit Office, *Ofsted's inspection of schools* (London: National Audit Office, 2018).

Rayner, D., *A Study of HM Inspectorate in England and Wales* (London: HMSO, 1982).

Roseveare, Sir Martin, *Final Report* (London: HMSO, 1956).

Tomlin Commission, *Royal Commission on the Civil Service, 1929–30*, Minutes of Evidence (London: HMSO, 1930).

Hansard, *The Parliamentary Debates: 1st session of the 28th Parliament of Great Britain and Ireland*, vol. CLXII, *Hansard Commons* (London: HMSO, May 1906).

Official publications – Wales

Andrews, L., *Teaching Makes a Difference* (Cardiff: Welsh Government (WG), 2011).

Bradshaw, J., Ager, R., Burge, B. and Wheater, R., *Achievement of 15-year-olds in Wales: PISA 2009 National Report* (Slough: National Foundation for Educational Research, 2010).

Bradshaw, J., Sturman, L., Vaopoula, H., Ager, R., Wheater, R., *Achievement of 15-year-olds in Wales: PISA 2006 National Report* (Slough: National Foundation for Educational Research, 2006).

Central Advisory Council for Education (Wales), *The Future of Secondary Education in Wales* (Cardiff: Central Advisory Council for Education (Wales), 1947).

Central Welsh Board (CWB), *Today and Tomorrow in Welsh Education* (Cardiff: CWB, 1916, Welsh Government Archive, WO 4559).

Committee of Council on Education, *Reports on Wales 1847*, vols I–III (London: HMSO, 1848).

Curriculum Council for Wales (CCW), *Developing a Cwricwlwm Cymreig* (Cardiff: CCW, 1993).

Curriculum Council for Wales, *The Whole Curriculum 5–16 in Wales* (Cardiff: CCW, 1991).

Donaldson, Graham, *A Learning Inspectorate: Independent Review of Estyn* (Cardiff: Estyn, 2018).

Donaldson, Graham, *Successful Futures: Independent Review of Curriculum and Assessment Arrangements in Wales* (Cardiff: WG, 2015).

Estyn, *Annual Reports of HMCI Wales* (Cardiff: OHMCI/Estyn, 1994–2020).

Estyn, *Estyn and the Centenary of the Welsh Inspectorate* (Cardiff: Estyn, 2007).

Estyn, *Estyn's Corporate Governance Framework* (Cardiff: Estyn, 2019).

Estyn, *Excellent Schools: A vision for schools in Wales in the 21st Century* (Cardiff: Estyn, 2002).

Estyn, *Guidance handbook for the inspection of primary schools* (Cardiff: Estyn, 2019).

Estyn, *Guidance for inspectors: What we inspect: Maintained schools and PRUs – for inspections from 2022* (Cardiff: Estyn, 2021).

Estyn, *Inspection framework and guidance handbooks* (Cardiff: Estyn, 2010, revised 2014).

Estyn, *Inspection framework and guidance handbooks* (Cardiff: Estyn, 2017 and 2019).

Estyn, *Transforming Schools: A Discussion Paper* (Cardiff: Estyn, 2007).

Further Education Funding Council for Wales (FEFCW), *Quality and Standards in Further Education in Wales 1993–1997* (Cardiff: FEFCW, 1997).

Hill, Robert, *The Future Delivery of Education Services in Wales* (Cardiff: WG, 2013).
Inspection Wales, *Briefing: Audit, Inspection and Regulation in Wales* (Cardiff: Inspection Wales, 2016).
Organisation for Economic Co-operation and Development (OECD), *Improving Schools in Wales: An OECD Perspective* (Paris: OECD, 2014).
OECD, *The Welsh Education Reform Journey: A Rapid Policy Assessment* (Paris: OECD, 2017).
OECD, *What makes a school a learning organisation?* (Paris: OECD, 2014).
OHMCI, *Inspection framework and guidance handbooks* (Cardiff: OHMCI, 1994).
Welsh Assembly Government (WAG), *Building Excellent Schools Together* (London: WAG, 2001).
WAG, *Dyfodol Dwyieithog: A Bilingual Future* (Cardiff: WAG, 2002).
WAG, *Iaith Pawb* (Cardiff: WAG, 2003).
WAG, *Inspection, Audit and Regulation Policy Statement* (Cardiff: WAG, 2008).
WAG, *Narrowing the gap in the performance of schools* (Cardiff: WAG, 2002).
WAG, *Narrowing the gap in the performance of schools project: Phase 2 primary schools* (Cardiff: WAG, 2005).
WAG, *The Learning Country* (Cardiff: WAG, 1997, 2001 and 2006).
WAG, *The School Effectiveness Framework* (Cardiff: WAG, 2008).
WG, *Cymraeg 2050: A million Welsh speakers* (Cardiff: WG, 2017).
WG, *Education in Wales: Our National Mission, Action Plan 2017–21* (Cardiff: WG, 2017).
WG, *Improving Schools* (Cardiff: WG, 2012).
WG, *Qualified for Life: An education improvement plan for 3 to 19 year olds in Wales* (Cardiff: WG, 2014).
WG, *Rewriting the future: Raising ambition and attainment in Welsh schools* (Cardiff: WG, 2014).
WG, *Successful futures: independent review of curriculum and assessment arrangements in Wales* (Cardiff: WG, 2015).
WG, *Taking Wales Forward 2016–2021* (Cardiff: WG, 2016).

Standing International Conference of Inspectorates (SICI)
SICI, *Bratislava Memorandum on Inspection and Innovation* (Brussels: SICI, 2013).
SICI, *Innovative practices of inspection* (Brussels: SICI, 2019).

SICI, *Supporting school improvement: the role of inspectorates across Europe* (Brussels: SICI, 2014).

Books

Andrews, L., *Ministering to Education* (Cardigan: Parthian, 2014).

Arnold, Matthew, *The Study of Celtic Literature* (London: Smith & Elder and Co., 1891).

Baxter, J. (ed.), *School Inspectors: Policy Implementers, Policy Shapers in National Policy Contexts* (Cham, Switzerland: Springer, 2017).

Bone, T. R., *School Inspection in Scotland 1840–1966* (London: University of London Press, 1968).

Boothroyd, H. E., *A History of the Inspectorate: Being a Short Account of the Origin and Development of the Inspecting Service of the Board of Education* (Board of Inspectors' Association, 1923).

Chapman, R., *W. J. Gruffydd* (Cardiff: University of Wales Press, 1993).

Daugherty, R., Phillips, R. and Rees, G. (eds), *Education Policy Making in Wales: Explorations in Devolved Governance* (Cardiff: University of Wales Press, 2000).

Davies, Cassie, *Hwb i'r Galon: Atgofion Cassie Davies* (Swansea: Gwasg John Penry, 1973).

Davies, Hazel Walford, *O. M. Cofiant Syr Owen Morgan Edwards* (Llandysul: Gomer Press, 2019).

Davies, Wynford, *The Curriculum and Organization of the County Intermediate Schools 1880–1926* (Cardiff: University of Wales Press, 1989).

Deacon, R., *The Governance of Wales* (Cardiff: Welsh Academic Press, 2002).

Dixon, Philip, *Testing Times: Success, Failure and Fiasco in Education Policy in Wales Since Devolution* (Cardiff: Welsh Academic Press, 2016).

Dunford, John E., *Her Majesty's Inspectors of Schools since 1944: Standard Bearers or Turbulent Priests?* (London: Woburn Press, 1998).

Edmonds, E. L., *The School Inspector* (London: Routledge and Kegan Paul, 1962).

Edwards, Owen M., *Clych Atgof* (Wrecsam: Hughes a'i Fab, 1921).

Elmore, Richard E., *School Reform from the Inside Out* (Cambridge, MA: Harvard Education Press, 2007).

Evans, Dorothy, *Women in the Civil Service: A History of the Development of the Employment of Women in the Civil Service* (London: Pitman, 1934).

Evans, G., *A Class Apart: Learning the Lessons of Education in Post-Devolution Wales* (Cardiff: Welsh Academic Press, 2015).

Evans, Leslie Wynne, *Studies in Welsh Education: Welsh Educational Structure and Administration, 1880–1925* (Cardiff: University of Wales Press, 1974).

Evans, W. Gareth, *Education and Emancipation: The Welsh Experience, 1847–1914* (Cardiff: University of Wales Press, 1991).

Gorard, S., *Education and Social Justice* (Cardiff: University of Wales Press, 2000).

Gordon, P. and Doughan, D., *Dictionary of British Women's Organisations, 1825–1960* (London: Woburn Press, 2001).

Gray, Adrian, *European School Inspection and Evaluation* (Retford: SICI, 2019).

Grier, Richard, *John Allen: A Memoir* (London: Rivingtons, 1889).

Gruffydd, W. J., *Owen Morgan Edwards: Cofiant* (Aberystwyth: Ab Owen, 1937).

Harrison, Wilfred, *Greenhill School Tenby 1896–1964: An Educational and Social History* (Cardiff: University of Wales Press, 1979).

Hattie, John, *Visible Learning: A synthesis of over 800 meta-analyses relating to achievement* (London: Routledge, 2009).

Horn, Pamela, *Education in Rural England 1800–1914* (Dublin: Gill & Macmillan, 1978).

Hughes, Dewi Rowland, *Cymru Fydd* (Cardiff: University of Wales Press, 2006).

Hughes, J. Elwyn, *Arloeswr Dwyieithedd: Dan Isaac Davies 1839–1887* (Cardiff: University of Wales Press, 1984).

Hunt, F., *Gender and Policy in English Education: Schooling for Girls, 1902–44* (Hemel Hempstead: Harvester Wheatsheaf, 1991).

Institute of Welsh Affairs, *Time to Deliver – The Third Term and Beyond: Policy Options for Wales* (Cardiff: Institute for Welsh Affairs, 2006).

James, C.R., Connolly, M., Dunning, G. and Elliott, T., *How Very Effective Primary Schools Work* (London: Paul Chapman Publishing, 2006).

Jenkins, Geraint H. (ed.), *Gwnewch Bopeth yn Gymraeg Yr Iaith Gymraeg a'i Pheuoedd 1801–1911* (Cardiff: University of Wales Press, 1999).

Jenkins, R. T. (ed.), *Y Bywgraffiadur Cymreig hyd 1940* (London: Honourable Society of Cymmrodorion, 1954).

Jones, Abel J., *I was privileged* (Cardiff: Abbrevia, 1943).

Jones, Abel J., *From an inspector's bag* (Cardiff: Abbrevia, 1944).

Jones, G. Arthur, *Bywyd a Gwaith Owen Morgan Edwards* (Aberystwyth: Cwmni Urdd Gobaith Cymru, 1958).
Jones, Gareth Elwyn, *Controls and Conflicts in Welsh Secondary Education* (Cardiff: University of Wales Press, 1982).
Jones, Gareth Elwyn and Roderick, Gordon Wynne, *A History of Education in Wales* (Cardiff: University of Wales Press, 2003).
Jones, Owen E. (ed.), *The Welsh Intermediate Education Act of 1889* (Cardiff: HMSO, 1990).
Jones, W. R., *Bilingualism in Welsh Education* (Cardiff: University of Wales Press, 1966).
Lawton, D. and Gordon, P., *HMI* (London: Routledge and Kegan Paul, 1987).
Maclure, J. Stuart, *The Inspectors' Calling* (London: Hodder & Stoughton, 2000).
Maclure, J. Stuart, *Educational Documents England and Wales 1816–1968* (London: Methuen Educational Ltd, 1965).
Major, Lee Elliot and Higgins, Steve, *What Works? Research and evidence for successful teaching* (London: Bloomsbury, 2019).
Matthews, Peter and Sammons, Pam, *Improvement through inspection: An evaluation of the impact of Ofsted's work* (London: Institute of Education and Ofsted, 2004).
Martin, J. and Goodman, J., *Women and Education, 1880–1980* (London: Palgrave Macmillan, 2004).
Morell, John R., *The case of Mr J. R. Morell* (privately published, 1864).
Morgan, Kenneth O., *Rebirth of a Nation, Wales 1880–1980* (Oxford: Oxford University Press, 1980).
Morgan, Kenneth O., *Wales in British Politics 1868–1922* (Cardiff: University of Wales Press, 1980).
Morgan, Prys, *Brad y Llyfrau Gleision* (Llandysul: Gwasg Gomer, 1991).
Morgan, R., 'Clear Red Water' speech to the National Centre for Public Policy, Swansea (Swansea: National Centre for Public Policy, 2002).
Morgan, T. J., *W. J. Gruffydd*, Writers of Wales Series (Cardiff: University of Wales Press, 1970).
Petty, David, *Two Centuries of Anglesey Schools* (Anglesey: Anglesey Antiquarian Society, 1977).
Richards, Colin and Robertson, Stewart (eds), *A Scrutiny of Inspectors: Her Majesty's Inspectors in England and Wales* (Association of Retired and Former HMI, Widows and Widowers, 2019).

Sahlberg, Pasi, *Finnish Lessons* (New York: Teachers College Press, 2011).
Selby-Bigge, Sir Lewis Amherst, *The Board of Education* (London: Putnam and Company Ltd, 1927).
Smelser, Neil, *Social Paralysis and Social Change: British Working-Class Education in the Nineteenth Century* (Berkeley, CA: University of California Press, 1991).
Smith, Frank, *The Life and Work of Sir James Kay-Shuttleworth* (London: James Murray, 1923).
Smith, Robert, *Schools, Politics and Society: Elementary Education in Wales, 1870–1902* (Cardiff: University of Wales Press, 1999).
Sneyd-Kynnersley, Edmund M., *H.M.I. Some Passages in the Life of One of H. M. Inspectors of Schools* (London: MacMillan & Co, 1908).
Taylor, C., Power S. and Powell, R., *Independent Review of Estyn's Contribution to Wales' Education Reform Programme, WISERD* (Cardiff: Cardiff University, 2018).
Thomas, Huw S., *Brwydr i Baradwys? Y Dylanwadau ar Dwf Ysgolion Cymraeg De-ddwyrain Cymru* (Cardiff: University of Wales Press, 2010).
Watkins, Percy, *A Welshman Remembers* (Cardiff: William Lewis Ltd, 1944).
Wilcox, Brian, *Making school inspection visits more effective: the English experience* (Paris: UNESCO, 2000).
Williams, G. Perrie, *Welsh Education in Sunlight and in Shadow* (London: Constable and Company Ltd, 1918).
Williams, Iolo Wyn (ed.), *Hanes Sefydlu Ysgolion Cymraeg 1939–2000* (Talybont, Ceredigion: Y Lolfa, 2002).
Williams, Jac L., *Owen Morgan Edwards: A Short Biography 1858–1920* (Aberystwyth: Swyddfa'r Urdd, 1959).

Chapters in books

Egan, D., 'School Effectiveness in The Learning Country', in C. Chapman et al. (eds), *School Effectiveness and Improvement: Research, Policy and Practice* (London: Routledge, 2012), pp. 109–25.
Egan, D., 'Shifting Paradigms: Can Education Compensate for Society?', in S. Gannon et al. (eds), *Resisting Educational Inequality: Reframing policy and practice in schools serving vulnerable communities* (London: Routledge, 2018), pp. 236–44.
Egan, D. and James, R., 'Education', in J. Osmond and B. Jones (eds), *Birth of Welsh Democracy: The First Term of the National Assembly*

for Wales (Cardiff: Institute for Welsh Affairs and Wales Governance Centre, 2003), pp. 99–114.

Egan, D. and James, R., 'Open government and inclusiveness', in B. Jones and J. Osmond (eds), *Institutional Change, Policy Development and Political Dynamics in the National Assembly for Wales* (Cardiff: Institute for Welsh Affairs, 2002), pp. 137–54.

Ehren, M., 'Accountability structures that support school self-evaluation, enquiry and learning', in D. Godfrey and C. Brown (eds), *An Ecosystem for Research-Engaged Schools: Reforming Education Through Research* (Abingdon: Routledge, 2019), pp. 41–55.

Ehren, M., Jones, K. and Perryman, J., 'Side effects of school inspection: motivations and contexts for strategic responses', in M. C. Ehren (ed.), *Methods and Modalities of Effective School Inspections* (Cham, Switzerland: Springer, 2016), pp. 87–109.

Evans, W. Gareth, 'Y Wladwriaeth Brydeinig ac Addysg Gymraeg 1914–1991', in Geraint H. Jenkins and Mari A. Williams (eds), *'Eu Hiaith a Gadwant'?* (Cardiff: University of Wales Press, 2000), pp. 331–56.

Goodman, J. and Harrop, S., '"The peculiar preserve of the male kind": women and the education inspectorate, 1893 to the Second World War', in J. Goodman and S. Harrop (eds), *Women, Educational Policy-Making and Administration in England: Authoritative women since 1880* (London: Routledge, 2000), pp. 137–55.

Lloyd, Wynne Ll., 'Owen M. Edwards (1858–1920)', in Glanmor Williams et al. (eds), *Pioneers of Welsh Education* (Swansea: University College Swansea Faculty of Education, 1962), pp. 83–99.

Phillips, R., 'Wales', in L. Gearson (ed.), *Education in the United Kingdom* (London: David Fulton, 2002), pp. 40–54.

Sahlberg, P., 'The Global Educational Reform Movement and Its Impact on Schooling', in Karen Mundy, Andy Green, Bob Lingard and Antoni Verger (eds), *The Handbook of Global Education Policy* (Hoboken, NJ: Wiley, 2016), pp. 128–44.

Williams, Cen, 'Addysg Uwchradd a'r Gymraeg yn yr Ugeinfed Ganrif', in Geraint H. Jenkins (ed.), *Cof Cenedl* XII (Llandysul: Gwasg Gomer, 1997), pp. 137–68.

Journal articles

Adams, S., 'The Inspection System in Wales', *Welsh Journal of Education*, 5/2 (1996), 105–17.

Altrichter, H. and Kemethofer, D., 'Does accountability pressure through school inspections promote school improvement?', *School Effectiveness and School Improvement*, 26/1 (2015), 32–56.

Ball, S., 'The teacher's soul and the terrors of performativity', *Journal of Education Policy*, 18/2 (2003), 215–28.

Brimblecombe, N., Ormston, M. and Shaw, M., 'Teachers' Perceptions of School Inspection: a stressful experience', *Cambridge Journal of Education*, 25/1 (1995), 53–61.

Case, P., Case, S. and Catling, S., 'Please Show You're Working: A critical assessment of the impact of OFSTED inspection on primary teachers', *British Journal of Sociology of Education*, 21/4 (2000), 605–21.

Davies, J. H., 'Atgofion', *Cymru Y Rhifyn Coffa*, LX (1921), 22–4.

Dedering, K. and Muller, S., 'School Improvement through Inspections? First Empirical Insights from Germany', *Journal of Educational Change*, 12/3 (2011), 301–22.

Edwards, O. M., (ed.), *Cymru* and *Wales* (various).

Egan, D., 'A Brief History of the Inspectorate in Wales', *Welsh Journal of Education*, 8/1 (1999), 7–24.

Egan, D., 'Educational Equity in Wales', *Wales Journal of Education*, 18/1 (2016), 21–44.

Egan, D. and James, R., 'Watching the Assembly: The subject committees and educational policy in Wales', *Welsh Journal of Education*, 10/1 (2001), 4–20.

Evans, W. G., 'The "Bilingual Difficulty": HMI and the Welsh Language in the Victorian Age', *Welsh History Review*, 16 (1992), 494–513.

Evans, W. G., 'The "Bilingual Difficulty": The Inspectorate and the Failure of a Welsh Language Teacher Training Experiment in Victorian Wales', *National Library of Wales Journal*, 28/3 (1993), 325–33.

Fletcher, L., 'A Further Comment on Recent Interpretations of the Revised Code, 1862', *History of Education Journal*, 10/1 (1981), 21–31.

Gipps, C., 'The debate over standards and the use of testing', *British Journal of Educational Studies*, 36/1, February 1988, 21–36.

Gordon, P., 'Katherine Bathurst: A Controversial Woman Inspector', *History of Education Bulletin*, 17/3 (1988), 193–207.

Grigg, R., '"Wading through children's tears": the emotional experiences of elementary school inspections, 1839–1911', *History of Education*, 49/5 (2020), 597–616.

Jones, E. D., 'The Journal of William Roberts ("Nefydd") 1853–1862', *National Library of Wales Journal*, X/3 (1953), 199–220.

Jones, G. E., 'Education and Nationhood in Wales: an Historiographical Analysis', *Journal of Educational Administration and History*, 38/3 (2006), 263–77.

Jones, J. C., 'A History of the Schools and Education in Buckley', *Flintshire Historical Society*, 55/15 (1954), 83–101.

Keane, A., 'O. M. Edwards: Ei Ddylanwad ar y Gymraeg mewn Ysgolion', *Wales Journal of Education*, 20/1 (2018), 26–45.

Knight, L. S., 'Welsh cathedral schools to 1600 AD', *Y Cymmrodor*, 29 (1919), 76–109.

Leithwood, K., Harris, A. and Hopkins, D., 'Seven strong claims about successful school leadership revisited', *School Leadership and Management*, 40, (2019), 1–18.

Matthews, P., Holmes, R., Vickers, P. and Corporaal, B., 'Aspects of the Reliability and Validity of School Inspection Judgements of Teaching Quality', *Educational Research and Evaluation*, 4/2 (2010), 167–88.

Perryman, J., 'Improvement after Inspection', *Improving Schools*, 13/2 (2010), 182–96.

Perryman, J., 'Inspection and Emotion', *Cambridge Journal of Education*, 37/2 (2007), 173–90.

Perryman, J., 'Inspection and the Fabrication of Professional and Performative Processes', *Journal of Education Policy*, 24/5 (2009), 611–31.

Perryman, J., 'Panoptic Performativity and School Inspection Regimes: Disciplinary Mechanisms and Life under Special Measures', *Journal of Education Policy*, 21/2 (2006), 147–61.

Power, S., 'The politics of education and the misrepresentation of Wales', *Oxford Review of Education*, 42/3 (2016), 285–98.

Rapple, B. A., 'Payment by Results (1862–1897): Ensuring a Good Return on Governmental Expenditure', *Journal of Educational Thought*, 25/3 (1991), 183–201.

Rees, G., 'Democratic Devolution and Education Policy in Wales: The Emergence of a National System', *Contemporary Wales*, 17 (2004), 28–43.

Rees, G. and Taylor, C., 'Is There a Crisis in Welsh Education?', *Transactions of the Honourable Society of Cymmrodorion* (2014), 97–113.

Reynolds, D., 'New Labour, Education and Wales: the devolution decade', *Oxford Review of Education*, 34/6 (2008), 753–65.

Webster, J. R., 'The First Reports of Owen M. Edwards on Welsh Intermediate Schools', *NLW Journal*, X/4 (1958), 390–4.

Wheldon, Sir Wynn and Thomas, Sir Ben Bowen, 'The Welsh Department, Ministry of Education, 1907–1957', *Transactions of the Honourable Society of Cymmrodorion* (1958), 2–35.

Williams, H. G., 'Longueville Jones and Welsh Education: The Neglected Case of a Victorian HMI', *Welsh History Review*, 15/3 (1991), 416–42.

Williams, H. G., 'Longueville Jones, Ralph Lingen and inspectors' reports: a tragedy of Welsh education', *History of Education*, 25/1 (1996), 19–36.

Unpublished theses

Hughes, Lowri, 'Writing the Welsh people: O. M. Edwards and the shaping of Welsh identity' (unpublished PhD thesis, Jesus College Oxford, 2007). Made available by the author.

Jenkins, Bethan, 'Women's Professional Employment in Wales, 1880–1939' (unpublished PhD thesis, Cardiff University, 2017).

Jones, O. G., 'Sylwadau O. M. Edwards ar Addysg' (unpublished MEd thesis, University of Wales College Bangor, 1973).

Mullins, C. A., '"Washtub Women": A Study of female school inspectors from the 1890s to the 1920s' (unpublished MEd thesis, University of Liverpool, 1999). Made available by the author.

Phillips, E., 'The History of the Development of the Teaching of Domestic Subjects between 1870 and 1944 with particular reference to Cardiff' (unpublished MEd thesis, University College Cardiff, 1979).

Webster, Roger, 'The Place of Secondary Education in Welsh Society 1800–1918' (unpublished PhD thesis, University College of Wales Swansea, 1959).

INDEX

A

Aberdare 67
Aberdare Committee (1881) 37
Aberdare National Eisteddfod 40
ACCAC 189
accountability 6–8, 13, 16, 17, 22, 135, 148, 150, 195–9, 207–9, 217–21, 230–3
Achievement and Under-Achievement in Secondary Schools in Wales (1991–3) 122–3
adult education 4, 72, 106, 134, 176
Adult Learning Inspectorate 140
Allen, John 25, 26, 31
Andrews, Leighton 195, 219
Anglican National Society (1811) 21, 22
annual reports 11, 52–3, 65, 71, 191, 201, 214, 220, 232
   1850 12–13
   1907 53
   1909 58–60, 62
   1910 60
   1911 61
   1913 67, 69, 165
   1914 67, 165
   1918 69
   1920 67
   1924 84
   1927–70 84–94
   1970s/80s 129–30
   1996–1997 143
   1999–2000 154
   2001–2002 143, 154
   2003 192
   2004–2005 143–4
   2005–2006 145
   2007–2008 155
   2009 196
   2010 149, 193
   2010–11 150, 197, 198
   2012 196
   2014 150
   2016 202
   2017 150, 155, 197
Anthony, Mary 178
Arnold, Matthew 27, 64
Assessment and Monitoring of Progress in Secondary Schools (1983) 115, 121
'athrawon bro' (peripatetic Welsh teachers) 114
Attendance and Achievement in Secondary Schools (1985) 121
Audit Wales 9

B

Baker, Colin 126
Baker, Kenneth 128, 132, 226
banding system (categorisation) 149–50, 195, 208, 219
Bathurst, Katherine (Kitty) 36, 161
Bellairs, H. W., report on schools in South Wales (1843) 23–4
Best Value inspections 9, 139
Black Paper writers 103

Blue Books see *Report of the Commissioners of Inquiry into the State of Education in Wales* (1847)
see also Johnson, Henry Vaughan; Lingen, Ralph; Symons, Jelinger C.
Board of Education 37, 39–40, 161, 225
    Welsh Department 3, 5, 21, 47–8, 68, 77, 78, 80, 87, 159, 160, 162, 167–8, 171, 173, 205
    see also Edwards, Owen M.
Bowen, Geraint 125
Bowstead, Joseph 29, 32–3
Bratislava Memorandum on Inspection and Innovation (2013) 209
British and Foreign School Society (1814) 21–2, 32, 35
Browne, Dr 80–1
Browne, Sheila 178
Bruce Committee (1920) 77–8
bullying, action on (2014) 216

C

Caernarvonshire 67
Callaghan, James, Ruskin College speech (1976) 103, 110
Callis, Miss C. 161
Cardiff school board 35–6
Cardiganshire 43, 67
Care and Social Services Inspectorate Wales (Care Inspectorate Wales) 9, 140
Carmarthenshire 33, 57, 66
Central Advisory Council for Education (Wales) 86, 98, 99
Central Welsh Board (CWB) 37, 48, 54, 58–61, 64, 69, 71, 77–8, 84, 86, 168

Children, Education and Lifelong Learning Committee 194
Children, Young People and Education (CYPE) Committee 10
Children's Commissioner 215
Circulars
    10/65 108
    153 63
    532 48–9, 55–6
Citizen's Charter (1991) 128, 132
Clarke, Kenneth 227
classroom organisation 118–19
Classroom organisation and teaching methods in primary schools in Wales (1992) 119–20
Coleg Harlech 169
Committee of the Privy Council on Education (CCE) 22, 25, 28
    Instructions (1840) 25–6
comprehensive schools 11, 77, 91–3, 103, 108–9, 111, 114, 120–1
compulsory attendance 34, 36, 109
Council of Welsh Training and Enterprise Councils (TECs) 139
'COVID-19: do we need to reimagine the purpose of school inspections?', webinar (2020) 229–30
Cross Committee (1887) 52, 64–5
Curriculum and the Community in Wales, The (1952) 99
Curriculum Council for Wales (CCW) 152
Cwricwlwm Cymreig, Y 3, 127, 133, 152, 153, 154
Cymraeg 2050: A million Welsh speakers 153

D

Darlington, Thomas 40
Davidson, Jane 193–4
Davies, Miss A. M. 168
Davies, Alfred T. 47, 58, 62, 63–4, 72, 78, 167, 168
Davies, Cathrin Jane (Cassie) 83, 96–7, 168, 171–2, 174, 175, 225
Davies, D. T. 79
Davies, Dan Isaac 40, 64, 225
Davies, E. M. (Betty) 176, 178
Davies, Gwilym 171
Davies, Jean E. (née Hughes) 174
Davies, Mrs Llywelfryn *see* Thomas, Mary C.
Davies, Mary 167, 168, 169, 171
Denbigh 38
Denbighshire 68
denominational challenges 28, 32–4, 42, 55
Department of Education and Science (DES) 77, 109
Department of Science and Art 37, 39
Departmental Committee on Rural Education in Wales Report (1930) 169–70
Departmental Organisation in Secondary Schools (1984) 121
Developing a Cwricwlwm Cymreig (1993) 152
Donaldson, Graham see *Learning Inspectorate* (2018); *Successful Futures* (2015)
Dyfodol Dwyieithog: A Bilingual Future (2002) 152

E

Education Acts
  1870 33–4
  1902 39–40
  1918 54
  1944 7, 82, 86, 88, 126, 173
  1988 3, 72, 120, 123–4, 126, 152
  1992 5, 8, 128, 132–3, 141, 143
  2005 3, 141, 142, 206, 215, 236
  see also Further and Higher Education Act (1992); Welsh Intermediate Education Act (1889)
Education and Learning Wales (ELWa) 139, 189
Education in Wales: Our National Mission (2017) 201
Education Scotland 9
Education Workforce Council 201
Edwards, E. C. (Betty) 178, 179
Edwards, Owen M. 3, 11, 42, 47–72, 91
  Board of Education 61–3
  Central Welsh Board 58–61
  committee man 60
  conferences 56
  elementary schools 64–8
  'Imperial Education Conference' address (1911) 64
  intermediate (secondary) schools 58–61, 68–70
  leadership and mission 48, 70–2
  notes of visit (NoVs) 50–1
  'Scheme of Educational Pamphlets' 62–3
  secondary schools 68–70
  Welsh language 48, 53, 64–70, 71–2, 225
  women inspectors 162, 164, 165
Edwards, William 36, 38, 40–1, 41–2, 58, 65, 78
elementary schools 4, 22, 29, 35, 36, 37, 40, 51, 64–8, 71, 78, 95, 225

Ellis, Mary Elizabeth 163–4, 165, 166, 168, 169, 171, 174
Emerson, Mrs E. 174
Estyn
  cyclical inspections 139–43, 212–13, 219, 227
  response to criticism 15–17
  role 5, 8, 9, 10, 12, 13, 135–7, 147–50, 156, 186, 189–202, 206, 207, 208, 209, 210, 211, 215, 216, 217, 218, 221, 228–9, 230–3
European countries 4, 10, 14, 17, 205–21
Evans, Beriah 52
Evans, Ellen 168
Evans, Gwyneth 173
evening classes 35, 36, 51, 162, 167
  Cadoxton 36
  Llangollen 36–7

F

Fleming, Lord David 79
Flintshire 68
Food Economy Campaign 165
Foundation Phase (FP) 12, 193, 194, 200
Framework for evaluation, improvement and accountability 230, 231–2
framework for inspection 8, 9, 133, 136–7, 140–1, 146, 149–51, 153, 155, 216
Framework for Inspection handbook 135
Fullan, Michael 16, 209
Fulton Committee Report (1968) 81
further and higher education (FHE) 4, 5, 51, 55, 81, 86, 103, 104, 106, 109, 111, 112, 134, 136–40, 180, 210, 211, 212

Further and Higher Education Act (1992) 136
Further Education Funding Council for Wales (FEFCW) 134, 136, 139, 145
Future of Secondary Education in Wales, The (1949) 91, 98

G

GCE performance outcomes 143
GCSE performance outcomes 15, 143, 144, 227
Gittins Report see *Primary Education in Wales* (1968)
Glamorgan 30, 54, 63, 68
Global Education Reform Movement (GERM) 13, 188
Godfrey, Mrs K. P. 174
Good Practice in A-level Courses 115
Gorst, Sir John 41
Gruffydd, W. J. 171

H

Hampton, Philip, review see *Reducing administrative burdens* (2005)
health education 91
Healthcare Inspectorate Wales 9
HMI Today and Tomorrow (1970) 6, 107, 108
Home-School Links (1983) 121
Homework in the Secondary School (1982) 121
Hopkins-Jones, Miss W. M. 176
Howells, Tudor, Wrexham 41

I

Iaith Pawb (2003) 152, 194

Improving Schools (2012) 195
in-service training 116, 118
industrialisation 22–5
initial teacher education (ITE) 1, 180, 190, 199, 201
Inspection, Audit and Regulation in Wales 8
'Inspection Wales' 9
inspectorate
   European comparisons 205–21
   future considerations 225–33
   history (1839–1907) 21–43; (1907–25) 47–72; (1925–70) 77–100; (1970–92) 103–28; (1992–2020) 131–56
   impact on provider improvement 12–15
   influence on education policy 10–12
   objectives 6–8
   policy context 8–9
   post-devolution education and policy making: a personal interpretation 187–202
   response to criticism 15–17
   structure 4–5
   women 159–83
Inspectorate and Inspection Arrangements in Wales (1941) 79
Institute of Welsh Affairs 189
intermediate schools 37, 39, 48, 58–61, 63–4, 68–70, 90

J
Jenkins, John 29
Johnson, Henry Vaughan 27
Jones, Abel J. 31, 49–50, 54–5, 162
Jones, D. E. Lloyd 80
Jones, Harry Longueville 2, 11, 26–8, 29, 31, 32, 33, 36, 40, 42
Jones, Mary Elizabeth Stanley 172–3

K
Kay-Shuttleworth, Dr James 22, 25, 26, 28, 35
Keane, Ann 182
Kelly, James, schoolmaster 30

L
Labour Proficiency Examination 53–4
Langland Bay conferences 56
Lawrence, Maude 36, 161–2, 165
league tables 193, 194, 208, 219, 231
Learning and Skills Act (2000) 3, 139
Learning and Skills Council (LSC) 139
Learning Country, The (2001) 189, 190, 208
Learning Country: Vision into Action, The (2006) 191
Learning Inspectorate, A (2018) 156, 208, 210, 228–9, 230–1
Learning Pathways (14–19) 12
Legard, Albert G. 39, 40, 41, 42
Lewis, Herbert MP 61
Lewis, Saunders 172
Lewis, Susan 179
Lifelong Learning Wales Record (LLWR) 145
Lingen, Ralph 27, 28, 30, 32
literacy and numeracy 32, 103, 121, 154, 195, 199, 208, 229
Literacy and Numeracy, occasional paper 115
Literacy and Numeracy Framework 195, 199

Llandrindod Wells conferences 56
Lloyd, Illtyd 127
Lloyd, Wynne Ll. 80
Lloyd George, David 47–8, 61
London Challenge, the 195
Lowe, Robert 28, 29, 32
　Revised Code (1862) 29, 32, 51, 209

M
Manpower Services Commission (MSC) 114, 116
Marshall, Steve 195, 208–09
Maurice, Henry 62
McCausland, Mrs M. K. 174
McDonnell Commission (1914) 166
Merioneth 29, 66–7
Millennium Cohort Study 198
Monkhouse, Miss R. L. 162
Monmouthshire 5, 22, 34, 40, 63, 67, 68
Morant, Robert L. 48–9, 52
Morell, J. D. 30
Morell, John Reynell 29, 30, 31
Morgan, Owen 43
Morris, Dominic 226–7

N
National Academy for Educational Leadership 201
National Council of Education for Wales 47, 58, 61, 70
National Curriculum (NC) 3, 12, 72, 104, 114, 116, 120, 123, 126, 128, 141, 148, 152, 154, 200, 209
National Evaluation and Improvement Resource (NEIR) 232
National Language Centre, Pontypridd 86
National Performance and Funding System (NPFS) 145
National School Categorisation System 150
National Strategy for Education Research and Enquiry 201
Neath 29, 66, 67
Nefydd *see* Roberts, William
Newcastle Commission on Popular Education in England (1858–61) 28–9
Newport 23, 30, 63, 66, 93
Norwood, Sir Cyril 79
notes of visit (NoVs) 84–6, 89, 107, 115, 117, 118
　see also Edwards, Owen M.
Nuffield Foundation 103, 118

O
Office of Her Majesty's Chief Inspector of Schools (England) (Ofsted) 5, 9, 14, 133, 140, 205–6, 211, 216, 227, 233
Office of Her Majesty's Chief Inspector of Schools (Wales) (OHMCI) 5, 12, 131, 133–5, 136, 140, 179, 205–6
Office of Public Services Reform 8
Ollivant, Bishop, Llandaff 28
outsourcing *see* privatisation
Organisation for Economic Co-operation and Development (OECD) 150, 195, 196, 200, 205, 212, 219, 220, 230, 232
Owen, Hugh 24
Owens, Owen 37

P

Parliamentary Select Committee on Education and Science, Review (1967) 87
Parry, Miss M. 172
Pastoral Care in Secondary Schools 115
Payment by Results scheme 6, 28, 35, 51–2, 225
Pickthorn, Kenneth, Minister for Education 88
'pioneer' schools 1
Place of Welsh and English in the Schools of Wales, The (1953) 99
Plaid Genedlaethol Cymru (Welsh National Party) 72, 172
Planning for Progress (1982) 12, 115, 121–3
Plowden Report (1967) 103, 178
post-16 education *see* further and higher education
Powis, Lord 34
primary education 81, 86, 87, 90, 98, 99, 100, 108, 115, 116, 124, 141, 144, 145, 146, 165, 174, 183, 199, 219
issues (1970s/1980s) 117–20
Primary Education in Wales (Gittins Report, 1968) 12, 86, 103, 108, 178
Principles in Public Service (1991) 132
privatisation 15, 131–6, 137, 143, 147–8, 156, 190
Programme for International Student Assessment (PISA) tests 13, 146–7, 195, 196, 197–8, 205, 207–8, 219, 227
Public Examinations in Wales: Attainment at 16+ (1982) 121
publication of reports (1983 onwards) 113
pupil teachers 37, 38–9, 54

Q

Qualified for Life (2014) 200
Quality and Standards in Further Education in Wales 1993–97 145

R

Radnor 66
Radnorshire 68
Rayner Report (1982) 7, 110–11, 114, 116, 128, 173, 213, 226
Reducing administrative burdens (2005) 8
Rees, Caleb 80
Report of the Commissioners of Inquiry for South Wales (1844) 23
Report of the Commissioners of Inquiry into the State of Education in Wales (1847) 2, 27, 64, 225
see also Johnson, Henry Vaughan; Lingen, Ralph; Symons, Jelinger C.
Report on the State of Elementary Education in the Mining District of South Wales (1840) 23
report on the teaching of art (1928) 83
Response to Underachievement (1984) 121
Revised Code (1862) 29, 32, 51, 209
see also Lowe, Robert
Rhyl 35
Rhŷs, Sir John 31

Roberts, L. J. 35, 38, 54, 65
Roberts, William (Nefydd) 22
Rogers, Annie 172, 173, 175
Role of Senior Staff in Comprehensive Schools 115
Roseveare, Sir Martin 5, 80
report (1956) 6, 80–1
Rowlands, Anna 163
Rowlands, Menai Jane 162, 163, 164, 165, 166, 167–8, 169, 170, 172
Royal Commission on the Civil Service (Tomlin Commission, 1929–30) 169

S
Sahlberg, Pasi 188
School Effectiveness Framework, The (SEF) (2008) 191, 200, 208–9
school leaving age (ROSLA) 36, 54, 103, 108, 109
school libraries 53, 91
school self-evaluation (SSE) 1, 156, 207, 212–13, 228
school subjects
  arithmetic 29, 50
  art 116, 127, 153
  domestic subjects 36, 50, 55, 161–2, 164, 165, 167, 169–70, 173, 176, 183
  drawing 37, 50
  English 3, 27–8, 40–1, 42, 50, 52, 53, 59, 61, 64, 65, 69–70, 90, 95, 98–9, 100, 148, 155, 165, 167, 178, 225
  French 36, 59, 68, 69, 98
  geography 50, 53, 66, 94, 96, 98, 116, 127, 153, 163
  handicrafts 50
  history 50, 153, 163
  history of Wales 3, 12, 53, 63, 66, 71, 94, 96, 97–8, 114, 116, 127
  hygiene 39, 50
  Latin 36
  mathematics 90, 92, 118, 120, 146, 198
  music 50, 53, 83, 91, 92, 116, 127, 153, 168
  physical exercise/training 26, 53, 92, 161, 167, 168, 172, 173, 176, 183
  reading 13, 29, 67, 124, 146, 219
  religious education/instruction 22, 25, 26, 32, 33, 116
  school gardens 50
  science 13, 39, 53, 90, 92, 118, 125, 146
  Welsh 12, 40, 48, 53, 65–70, 79, 86, 90, 94–100, 116, 117, 124, 127, 152–5
    see also Welsh language, the
  writing 29
school visits 6, 11, 30, 38, 50, 51, 57–8, 71, 78, 81, 87, 89, 91, 100, 106, 107–8, 109–10, 111, 115, 127, 147, 164, 165, 178, 218, 226, 229, 230–1
  see also notes of visit (NoVs)
schools
  Abergynolwyn 86
  Bishopston School 85
  Bistre School (Flintshire) 43
  Bontddu School 85
  Caernarfon Girls' County School 163
  Cardiff school for the blind and deaf 35
  Carmarthen Borough Roman Catholic School 86
  Dr Williams School, Dolgellau 163, 166

Garnswllt 85
grant-maintained schools 116
Howells School, Denbigh 165
Llanelli 33
Llanfairfechan National School 33
Llangollen Evening School 36–7
Llanidloes 27
Llwynypia Colliery Infant School 31–2
Newport 93
Pwllheli 27
Reynoldston School 85
Rhiwfawr 85
Rhondda 96; Rhondda Fach Higher Grade School, Ferndale 36
Roman Catholic schools 29, 33
rural schools 116, 119, 124
Ruthin Girls' County School 163
St David's Roman Catholic School, Cardiff 30
Swansea 91; school for the blind and deaf 35
Trecastle, Carmarthenshire 33
Welshpool 34
Ysgol Gymraeg, Aberystwyth 98
see also comprehensive schools; elementary schools; further and higher education; intermediate schools; primary education; secondary education
Schools Council Committee for Wales 82, 86, 103, 106, 116, 118, 124, 125
secondary education 11, 37, 39, 51, 62, 68–70, 71, 77, 78, 81, 87, 88, 90, 91, 92, 94, 95, 98, 106, 108, 114, 115, 117, 118, 126–7, 137, 141, 191–2, 211, 216

examination issues 144–5, 196, 199
issues (1970s/1980s) 120–3
Selby-Bigge, Sir Lewis Amherst 51, 52, 56
Sex Disqualification (Removal) Act (1919) 166
Sharpe, Revd T. W. 38
Shaw, Captain T. B. 39
Short, Edward H. 43
Sillitoe, Miss H. 55, 162
Sneyd-Kynnersley, Edmund M. 29
Social Services and Well-being (Wales) Act (2014) 216
Society for the Promotion of Christian Knowledge (1699) 21
Society for the Utilisation of the Welsh Language (1885) 40, 64
South Pembrokeshire 68
South Wales and Monmouthshire Training College (Carmarthen) 28
Spens, Sir Will 79
Standardised Assessment Tests 219
Standing International Conference of Inspectorates (SICI) 13, 206, 209, 212
Standing Reference Committee 82
substance misuse, survey (2007) 216
Successful Futures (2015) 199, 200, 229
Sunday schools 24
Swansea 66
Symons, Jelinger C. 27

T
Taking Wales Forward 2016–2021 (2016) 152–3

Taunton Commission Report (1868) 37
teacher education/training 39, 79, 81, 104, 134, 155
teacher training colleges 4, 37–8, 51, 54, 172
  Bangor (1862) 38
  Caernarfon (1856) 38
  Carmarthen (1848) 37
  Swansea (1872) 38
'Teaching through the medium of a second language', (Canadian/Welsh) seminar (1979) 123
Technical and Vocational Education Initiative 116
technical education 4, 37, 51, 55, 83, 90
Temple, Robert 40
Thomas, Iola 179
Thomas, Mary C. (Mrs Llywelfryn Davies) 173, 174
Thomas, Peter MP 88
Thomas, T. C., Bedlinog 41
'three Rs' 29, 51, 53, 117, 118
Tomlin Commission *see* Royal Commission on the Civil Service
'total quality management' 218
Training and Enterprise Councils (TECs) 116, 139
Tremenheere, Hugh Seymour 23, 25, 26
  see also Report on the State of Elementary Education in the Mining District of South Wales (1840)

U

Undeb Athrawon Cymreig (UCAC, Union of Welsh Teachers) 72

United Nations Convention on the Rights of the Child (1989) 151, 215
university colleges
  Aberystwyth 39; day training college 38
  Bangor 38
  Cardiff 39; day training college 38
Urdd Gobaith Cymru 72, 154

V

virtual inspection rooms (VIR) 15, 149

W

Wakefield, HMI 36
Wales Audit Office (Audit Wales) 9
Wales Education Office 82
Wales Institute of Social & Economic Research, Data & Methods (WISERD) 16
War Savings scheme 54, 165
Wark, Miss 169
Watts, Revd E. T., Anglesey 34
well-being 215–17
Well-being of Future Generations (Wales) Act (2015) 151, 216
Welsh Assembly Government (WAG), later named Welsh Government 3, 8, 9, 141, 155, 187, 188, 189, 191, 194, 206, 207, 208, 213, 215, 216, 219, 220, 221
Welsh Baccalaureate 12, 193, 200
Welsh Books Council, later named Books Council of Wales 126
Welsh Department *see* Board of Education

Welsh in Education and Life (1927) 63, 68, 69, 78–9, 94–5, 97
Welsh in the primary schools of Gwynedd, Powys and Dyfed (1977) 124
Welsh Intermediate Education Act (1889) 37, 52–3, 84
Welsh Joint Education Committee (WJEC) 78, 86, 109, 116, 124, 126
Welsh language, the 2, 27, 40–2, 51–2, 53, 63, 64–72, 105, 133, 168, 171–2, 225
  bilingualism 11, 94, 123–7, 131, 151–5, 171
  see also *Curriculum and the Community in Wales, The*; Cwricwlwm Cymreig, Y; *Cymraeg 2050: A million Welsh speakers*; *Dyfodol Dwyieithog: A Bilingual Future*; *Iaith Pawb*; *Place of Welsh and English in the Schools of Wales, the*; *Report of the Commissioners of Inquiry into the State of Education in Wales*; *Welsh in Education and Life*; school subjects: Welsh; Welsh-medium education
Welsh Language Act (1993) 152
Welsh League of Nations Union (WLNU) 169
Welsh-medium education 3, 10, 77, 94–100, 117, 119, 124–7, 151–5, 164, 183, 198
Welsh National Party, the see Plaid Genedlaethol Cymru
Welsh Office, the (WO) 11, 12, 77, 82, 104–5, 106, 109, 111, 115, 124, 133, 187, 189, 193, 205, 227
Welsh School of Social Service 169
Welsh Women's Peace Memorial 169
White, Angharad 167, 169
Whitmell, C. T. 160
Whole Curriculum 5–16 in Wales, The (1991) 152
Williams, G. Prys 57, 58, 63, 64, 65, 94
Williams, William, principal of Swansea Training College 34–5, 41, 42
Williams, William J. 63, 64, 65, 80
women 4, 35–6, 55, 63, 79, 80, 82, 105, 159–83
  'Aggregation' 170, 173, 174
  gender composition of the Welsh inspectorate (1952–82) 177
  marriage bar 79, 166, 170–1, 174, 175, 182
  pay scales 161, 165–6, 170, 175, 182
  personal perspectives on gender into the 21 century 179–82
  training colleges 38, 167
  see also names of individual inspectors

Y
Years 1–3 in Comprehensive Schools 115
Years 4–5 in Comprehensive Schools 115
Youth Training Schemes (YTS) 114